Organizational Perspectives on Environmental Migration

Over the past decade, international organizations (IOs) and non-governmental organizations (NGOs) have increasingly focused their efforts on the plight of environmental migrants in both industrialized and developing countries. However, to date very few studies have analysed the influence and rhetoric of advocacy groups in the debates on environmental migration.

Organizational Perspectives on Environmental Migration fills this lacuna by drawing together and examining the related themes of climate change and environmental degradation, migration and organizational studies to provide a fresh perspective on their increasing relevance. In order to assess the role of IOs and NGOs in the environmental migration discourse and to understand their interaction and their ways of addressing the topic, the book contains a wide-range of contributions covering the perspectives of organizational sociologists, political scientists, anthropologists, geographers, lawyers and practitioners. The chapters are organized thematically around the perspectives of key actors in the area of environmental migration, including IOs, courts and advocacy groups. The geographically diverse and interdisciplinary range of contributions makes this volume an essential foundational text for organizational responses to environmental migration.

This volume will be of great interest to students and scholars of migration studies, international relations, organizational sociology, refugee law and policy, and development studies.

Kerstin Rosenow-Williams is a postdoctoral researcher at the Institute for International Law of Peace and Armed Conflict and at the Chair for Sociology/ Organisation, Migration, Participation, Ruhr University Bochum, Germany.

François Gemenne is a research fellow in Political Science (FNRS/CEDEM – University of Liège/CEARC – University of Versailles), and an associate expert with CERI – Sciences Po, France.

Routledge Studies in Development, Mobilities and Migration

This series is dedicated to the growing and important area of mobilities and migration within Development Studies. It promotes innovative and inter-disciplinary research targeted at a global readership.

The series welcomes submissions from established and junior authors on cutting-edge and high-level research on key topics that feature in global news and public debate.

These include the Arab spring; famine in the Horn of Africa; riots; environmental migration; development-induced displacement and resettlement; livelihood transformations; people-trafficking; health and infectious diseases; employment; South–South migration; population growth; children's well-being; marriage and family; food security; the global financial crisis; drugs wars; and other contemporary crises.

Organizational Perspectives on Environmental Migration

Edited by Kerstin Rosenow-Williams and
François Gemenne

Routledge
Taylor & Francis Group

LONDON AND NEW YORK

earthscan
from Routledge

First published 2016
by Routledge
2 Park Square, Milton Park, Abingdon, Oxon OX14 4RN

and by Routledge
711 Third Avenue, New York, NY 10017

First issued in paperback 2017

Routledge is an imprint of the Taylor & Francis Group, an informa business

British Library Cataloguing-in-Publication Data
A catalogue record for this book is available from the British Library

Library of Congress Cataloging-in-Publication Data
Organizational perspectives on environmental migration / edited by
François Gemenne and Kerstin Rosenow-Williams.
pages cm. -- (Routledge studies in development, mobilities, and
migration)
Includes bibliographical references.
ISBN 978-1-138-93966-0 (hb) -- ISBN 978-1-315-67480-3 (e-book)
1. Environmental refugees. 2. Emigration and immigration--
Environmental aspects. 3. Environmental degradation--Social aspects. 4.
Climatic changes--Social aspects. 5. International agencies. 6. Non-
governmental organizations. I. Gemenne, François, 1980- editor of
compilation. II. Rosenow-Williams, Kerstin, editor of compilation.
HV640.O75 2016
363.738'74086914--dc23
2015019496

ISBN 13: 978-1-138-10420-4 (pbk)
ISBN 13: 978-1-138-93966-0 (hbk)

Typeset in Goudy
by Saxon Graphics Ltd, Derby

Contents

Acknowledgements

In October 2013, we discussed our current research on organizational perspectives at the 'Climate Change, Migration and Conflict: Humanitarian Perspectives and Responses' panel at the Third World Conference on Humanitarian Studies in Istanbul. We agreed with the audience that not only have academics and politicians increasingly addressed the challenge of environmental migration but also many types of organizations ranging from small non-governmental organizations and international non-governmental organizations, to international organizations, such as various United Nations bodies or the International Organization for Migration.

However, organizational perspective on environmental migration had so far received limited attention in academic discourses. It was this observation that led to the idea to gather a group of academics and practitioners working in the field of migration to discuss the current state of affairs both from a scholarly and practical perspective. The aim was to outline where the academic, legal, public and political discussions currently stand and how these debates are related to the experiences of those actors who advocate for the rights and the protection of environmental migrants.

In November 2014, 28 participants from 13 different countries and three different continents gathered in Rome to participate in well-informed, up-to-date and lively discussions that comparatively addressed the organizational challenges and possible solutions for people being displaced by environmental or climate change-related factors. We deeply thank each participant for their contribution and valuable input that helped advance each of the chapters that are now presented in this volume.

The workshop benefited from the support of the Academia Belgica, and was funded by the COST Action 'Climate Change and Migration: Knowledge, Law and Policy, and Theory', which provides opportunities for experts, practitioners, researchers and policy-makers to exchange, develop and improve on knowledge and tools surrounding issues of climate change and environmental migration. We thank the COST secretariat, especially Catherine Alexander and Andrew Baldwin, in helping us organize this event.

The publication process was extremely swift and we have to acknowledge the support of those that helped us, especially during the early months of 2015.

Foremost, we thank our authors, who agreed to work with us on this volume and who made it possible to deliver the final manuscript within six months of the workshop. We also thank Thea Coventry and Dilan Khoshnaw for their help in editing and formatting the text. Annabelle Harris and Margaret Farrelly from Routledge and our anonymous reviewers also did a great job in pushing this project forward. Finally, we thank our families and colleagues who supported us not only during this last year.

Kerstin Rosenow-Williams and François Gemenne
Cologne, Germany and Princeton, USA

Abbreviations

AU	African Union
AWG-LCA	Ad Hoc Working Group on Long-term Cooperative Action under the Convention
BBS	Bangladesh Bureau of Statistics
BCCSAP	Bangladesh Climate Change Strategy and Action Plan
CAF	Cancun Adaptation Framework
CAMM	Common Agenda for Migration and Mobility
CBDR	Common but Different Responsibilities
CCA	Climate Change Adaption
CCCM	Camp Coordination and Camp Management
CCEMA	Climate Change, Environment and Migration Alliance
CCIS	Joint Paper on Climate Change and International Security
CEARC	Cultures Environments Arctic Representations Climate
CEDEM	Center for Ethnic and Migration Studies
CEGIS	Centre for Environment and Geographic Information Services
CELAC	Community of Latin American and Caribbean States
CEN	Center for Earth System Research and Sustainability
CERI	Center for International Studies and Research
CMP	Conference of the Parties Serving as the Meeting of the Parties to the Kyoto Protocol
CNA	Center for Naval Analyses
COAST	Coastal Association for Social Transformation
COHRE	Centre on Housing Rights and Evictions
COP	Conference of the Parties
COREPER	Committee of Permanent Representatives
CSO	Civil Society Organization
DAAD	German Academic Exchange Service
DG	Directorate-General
DG CLIMA	Directorate-General for Climate Action
DG DEVCO	Directorate-General for International Cooperation and Development
DRM	Disaster Risk Management
DRR	Disaster Risk Reduction

DTM	Displacement Tracking Matrix
EASO	European Asylum Support Office
ECHO	European Commission's Humanitarian Aid and Civil Protection Department
ECHR	European Convention on Human Rights
ECJ	Court of Justice of the European Union
ECOWAS	Economic Community of West African States
ECtHR	European Court of Human Rights
EDP	Environmentally Displaced Person
EEAS	European External Action Service
EFMSV	Environmentally Forced Migration and Social Vulnerability
EIA	Environmental Impact Assessment
EMSVA	Environmental Migration, Social Vulnerability and Adaptation Section
EPSRC	Engineering and Physical Sciences Research Council
EU	European Union
FAO	Food and Agriculture Organization of the United Nations
FRONTEX	European Agency for the Management of Operational Cooperation at the External Borders of the Member States of the European Union
GAM	Global Approach to Migration: Priority Actions Focusing on Africa and the Mediterranean
GAMM	Global Approach to Migration and Mobility
GHG	Greenhouse Gases
GRC	German Red Cross
GRCY	German Red Cross Youth Organization
HELIX	High-End cLimate Impact eXtremes
HFA	Hyogo Framework for Action on Disaster Risk Reduction
HRC	Human Rights Council
HRUFASP	High Representative of the Union for Foreign Affairs and Security Policy
IASC	Inter-Agency Standing Committee
ICCPR	International Covenant on Civil and Political Rights
ICESCR	International Covenant on Economic, Social and Cultural Rights
ICRC	International Committee of the Red Cross
IDM	International Dialogue on Migration
IDMC	Internal Displacement Monitoring Centre
IDP	Internally Displaced Person
IEE	Institute of Development Research and Development Policy
IEO	International Epistemic Organization
IFAD	International Fund for Agricultural Development
IFHV	Institute for International Law of Peace and Armed Conflict
IFRC	International Federation of Red Cross and Red Crescent Societies

ILO	International Labour Organization
INGO	International Non-Governmental Organization
IO	International Organization
IOM	International Organization for Migration
IPCC	Intergovernmental Panel on Climate Change
IUCN	International Union for Conservation of Nature
JHA	Justice and Home Affairs
KNOMAD	Global Knowledge Partnership on Migration and Development
LDC	Least Developed Countries
LiSER	Living Space for Environmental Refugees
MDG	Millennium Development Goal
MECC	Migration, Environment and Climate Change
MECLEP	Migration, Environment and Climate Change: Evidence for Policy
MoEF	Ministry of Environment and Forest
MP	Mobility Partnership
NATO	North Atlantic Treaty Organization
NGO	Non-Governmental Organization
NRC	Norwegian Refugee Council
OAS	Organization of American States
OAU	Organization of African Unity
ODA	Official Development Assistance
ODID	Oxford Department of International Development
OWG	Open Working Group
QD	Qualification Directive
RC/RC	Red Cross/Red Crescent
SAPRSO	Space Research and Remote Sensing Organization
SCPF	Standing Committee on Programmes and Finance
SDG	Sustainable Development Goal
TPD	Temporary Protection Directive
UK	United Kingdom (of Great Britain and Northern Ireland)
UKCCMC	UK Climate Change and Migration Coalition
UN	United Nations
UNCCD	United Nations Convention to Combat Desertification
UNDP	United Nations Development Programme
UNEP	United Nations Environment Programme
UNFCCC	United Nations Framework Convention on Climate Change
UNHCR	United Nations High Commissioner for Refugees
UNISDR	United Nations International Strategy for Disaster Reduction
UNU	United Nations University
UNU-EHS	United Nations University Institute for Environment and Human Security
ZLHR	Zimbabwe Lawyers for Human Rights

Contributors

Elmond Bandauko is an urban policy science intern and researcher with the Zimbabwe Democracy Institute in Harare. His research interests are urban systems, urban management and strategic urban planning.

Barbara Bendandi works as a migration and environment policy officer for the International Organization for Migration (IOM). Previously, she worked for other international organizations in the field of environmental conservation (United Nations Convention to Combat Desertification [UNCCD] and International Union for Conservation of Nature (IUCN)) and advised the Italian government for the G8/G20 Office. She earned a Master's degree in Public Administration from the School of International and Public Affairs at Columbia University (New York) and is pursuing a PhD in Economics at Ca' Foscari University (Venice).

Julia Blocher is a PhD candidate at the Center for Ethnic and Migration Studies (CEDEM) at the University of Liège and a research assistant for the "Politics of the Earth" research programme at Sciences Po Paris. She previously worked for the Internal Displacement Monitoring Centre (IDMC) and the United Nations High Commissioner for Refugees (UNHCR).

Lena Brenn has been a programme coordinator on disasters and climate change at the Partnership and Policy Department of the Norwegian Refugee Council (NRC) since 2014. Previously, from 2012, she worked on displacement and humanitarian policy at the Swiss Federal Department of Foreign Affairs.

Innocent Chirisa is an urban and regional planner. Since 2007, he has been researching urbanization, environment and housing among other related subjects. He completed his doctoral thesis on the stewardship of peri-urban areas and housing in Zimbabwe at the University of Zimbabwe in 2013. He has published several articles.

Thea Coventry is an admitted lawyer in Australia, and is currently completing a Master of Law in Human Rights at Maastricht University, as well as working as a graduate research assistant at the Institute for International Law of Peace and Armed Conflict (IFHV), Ruhr University Bochum. She previously worked at the Administrative Appeals Tribunal in Sydney.

Clara Crimella works as a migration and environment project officer for the International Organization for Migration (IOM). Prior to joining IOM, Clara worked as a consultant for the Food and Agriculture Organization of the United Nations (FAO) in Rome. She holds a Bachelor's degree in Political Philosophy from La Sapienza University Rome and a Master's degree in International Security from the Paris School of International Affairs (Sciences Po, Paris). She is a specialist in Migration Studies.

François Gemenne, is a research fellow in Political Science (Center for Ethnic and Migration Studies (CEDEM), University of Liège, and Cultures Environments Arctic Representations Climate [CEARC], University of Versailles), and an associate expert with the Center for International Studies and Research (CERI) – Sciences Po. He is a specialist of environmental geopolitics and migration governance, and lectures on these issues at various universities.

Sinja Hantscher is a research fellow at the Chair of International Governance at the University of Münster. Her current research explores how international organizations, such as the United Nations High Commissioner for Refugees (UNHCR), approach climate change and environmental migration. She completed a Bachelor's degree in International Relations and specialized in Conflict Studies for her Master's degree.

Aminul Hoque is the deputy director of the Bangladeshi non-governmental organization Coastal Association for Social Transformation (COAST) Trust. He works as a policy researcher and has experience in development campaigns and policy advocacy in the field of economic, climate change and environmental issues.

Dina Ionesco is the head of the Migration, Environment and Climate Change (MECC) Division at the International Organization for Migration (IOM). She has been coordinating and developing IOM's MECC thematic portfolio since 2011, including policy, research, capacity-building and communication activities.

Charlotte Lülf, LL.M., M.A. is a research associate at the Institute for International Law of Peace and Armed Conflict (IFHV), and is completing her PhD at the Institute of Development Research and Development Policy (IEE) at the Ruhr University Bochum.

Sarah Nash is a PhD student in Political Science at the University of Hamburg. She is based in the research group 'Climate Change and Security' within the

Center for Earth System Research and Sustainability (CEN). Her research is funded by a scholarship from the German Academic Exchange Service (DAAD).

Angela Pilath is a DPhil candidate at the Oxford Department of International Development (ODID) at the University of Oxford. She holds an MSc in Refugee and Forced Migration Studies from the University of Oxford and a BA (Hons) in European Studies from Maastricht University. Her current research examines the politics of environmental migration focusing on the influence of epistemic actors, the political effects of causal claims and the political economy of knowledge production in the environment-migration nexus.

Alex Randall coordinates the UK Climate Change and Migration Coalition (UKCCMC), a network of refugee and migration rights organizations working together on migration linked to climate change. The coalition aims to alter the media and public discourse around migration and climate change to make it reflect the needs of affected communities.

Kerstin Rosenow-Williams, is a postdoctoral researcher at the Institute for International Law of Peace and Armed Conflict (IFHV) and at the Chair for Sociology/Organisation, Migration, Participation, Ruhr University Bochum, Germany. Her current research focuses on international migration, climate change, humanitarian action and civil society organizations.

Lars Thomann, works as a development consultant, including for the International Fund for Agricultural Development (IFAD) and the Food and Agriculture Organization of the United Nations (FAO).

Mariam Traore Chazalnoël has been working with the International Organization for Migration (IOM) since 2011. She currently serves as the Organization's associate expert on migration, environment and climate change.

Sven Walter works as programme officer for the Global Mechanism of the United Nations Convention to Combat Desertification's (UNCCD) Liaison Office on Land, Security and Resilience housed by the Food and Agriculture Organization of the United Nations (FAO).

1 Introduction

Organizational perspectives on environmental migration

Kerstin Rosenow-Williams

Introduction

Over the past few years several civil society organizations have emerged that are specifically devoted to the plight of environmental migrants, both in industrialized and developing countries. In addition, most large international non-governmental organizations (INGOs) and international organizations (IOs) have also developed advocacy work with regard to environmental migration. What is their role in shaping the discourse on environmental migration? How do they interact with other organizations? Very few studies have yet analysed the influence and rhetoric of advocacy groups in the debates on environmental migration.

In order to both address and close this research gap, this publication unites researchers that work on these questions from various disciplinary contexts, including sociology, political science, geography, anthropology, and conflict studies. Contributions also come from members of non-governmental organizations (NGOs), INGOs, and IOs who reflect on their organizational needs and challenges to address the topic of environmental migration efficiently in order to reach the targeted audiences (e.g., the general public, policy makers, migrants, or other stakeholders both in the countries affected by environmental migration internally and destination countries worldwide).

To situate the chapters collected in this volume within the current debates on environmental migration, this chapter gives a threefold overview of the state-of-the-art academic, political and legal debates on environmental migration, outlining the main points of departure and remaining gaps. The main contributions and their linkages to these debates, including their theoretical approaches to the study of organizational perspectives on environmental migration, are then briefly introduced.

Academic debates on environmental migration[1]

Various empirical studies in the field have been conducted clearly establishing the impact of changing climate patterns on local responses, with migration emerging as one adaptation strategy across the globe (Ferris 2013; Ferris *et al.* 2011; Gemenne *et al.* 2011; Kolmannskog 2009a; Rasmusson 2009; UNEP 2012; Warner *et al.* 2009, 2012). In describing the future development of environmental migration, the latest International Panel on Climate Change (IPCC) report of Working Group II concluded:

> Climate change over the 21st century is projected to increase displacement of people (medium evidence, high agreement). Displacement risk increases when populations that lack the resources for planned migration experience higher exposure to extreme weather events, in both rural and urban areas, particularly in developing countries with low income. Expanding opportunities for mobility can reduce vulnerability for such populations. Changes in migration patterns can be responses to both extreme weather events and longer-term climate variability and change, and migration can also be an effective adaptation strategy. There is low confidence in quantitative projections of changes in mobility, due to its complex, multi-causal nature.
>
> (IPCC 2014: 20)

While the figures on the extent of environmental migration are highly 'contentious' and 'not satisfactory' (Gemenne 2011), the known numbers especially for internally displaced persons (IDPs) have been steadily increasing. By the end of 2013, 51.2 million people were forcibly displaced worldwide including 16.7 million refugees and 33.3 million IDPs (UNHCR 2014: 2–3).

The literature has generally stressed the need to differentiate between national and international environmental migration, temporary and permanent environmental migration (Williams 2008), and environmental migration caused by sudden-onset weather-related extremes, such as heat waves, floods, and cyclones, or by slow-onset deterioration of the environment such as rising sea levels, desertification and permafrost melt (Brown and McLeman 2013; IPCC 2014; Kolmannskog and Trebbi 2010; Warner *et al.* 2013). Displacement has also been identified from conflicts over scarce resources following environmental change or through development projects (Drydyk 2007; Ferris 2011, 2012; Kolmannskog and Trebbi 2010).

The urgency of environmental migration will depend on the combination of factors present described above. Accordingly Renaud *et al.* (2011) differentiate between *environmental emergency migrants*, due to floods or cyclones, *environmentally forced migrants*, due to deteriorating environments such as coastal erosions or sea level rise, and *environmentally motivated migrants*, who might leave a deteriorating environment, such as in cases of desertification or salinification of water supplies, to pre-empt the worst case scenario. Similarly Brown and McLeman (2013) distinguish *distress migration* and *adaptive or amenity seeking migration* patterns which also include movements to regions that have become more habitable due to climatic changes such as is occurring in the Arctic tundra.

Researchers furthermore agree that most migration caused by climate change takes place within nation states (McAdam 2011: 8). Moreover, climate and environmental change is often just one driver for migration among many (Kolmannskog 2008), and while having a limited direct role has a strong effect on various other drivers of migration (Foresight 2011a: 43ff.). The interrelationship between the varieties of changing climate-related factors and the possible human responses creates a continuum of scenarios that have been summarized under the umbrella term environmental migration. Although freedom of choice as a factor is hard to measure empirically (Renaud *et al.* 2011), the term environmental migration also encompasses voluntary migration patterns that pre-empt forced displacement due to natural or manmade causes. Overall, 'migration can be seen as a form of adaptation and an appropriate response to a variety of local environmental pressures' (World Bank 2013: 95).

The most often cited definition on environmental migrants, provided by the International Organization for Migration (IOM) (2007), also encompasses both voluntary and involuntary migration, making it difficult to incorporate into legal responses as outlined below:

> Environmental migrants are persons or groups of persons who, for compelling reasons of sudden or progressive change in the environment that adversely affects their lives or living conditions, are obliged to leave their habitual homes, or choose to do so, either temporarily or permanently, and who move either within their country or abroad.
>
> (IOM 2007: 2–3)

Within the environmental migration research arena, the concepts of vulnerability and resilience, as related to local populations affected by climate change, have received increasing research attention (Afifi and Jäger 2010; Boano *et al.* 2007; Laczko and Aghazarm 2009; Oliver-Smith 2009; Warner *et al.* 2012). According to Brown and McLeman (2013) populations are vulnerable to *biophysical conditions* due to their geographic location, such as flood or drought prone areas. Secondly, vulnerability is affected by the level of household *sensitivity*, that is, particular social, economic and livelihood practices. Thirdly, the individual and community *capacity* to adapt or cope with the changes impacts on the level of vulnerability. Taking these conditions into account, the level of vulnerability differs considerably with, for example, elderly and handicapped people being more vulnerable in emergency evacuations and poorer households being often less capable of adapting their livelihoods to changing climate patterns. This knowledge is of importance to provide targeted assistance and protection.

In their comparative study of changing rainfall patterns in eight countries across several continents, a research team from the United Nations University Institute for Environment and Human Security (UNU-EHS) in Bonn observed four different migration patterns in the context of changing climate conditions (Warner *et al.* 2012). On the one hand, migration takes place as a positive risk management strategy that can improve the resilience of households, such as through remittances or through new livelihood options in the destination area. On the other hand, migration can be less successful, or even not possible at all due to lack of the resources allowing for relocation. As in many forced migration contexts, the people left behind might require as much humanitarian attention as those migrating due to environmental stress (Foresight 2011b: 6).

Overall, the main challenges highlighted by the academic debates on the topic are the need for more research and for consensus on common definitions, which will in turn allow for a comparative approach between different global case studies. Moreover, since the first studies proved the increasing relevance of environmental migration in a globally warming world, calls have been made for policies that adequately address the challenges of environmental migration, including the issues of legal protection and individual rights in cases of displacement (cf. CSC 2013).

Political debates on environmental migration

Environmental migration has been addressed as a topic by international politics since the mid-1990s. In the mid-1980s, the United Nations Environment Programme (UNEP) commissioned a report on 'Environmental Refugees' (El-Hinnawi 1985) referring to 'those people who have been forced to leave their traditional habitat, temporarily or permanently, because of a marked environmental disruption (natural and/or triggered by people) that jeopardized their existence and/or seriously affected the quality of their life'. Since then, the use of the refugee terminology in the context of climate change has been controversially discussed.

The United Nations High Commissioner for Refugees (UNHCR) underlines that the Geneva Convention on Refugees provides no basis for claims of climate-induced migrants. The UNHCR and the International Red Cross/Red Crescent (RC/RC) Movement therefore oppose the term 'climate refugee' because of its potential to undermine the existing refugee protection system (IFRC 2012; UNHCR 2008). Consequentially, the terms 'environmental migration' or 'environmental displacement' have gained acceptance in international policy debates.

Throughout the first decade of the twenty-first century, UNHCR strengthened its advocacy work on environmental migration (UNHCR 2009a, 2009b), pressing the international community of nation states to collaborate on the issue and add it to the official UNHCR mandate. One of the tangible outcomes of this advocacy work was the Cancun Outcome Agreement in 2010 at the Conference of Parties to the Kyoto Protocol. It was the first time that the international community of nation states recognized 'climate change-induced migration, displacement and planned relocation' as an adaption challenge and agreed 'to enhance [their] understanding, coordination and cooperation' on the issue (UNFCCC 2010: para. 14[f]).

In December 2011, however, at the UNHCR Ministerial Conference, the international community of nation states refused to extend the UNHCR mandate to address environmental migration at the United Nations (UN) level (Hall 2013; Ministerial Communiqué 2011; McAdam 2013: 15–6). As an alternative response, the Nansen Initiative was established under the leadership of Switzerland and Norway who pledged to address disaster-induced cross-border displacement (The Nansen Initiative 2014a). The first Nansen Conference on

Climate Change and Displacement was held in Oslo in June 2011 and the Nansen Initiative was officially launched in October 2012. With a projected duration of three years, five sub-regional consultative groups from the most affected regions (the Pacific, Central America, Horn of Africa, South Asia and South-East Asia) have taken place leading up to a global consultative meeting in October 2015.

The main goal of the Nansen Initiative is to find new ways to strengthen the international cooperation among states in protecting displaced people. The envisioned protection agenda is based on three pillars: 'i) international cooperation and solidarity; ii) standards for admission, stay and status; and iii) operational responses, including funding mechanisms and responsibilities for international humanitarian and development actors' (The Nansen Initiative 2014b: 1). The Nansen Initiative therefore highlights key legal and policy gaps concerning the international responsibility of states to accept migrants crossing their borders due to sudden-onset or slow-onset natural disasters.

At the same time, the Inter-Agency Standing Committee (IASC)[2] has also addressed the issue through various subsidiary bodies. A former IASC Task Force on Climate Change, established in 2008, addressed the topic of environmental migration when outlining the general challenges posed to humanitarians by a changing climate:

> Climate change increases the frequency, intensity and uncertainty of weather and climatic hazards such as floods, tropical cyclones, heat waves and droughts. It can also lead to ecosystem degradation, reduced availability of water and food, increase of insect plagues and health threats such as malnutrition and diseases like malaria, diarrhoea and dengue, impact on livelihoods, and may provoke conflict and migration and displacement. Few people will be unaffected by climate change, with the poorest and most vulnerable populations most at risk.
>
> (IASC 2010: 1)

A sub-committee of the IASC Task Force entitled 'Climate Change and Migration' was also established. Its goal was to develop a joint position in order to best influence the United Nations Framework Convention on Climate Change (UNFCCC) negotiations in Poznan (2008), Copenhagen (2009) and Cancun (2010), identifying, for example, existing legal protection gaps for those 'directly affected by the effects of climate change' (IASC 2008: 1; cf. Hall forthcoming).

International legal debates on environmental migration

The third context in which environmental migration has been debated is within the framework of international law (Kälin and Schrepfer 2012; Kolmannskog 2009b; Kolmannskog and Myrstad 2009; McAdam 2011, 2012). Legal protection mechanisms for environmental migration are discussed in the context of national legislations, regional frameworks and international treaties such as the Geneva

Convention on Refugees and its additional protocols (UNHCR 2010) or international human rights law (UNHCR 2011). As Leighton explains,

> Human rights law, as a general matter, obligates states to safeguard the life and property of those within a state's territory against threats of disaster and foreseeable harm. It requires states to mitigate the negative impacts of disaster when these occur, including through legal and administrative mechanisms, evacuation and possible temporary or permanent relocation of affected persons consonant with the right of freedom of movement. It further obligates governments to be particularly sensitive to the needs of vulnerable groups, such as women, children, minorities and indigenous peoples.
>
> (2010: 2)

As outlined in the policy debates, gaps in the legal framework mainly concern environmental migrants crossing international borders. Climate change as a ground for 'well-founded fear of persecution' is not included in the 1951 Geneva Convention for Refugees or its additional protocols (UNHCR 2010), but only applies to people being persecuted for reasons of race, religion, nationality, membership of a particular social group, or political opinion (UNHCR 2010). Victims of natural disasters could only be protected if their government consciously withheld assistance following the natural disaster because the person belonged to one of the five protection grounds (UNHCR 2009a).

Refugee law is therefore clearly linked to the state's responsibility either for the act of persecution, the failure to prevent such persecution, or the failure to provide adequate protection for victims (UNHCR 2009a). In the context of climate change, however, it is not possible to assign a single state the responsibility for a certain extreme weather event. Moreover, the logic to provide refugee status in industrialized countries would be:

> A complete reversal of the traditional refugee paradigm: whereas Convention refugees flee their own government (or private actors that the government is unable or unwilling to protect them from), a person fleeing the effects of climate change is not escaping his or her government but rather is seeking refuge from—yet within—countries that have contributed to climate change.
>
> (McAdam 2011: 12–3)

This position has also been taken by the High Court in New Zealand in 2013 when rejecting the appeal of a Kiribati islander, who claimed asylum as an environmental refugee under the Geneva Convention for Refugees (NZHC 2013).

With regards to the international human rights doctrine, it has been agreed that climate change will negatively affect various human rights, including civil and political rights (UNGA 1966a) and economic, social and cultural rights, such as the right to adequate food, water and the highest attainable level of health (OHCHR 2009; UNGA 1966b). Therefore, while there is no recognized right to a safe and healthy environment, UN conventions recognize the intrinsic link between a healthy environment and the realization of rights.

Generally, human rights apply differently to migrants being displaced within or across national borders. With regard to internal displacement, human rights and state obligations have been summarized in the 1998 Guiding Principles on Internal Displacement (UN 2004). However, as the principles are a soft law instrument, the implementation of national protection measures against arbitrary and forced displacement, provisions for housing and restitution and for the freedom of movement lie in the power of national executives.

People moving across borders also enjoy general human rights protection, but human rights law does not regulate their admission to foreign territories. Currently, climate change is not perceived as activating non-*refoulement* obligations through state-based complimentary protection mechanisms in domestic refugee law, normally triggered when the right to life and the right not to be subjected to cruel, inhuman or degrading treatment are threatened (Kolmannskog and Myrstad 2009; McAdam 2011, 2012).

Legal discussions on progressing environmental migration protection mechanisms have suggested the establishment of new conventions: internationally, in the form of a new UN convention for persons displaced by climate change both internally and across state borders (Hodgkinson and Young 2012); regionally, in the form of protection mechanisms such as those established in the European Union (EU),[3] the African Union (AU),[4] and in Latin America,[5] or nationally, as in the case of Finnish and Swedish legislation on temporary protection for people affected by serious environmental disruptions, or the Danish law that expands protection for victims and their families seeking humanitarian asylum from drought disasters (Leighton 2010: 6–7).

Contributions to this volume

Due to the diverse range of debates surrounding the concept of environmental migration and the diversity of actors in this organizational field, this book analyses organizational perspectives upon this topic from five different angles. The first part disentangles the 'Complex regime of environmental migration', the second part pays close attention to the 'Role of courts', followed by a third part that summarizes the 'Role of international organizations' including analyses of the main IOs in the field. The fourth part switches from an analytical perspective to 'The point of view of practitioners', highlighting the daily challenges encountered by international NGOs and IOs working on the topic of environmental migration. The fifth part focuses on 'The role of advocacy work' in the context of environmental migration outlining recent shifts in both discourse and related practices by epistemic communities and civil society organizations. The 'Conclusion' part summarizes the roles of the main actors in the environmental migration complex.

In Part 1, the two authors use differing theoretical lenses to discuss 'The complex regime of environmental migration' (Part 1). While Lars Thomann looks at the environmental migration concept from an international relations perspective to explain why IOs embrace this relatively new issue or not; Julia Blocher applies the concept of organizational fields within an intra-organizational approach to trace the issue of environmental migration and its institutional location within EU structures. Thomann concludes, after reviewing the ongoing negotiations for a post-2015 sustainable development agenda and a post-Kyoto climate change agreement, that environmental migration, at best, plays a minor role in both processes. He explains this situation with reference to realist, institutionalist and constructivist schools of international relations, pointing to differences in the distribution of power, interests and identities. Blocher argues in her analysis that responses towards the topic of environmental migration have been shaped by security actors within the EU. Despite this she has also observed a slow integration of the debates into the fields of climate change adaptation and development cooperation with third countries. Although the integration of the topic in the climate adaptation and development portfolios of the EU is still in its early stages, she evaluates this approach as 'a more promising avenue than through the EU's external migration and asylum policy'. Both authors therefore explore the range of discourse and policy opportunities that the debate on environmental migration entails.

The second pair of authors focus on 'The role of courts' (Part 2) within this complex regime of actors. While Charlotte Lülf focuses on the European Court of Human Rights and the European Court of Justice and their role as 'pacemakers for defining, redefining and potentially expanding climate refugee protection in European asylum laws', Thea Coventry analyses national courts and tribunals in the common law countries of New Zealand, Australia and Canada with regards to a possible expansion of the protection space within the still restrictive complementary protection regimes for displaced persons. Both authors analyse the strategies used by the courts to find legal solutions for the claims raised by people crossing international borders due to environmental or climate change-induced changes in their countries of origin. As the 1951 Refugee Convention and its 1967 Protocol are not applicable in these cases, issues of complimentary and subsidiary protection under international human rights law, EU asylum law and the EU qualification directive are comparatively assessed. Since an international law framework that recognizes state responsibility for persons displaced because of natural disasters or environmental degradation is not yet in place and not likely to develop in the near future, individual court cases, which generate public discussion and which might eventually influence governments' policy positions, remain the main source of legal analysis and legal development.

Part 3 of the book addresses 'The role of IOs' in the environmental migration discourse, presenting current case studies on UNHCR, IOM, and the International RC/RC Movement. Sinja Hantscher discusses UNHCR's role from the perspective of security studies. The frameworks of the Copenhagen school and the Paris school are used as a theoretical background to analyse how UNHCR as a humanitarian organization uses the language of securitization for environmental migrants. Dina Ionesco and Mariam Traore Chazalnoël describe the role of IOM in the international governance of environmental migration, tracing historic and recent developments within the organization as well as the challenges related to this endeavour. Kerstin Rosenow-Williams traces the developments within the International RC/RC Movement from an organizational sociology perspective. Humanitarians had to first learn how to position themselves towards this new challenge of environmental migration despite their long-term experience in the field of displacement and protection. She highlights both external and internal expectations as explanatory factors for the organization's position towards environmental migration as a humanitarian challenge. All four authors provide a detailed analysis of the recent developments in three IOs that have become central actors within the policy debates on environmental migration leading to increasing cooperation, as well as sometimes competing points of view that have influenced the discourses on this topic since the turn of the twenty-first century.

Part 4 of this volume introduces 'The point of view of practitioners', the views of NGOs and IOs in the field of environmental migration through the eyes of their representatives. These shorter opinion-based chapters are intended to provide an overview on the scale of arguments and practical organizational experiences that make up the complex regime of environmental migration. First, Lena Brenn from the Norwegian Refugee Council (NRC) reflects on the historic and current activities of the NRC in the context of disasters, climate change and environmental degradation. She also introduces the newly established links between the NRC and the Nansen Initiative on disaster-induced cross-border displacement. Second, Barbara Bendandi, Clara Crimella and Sven Walter outline a new partnership between the United Nations Convention to Combat Desertification (UNCCD) and IOM on 'addressing land, sustainable development and human mobility'. Their description of a pilot project on the land-migration nexus in West Africa sheds light on inter-agency cooperation benefits and practical challenges. Third, Alex Randall from the UK Migration and Climate Change Coalition discusses his perceptions on current discourses surrounding environmental migration from an activist position. He describes a deeply divided field of environmental activists including their diverse strategies and actions, along with opposing arguments raised by security actors. Fourth, Aminul Hoque presents an NGO point of view from Bangladesh on climate-induced migration. While presenting the position of the civil society organization EquityBD, he critically discusses the Bangladesh Climate Change Strategy and Action Plan, identifies protection gaps and makes recommendations for adopting new policies to protect environmental migrants.

Part 5 of the volume presents three chapters that extend the discussion on 'The role of advocacy work' to advance the topic of environmental migration from an organizational perspective. Innocent Chirisa and Elmond Bandauko present a case study on 'civil society advocacy and environmental migration in Zimbabwe'. Drawing on the concepts of public policy and spatial planning, the authors outline the tensions between the state's argument on equity, investment and employment creation with regard to environmental migration and displacement versus the concern of civil society organizations concerning the protection of the affected households and communities. In contrast to the situation in Zimbabwe, Sarah Nash argues in her global discourse analysis that a discursive turn towards environmental migration management has taken place within the environmental migration advocacy discourse. Migration is conceptualized in this discourse as a normal and potentially positive phenomenon and a potential climate change adaptation strategy in itself. However, although this discourse is gaining ground, the environmental migration management discourse has not directly replaced the securitized discourse on environmental migration. Nash also outlines other competing discourse and advocacy threats, for example, with regard to protection issues that are also discussed in Parts 2 and 3 of this volume. The third chapter by Angela Pilath introduces international epistemic communities (knowledge actors, such as academics and researchers representing universities, think tanks and research centres) as another important set of actors in the advocacy context of environmental migration. She thereby explores an understudied field concerning their influence on international politics and policy networks, as international epistemic communities have often been ignored by international relations. She shows in particular that these communities can be highly influential through expert authority and loyalty networks.

The final part of the volume on 'The actors involved in the environmental migration complex' brings together the main results of the volume and the current state-of-the-art research results on organizational perspectives on environmental migration. François Gemenne and Kerstin Rosenow-Williams discuss the role of various types of organizations in shaping the discourse on environmental migration, outlining their interaction processes, and their strategies to reach their targeted audiences, such as the general public, policy makers, migrants or other stakeholders both in the countries affected by environmental migration internally and destination countries worldwide.

Theoretical approaches to study the evolving landscape of actors

This volume brings together an interdisciplinary set of scholars along with practitioners from selected organizations. Theoretical approaches presented in the chapters range from political science, to sociology and international law. The variety of theoretical approaches used to study organizational perspectives on environmental migration can be attributed on the one hand to the scope of organizations – ranging from courts to civil society organizations, such as local NGOs or INGOs, to intergovernmental organizations such as the main IOs involved in the organizational field of migration; and on the other hand to the differing theoretical approaches applied to the research questions posed in each chapter. While political scientists ask about the role of coalitions between different actors within the realms of international relations, i.e. processes of (international) policy negotiation, organizational sociologists rather focus on internal dynamics taking place within an organization, which are, however, also influenced by external dynamics and changes in their organizational environment.

Legal scholars finally trace the current state-of-the-art within existing case law to distinguish trends for future jurisdiction on the issue.

In particular, the chapters in this volume use the following theoretical frameworks that can guide future research but also help us to understand the current status quo in the dynamic field of debate surrounding the topic of environmental migration.

Thomann compares the explanatory powers of the realist, institutionalist and constructivist schools of international relations when analysing the question why environmental migration, at best, plays a minor role in the post-2015 sustainable development agenda and a post-Kyoto climate change agreement. He comes to the following conclusion:

> Realists would argue that powerful states simply are not interested in pushing the concept further, unless it is framed in a manner that addresses their security concerns. Institutionalists in contrast would point to the distributional problems between migration sending and receiving countries, aggravating an institutional solution to effectively addressing environmental migration. Constructivist approaches could be viewed as the most 'realistic' as they would point to the need for further deliberations and arguing over the validity of the concept, on the basis of sound scientific evidence. All this leaves the question open of what would really be in the real and genuine interest of environmental migrants.
>
> (Thomann in this volume)

Blocher applies the concept of organizational fields to trace the issue of environmental migration and its institutional location within EU structures. She utilizes a neo-institutional perspective, following Baker and Faulkner (2005) who argue that the shape of fields may be deduced by examining the character and extent of organizations' involvement in particular interest areas. She concludes that policies on environmental migration have traditionally been shaped by security actors within the EU, followed by a slow integration of the debates into the fields of climate change adaptation and development cooperation with third countries.

> Relating back to our definition of organizational fields, a distinct separation between climate change actors and development actors is difficult to draw. It further cuts across EU bodies and incorporates external scholars and partners. The shape and extended reach of a unified field, which one may identify as the climate resilience field, is discernable.
>
> (Blocher in this volume)

Rosenow-Williams also applies an organizational sociology perspective. Combining literature on neo-institutionalism with Buchanan and Badham's definition of 'change agents' as 'any individual seeking to reconfigure an organization's roles, responsibilities, structures, outputs, processes, systems, technology, or other resources' (1999: 610) she examines both external and internal expectations as explanatory factors for her analysis of the advocacy work of the International RC/RC Movement on environmental migration as a humanitarian challenge.

> The analysis showed that the question, how humanitarian organizations address the topic of environmental migration, depends on the one hand, on individual actors within the organization and their perception of local needs and organizational capacities and on the other hand, on the overall discourse development at the national and international level which can have a decisive influence on both organizational projects and advocacy work.
>
> (Rosenow-Williams in this volume)

Sabatier and Jenkins-Smith (1993) had already shown how policy-making is determined by a wide range of stakeholders, organized in what they called 'advocacy coalitions'. They posited that researchers, experts, practitioners and NGOs were coalescing around common positions on policy issues, and working together to advance their positions. This volume has tried to show how a similar conclusion can be drawn from the perspectives of diverse organizations active with regard to the topic of environmental migration.

This development of common positions has become evident, as found in the four chapters provided in Part 4 on 'The point of view of practitioners', which outlines various types of coalitions. At the same time, these accounts also highlight opposing points of views, e.g. concerning environmental protection, climate justice, individual protection rights versus state sovereignty and security, or migration management approaches, and the migration-development context. These different points of view or organizational traditions can lead to conflicts between the advocacy coalitions and nation states, as well as between the advocacy coalitions themselves.

Part 5 on 'The role of advocacy work' also addresses the challenges of civil society organizations between efforts of cooperation and protest. Chirisa and Bandauko refer to the concepts of public policy and spatial planning when outlining the tensions between the state's argument on equity, investment and employment creation with regard to environmental migration and displacement versus the concern of civil society organizations concerning the protection of the affected households and communities. They conclude:

> Public policy and spatial planning can be used to an advantage instead of being misused, as seems to be the case in Zimbabwe. Spatial planning should ensure that before people are displaced, compensation and relocation plans are in place.
>
> (Chirisa and Bandauko in this volume)

In contrast to the situation in Zimbabwe, Nash shows in her global discourse analysis that a discursive turn towards environmental migration management has taken place within the environmental migration advocacy, although it has not yet replaced the dominant securitized discourse. Following the definition by Wodak and Fairclough, she argues that a discourse is 'constitutive both in the sense that it helps to sustain and reproduce the status quo, and in the sense that it contributes to transforming it' (1997: 258). The existing contradictions in the current debates are also apparent in her conclusion:

> Environmental migration is no longer a phenomenon to be avoided at all costs, but is perceived as normal and potentially positive. This signifies a distinct move away from the securitized discourse which has previously dominated [...]. However, it does not mean that there is complete discursive agreement among actors. Within academia, there is an emerging critical discourse in response to the environmental migration management discourse, and among actors having a specific protection mandate, there is still a focus on the protection regimes for forced migrants.
>
> (Nash in this volume)

Finally, Pilath addresses international epistemological organizations through the prism of epistemic community theory, which was first developed by Haas (1992). Through expert authority and loyalty networks, these organizations, such as *think tanks*, for example, manage to exert considerable influence in policy processes. Yet they are often overlooked in international relations theory. Pilath uses the case of UNU-EHS to show how its influence was crucial in the adoption of paragraph 14(f) of the Cancun Adaptation Framework, which formally recognizes migration as an adaptation strategy in the negotiations on climate change.

Who this volume is intended for

To date, very few studies have analysed the influence and rhetoric of advocacy groups in the debates on environmental migration, thus this contribution both addresses and closes an important research gap, as well as contributing to the debate on possible solutions for people being displaced by environmental or climate change-related factors. The book draws together and examines the related themes of climate change and environmental degradation, migration and organizational studies to provide a fresh perspective on their increasing relevance.

In addition, the interdisciplinary and geographically varied focus on this volume means it provides a broad and overarching perspective useful as a textbook for students, as well as a resource for both academic researchers and practitioners alike working in the areas of migration, development, environmental change, international law and related policy fields. Its interdisciplinary approach makes it suitable for a wide audience with differing levels of relevant knowledge. The volume's authors include both specialized researchers and expert staff from IOs and NGOs, while being written and formatted in an accessible language and style.

The topical introduction to the field of environmental migration, as well as the conclusion on the main actors involved in this policy field, provides important up-to-date guidance both to scholars interested in the topic as well as politicians and practitioners. While the book is valuable also for students at the master or doctoral level, it is also accessible to undergraduate students specializing in migration studies, environmental management, political science, international law or sociology. This overlap means the general area is both widely taught and researched, with the attention on environmental migration being very likely to increase even further over the next decade.

Notes

1   The three literature review chapters are based on Rosenow-Williams (2015, forthcoming).
2   'The Inter-Agency Standing Committee (IASC) is a unique inter-agency forum for coordination, policy development and decision-making involving the key UN and non-UN humanitarian partners. The IASC was established in June 1992 in response to United Nations General Assembly Resolution 46/182 on the strengthening of humanitarian assistance' (PreventionWeb n.d.).
3   The EU Council Directive 2001/55 provides temporary protection status in 'situations of a mass influx due to armed conflict and where the disruption prevents return to the country of origin or the persons would be subject to serious human rights violations and would not qualify otherwise under the 1951 Convention' (EU 2001).
4   The AU Convention for the Protection and Assistance of Internally Displaced Persons in Africa ('Kampala Convention') (AU 2009) recognizes that climate change may cause internal displacement and provides a detailed description of government obligations.
5   The 1969 Organization of African Unity (OAU) Convention (OAU 1969) and the Organization of American States (OAS) 1984 Cartagena Declaration (OAS 1984) have already extended refugee definitions, which include flight from aggression, conflict, situations seriously disturbing public order, generalized violence and massive human rights violations. These extended grounds provide significantly more definitional space for environmentally-induced displacement. The Cartagena Declaration is non-binding and has to be implemented in national laws. Cf. San José Declaration on Refugees and Displaced Persons (International Colloquium in Commemoration of the 'Tenth Anniversary of the Cartagena Declaration on Refugees' 1994) and Mexico Declaration and Plan of Action to Strengthen International Protection of Refugees in Latin America (OAS 2004).

References

Afifi, T. and Jäger, J. (2010) *Environment, forced migration and social vulnerability*. Berlin, Heidelberg: Springer.
African Union (AU) (2009) *African Union Convention for the Protection and Assistance of Internally Displaced Persons in Africa (Kampala Convention)* [online]. Adopted by the Special Summit of the Union held in Kampala, Uganda, 22 October 2009. Available: www.au.int/en/sites/default/files/AFRICAN_UNION_CONVENTION_FOR_THE_PROTECTION_AND_ASSISTANCE_OF_INTERNALLY_DISPLACED_PERSONS_IN_AFRICA_(KAMPALA_CONVENTION).pdf [Accessed 24 March 2014].
Baker, W.E. and Faulkner, R.R. (2005) Interorganizational networks. In *The Blackwell companion to organizations*, ed. J.A.C. Baum. Malden: Blackwell Publishing.

Boano, C., Zetter, R. and Morris, T. (2007) *Environmentally displaced people: understanding the linkages between environmental change, livelihoods and forced migration*. Oxford: Refugee Studies Centre.

Brown, O. and McLeman, R. (2013) Climate change and migration: an overview. In *The encyclopedia of global human migration*, ed. I. Ness. Oxford: Blackwell Publishers.

Buchanan, D. and Badham, R. (1999) Politics and organizational change: the lived experience. *Human Relations*. 52(5): 609–29.

Climate Service Center (CSC) (2013) *The Hamburg Conference Declaration* [online]. Available: www.hzg.de/imperia/md/content/csc/workshopdokumente/hamburgconfer ence/hamburg_declaration.pdf [Accessed 24 January 2015].

Drydyk, J. (2007) Unequal benefits: the ethics of development-induced displacement. *Georgetown Journal of International Affairs*. 8(1): 105–13.

El-Hinnawi, E. (1985) *Environmental refugees*. Nairobi: UNEP.

European Union (EU) (2001) Council directive 2001/55, 2001. *Official Journal* (O.J.) (L.212) 12 E.C.

Ferris, E. (2011) *Climate change and internal displacement: a contribution to the discussion*. Bern: Brookings Institution.

Ferris, E. (2012) *Protection and planned relocations in the context of climate change, legal and protection policy research series* [online]. Available: www.unhcr.org/5024d5169.html [Accessed 21 August 2014].

Ferris, E. (2013) *A complex constellation: displacement, climate change and Arctic peoples* [online]. Available: www.brookings.edu/~/media/Research/Files/Papers/2013/1/30%20 arctic%20ferris/30%20arctic%20ferris%20paper.pdf [Accessed 17 April 2014].

Ferris, E., Cernea, M. and Petz, D. (2011) *On the front line of climate change and displacement: learning from and with Pacific island countries* [online]. Available: www.brookings.edu/~/ media/research/files/reports/2011/9/idp%20climate%20change/09_idp_climate_ change.pdf [Accessed 17 April 2014].

Foresight (2011a) *Migration and global environmental change: future challenges and opportunities*. London: The Government Office for Science.

Foresight (2011b) *Migration and global environmental change: future challenges and opportunities*. Final project report: executive summary. London: The Government Office for Science.

Gemenne, F. (2011) Why the numbers don't add up: a review of estimates and predictions of people displaced by environmental changes. *Global Environmental Change: Human and Policy Dimensions*. 21(S1): S41–9.

Gemenne, F., Brücker, P. and Glasser, J. eds. (2011) *The state of environmental migration 2010*. Paris: IDDRI.

Haas, P.M. (1992) Epistemic Communities and International Policy Coordination. *International Organization*. 46(1): 1–35.

Hall, N. (2013) Moving beyond its mandate? UNHCR and climate change displacement. *Journal of International Organizations Studies*. 4(1): 91–108.

Hall, N. (forthcoming) A catalyst for cooperation? The Inter-Agency Standing Committee and the humanitarian response to climate change. *Global Governance*.

Hodgkinson, D. and Young, L. (2012) '*In the face of looming catastrophe*': *a convention for climate change displaced persons* [online]. Available: www.ccdpconvention.com/ documents/Climate%20change%20displacement%20treaty%20proposal.pdf [Accessed 2 February 2014].

Inter-Agency Standing Committee (IASC) (2008) *Climate change, migration and displacement: who will be affected?* [online]. Working paper submitted by the informal group on migration/ displacement and climate change of the IASC – 31 October 2008. Available: http://unfccc.int/resource/docs/2008/smsn/igo/022.pdf [Accessed 10 March 2015].

Inter-Agency Standing Committee (IASC) (2010) *Quick guide to climate change adaptation* [online]. Available: www.humanitarianinfo.org/iasc/downloaddoc.aspx?docID=5436& type=pdf [Accessed 16 April 2015].

Intergovernmental Panel on Climate Change (IPCC) (2014) *Climate change 2014: impacts, adaptation, and vulnerability. Summary for policymakers* [online]. WGII AR5 Phase I Report Launch 1, 31 March 2014. Available: https://ipcc-wg2.gov/AR5/images/ uploads/WG2AR5_SPM_FINAL.pdf [Accessed 10 March 2015].

International Colloquium in Commemoration of the 'Tenth Anniversary of the Cartagena Declaration on Refugees' (1994) *San Jose Declaration on Refugees and Displaced Persons: conclusions and recommendations* [online]. Adopted by the International Colloquium in Commemoration of the 'Tenth Anniversary of the Cartagena Declaration on Refugees', San José, 5–7 December 1994. Available: www.refworld.org/pdfid/4a54bc3fd.pdf [Accessed 29 March 2014].

International Federation of Red Cross and Red Crescent Societies (IFRC) (2012) *World disasters report 2012: focus on forced migration and displacement* [online]. Available: www. ifrcmedia.org/assets/pages/wdr2012/resources/1216800-WDR-2012-EN-FULL.pdf [Accessed 17 April 2014].

International Organization for Migration (IOM) (2007) *Discussion note: migration and the environment*. 94th session, Doc. No. MC/INF/288.

Kälin, W. and Schrepfer, N. (2012) *Protecting people crossing borders in the context of climate change: normative gaps and possible approaches* [online]. Legal and Protection Policy Research Series. Available: www.unhcr.org/4f33f1729.html [Accessed 17 April 2014].

Kolmannskog, V. (2008) *Future floods of refugees: a comment on climate change, conflict and forced migration* [online]. Available: www.nrc.no/arch/_img/9268480.pdf [Accessed 17 April 2014].

Kolmannskog, V. (2009a) *Climate change, disaster, displacement and migration: initial evidence from Africa* [online]. New Issues in Refugee Research Working Paper. Available: www.unhcr.org/4b18e3599.html [17 April 2014].

Kolmannskog, V. (2009b) The point of no return: exploring law on cross-border displacement in the context of climate change. *Refugee Watch*. 34: 28–41.

Kolmannskog, V. and Myrstad, F. (2009) Environmental displacement in European asylum law. *European Journal of Migration and Law*. 11(4): 313–26.

Kolmannskog, V. and Trebbi, L. (2010) Climate change, natural disasters and displacement: a multi-track approach to filling the protection gaps. *International Review of the Red Cross*. 92(879): 713–30.

Laczko, F. and Aghazarm, C. eds. (2009) *Migration, environment and climate change: assessing the evidence*. Geneva: International Organization for Migration.

Leighton, M. (2010) *Climate change and migration: key issues for legal protection of migrants and displaced persons* [online]. Available: www.ehs.unu.edu/file/get/7102 [Accessed 19 August 2011].

McAdam, J. (2011) *Climate change displacement and international law: complementary protection standards* [online]. Legal and Protection Policy Research Series. Available: www.unhcr.org/4dff16e99.html [Accessed 17 April 2014].

McAdam, J. (2012) *Climate change, forced migration, and international law*. Oxford: Oxford University Press.

McAdam, J. (2013) Creating new norms on climate change, natural disasters and displacement: international developments 2010–2013. *Refuge.* 29(2): 11–26.

Ministerial Communiqué (2011) *Intergovernmental event at the ministerial level of member states of the United Nations on the occasion of the 60th anniversary of the 1951 Convention relating to the Status of Refugees and the 50th anniversary of the 1961 Convention on the Reduction of Statelessness, 7–8 December 2011.* HCR/MINCOMMS/2011/6.

New Zealand High Court (NZHC) (2013) *Teitiota v. Chief Executive of the Ministry of Business, Innovation and Employment.* NZHC 3125.

Office of the United Nations High Commissioner for Human Rights (OHCHR) (2009) *Report of the Office of the United Nations High Commissioner for Human Rights on the relationship between climate change and human rights.* UN Doc. A/HRC/10/61.

Oliver-Smith, A. (2009) Sea level rise and the vulnerability of coastal peoples: responding to the local challenges of global climate change in the 21st century [online]. *Intersections.* (7). Available: http://d-nb.info/102969186X/34 [Accessed 6 February 2014].

Organization of African Unity (OAU) (1969) *OAU convention governing the specific aspects of refugee problems in Africa* [online]. Addis Ababa, 10 September 1969. UN Treaty Series No. 14691. Available: www.unhcr.org/45dc1a682.pdf [Accessed 16 April 2015].

Organization of American States (OAS) (1984) *Cartagena Declaration on Refugees* [online]. Colloquium on the international protection of refugees in Central America, Mexico and Panama. Available: www.oas.org/dil/1984_Cartagena_Declaration_on_Refugees. pdf [Accessed 16 April 2015].

Organization of American States (OAS) (2004) *Mexico declaration and plan of action to strengthen the international protection of refugees in Latin America* [online]. Mexico City, 16 November 2004. Available: www.oas.org/dil/mexico_declaration_plan_of_action_16nov2004.pdf [Accessed 29 March 2014].

PreventionWeb (n.d.) *Inter-Agency Standing Committee (IASC): organization profile* [online]. Available: www.preventionweb.net/english/professional/contacts/profile. php?id=2747 [Accessed 25 August 2014].

Rasmusson, E. (2009) *Climate changed: people displaced.* Oslo: Norwegian Refugee Council.

Renaud, F.G., Dun, O., Warner, K. and Bogardi, J. (2011) A decision framework for environmentally induced migration. *International Migration.* 49(S1): e5–29.

Rosenow-Williams, K. (2015, forthcoming) Environmental migration as a humanitarian challenge. In *From Cold War to Cyber War. The evolution of the International Law of Peace and Armed Conflict over the last 25 years,* eds. H.-J. Heintze and P. Thielbörger. Baden Baden: Springer: 87-104.

Sabatier, P.A. and Jenkins-Smith, H.C. (1993) *Policy change and learning: an advocacy coalition approach.* Boulder: Westview Press.

The Nansen Initiative (2014a) *About us* [online]. Available: www2.nanseninitiative.org/ secretariat/ [Accessed 18 February 2014].

The Nansen Initiative (2014b) *Strategic framework and work plan 2014–15: Nansen Initiative* [online]. Version 29 January 2014. Available: www.nanseninitiative.org/sites/default/ files/Nansen%20Initiative%20Work%20Plan%202014%20%2829%20January%20 2014%29.pdf [Accessed 11 February 2014].

United Nations (UN) (2004) *Guiding principles on internal displacement.* Geneva: United Nations.

United Nations Environment Programme (UNEP) (2012) *Livelihood security: climate change, migration and conflict in the Sahel.* Châtelaine, Geneva: UNEP.

United Nations Framework Convention on Climate Change (UNFCCC) (2010) *Report of the conference of the parties on its sixteenth session, held in Cancun from 29 November to 10 December 2010.* UNFCC/CP/2010/7/Add.1.

United Nations General Assembly (UNGA) (1966a) *International Covenant on Civil and Political Rights, opened for signature 16 December 1966,* 999 UNTS 171 (entered into force 23 March 1976).

United Nations General Assembly (UNGA) (1966b) *International Covenant on Economic, Social and Cultural Rights, 16 December 1966,* 993 UNTS 3 (entered into force 3 January 1976).

United Nations High Commissioner for Refugees (UNHCR) (2008) *Climate change, natural disasters and human displacement: a UNHCR perspective* [online]. Final version: 23 October 2008. Available: www.unhcr.org/4901e81a4.html [Accessed 19 February 2014].

United Nations High Commissioner for Refugees (UNHCR) (2009a) *Forced displacement in the context of climate change: challenges for states under international law* [online]. Available: www.unhcr.org/4a1e4d8c2.html [Accessed 17 April 2014].

United Nations High Commissioner for Refugees (UNHCR) (2009b) *Climate change and statelessness: an overview* [online]. Available: www.unhcr.org/4a1e50082.html [Accessed 17 April 2014].

United Nations High Commissioner for Refugees (UNHCR) (2010) *Convention and protocol relating to the status of refugees.* Geneva: UNHCR.

United Nations High Commissioner for Refugees (UNHCR) (2011) *Expert meeting on complementarities between international refugee law, international criminal law and international human rights law: summary conclusions.* Geneva: UNHCR.

United Nations High Commissioner for Refugees (UNHCR) (2014) *Global trends 2013* [online]. Available: www.unhcr.org/5399a14f9.html [Accessed 25 July 2014].

Warner, K., Ehrhart, C., de Sherbinin, A., Adamo, S. and Chai-Onn, T. (2009) *In search of shelter: mapping the effects of climate change on human migration and displacement* [online]. Available: www.careclimatechange.org/files/reports/CARE_In_Search_of_Shelter.pdf [Accessed 25 August 2014].

Warner, K., Afifi, T., Henry, K., Rawe, T., Smith, C. and de Sherbinin, A. (2012) *Where the rain falls: climate change, food and livelihood security, and migration.* Bonn: United Nations University and CARE.

Warner, K., Afifi, T., Kälin, K., Leckie, S., Ferris, B., Martin, S.F. and Wrathall, D. (2013) Changing climate moving people: framing migration, displacement and planned relocation [online]. *Policy Brief.* (8). Available: www.ehs.unu.edu/file/get/11213.pdf [Accessed 5 March 2014].

Williams, A. (2008) Turning the tide: recognizing climate change refugees in international law. *LAW & POLICY.* 30: 502–29.

Wodak, R. and Fairclough, N. (1997) Critical discourse analysis. In *Discourse as social interaction,* ed. T.A. van Dijk. London: Sage.

World Bank (2013) *Turn down the heat: climate extremes, regional impacts, and the case for resilience* [online]. Available: www.worldbank.org/en/topic/climatechange/publication/turn-down-the-heat-climate-extremes-regional-impacts-resilience [Accessed 11 March 2015].

Part 1

The complex regime of environmental migration

2 Environmental migration

A concept between complexes and complexities

Lars Thomann

Introduction

One way of studying how international organizations treat and deal with the concept of environmental migration is by having a closer look at what international relations scholars have to say about the role, causes and effects of international organizations. International organizations and international regimes are international institutions characterized by principles, norms and rules that set common standards for converging states' behaviour around a given issue area. Whereas regimes typically are issue-specific, international organizations in contrast act beyond the boundaries of a given topic. In addition, international regimes merely provide behavioural guidelines without exerting any actor qualities of their own; international organizations and their bodies in contrast act on their own, for instance when passing judgment on a particular state behaviour (Rittberger *et al.* 2013: 20). Taking a step back and viewing the world from different perspectives of international relations theory, allows us to better understand how new issues and topics such as environmental migration emerge, diffuse and eventually enter the international political agenda. But it also helps us to gain a fuller picture of what actually drives the behaviour of international organizations, and to what extent they exert actor qualities of their own.

Realist accounts, for example, view international organizations as epiphenomenal to state power, without, however, denying that international organizations can play a useful role in joint problem solving (Waltz 1979). For most realists international organizations merely reflect the interests of the most powerful states when setting common standards and do not exert any actor qualities of their own. Institutionalist approaches, on the other hand, perceive commonly with realists that states play an important role in international relations, but at the same time view international institutions as a crucial instrument in achieving 'cooperation under anarchy' (Axelrod and Keohane 1985; Oye 1985) by shaping and changing states' preferences and interests through making defection costly and providing incentives for cooperating. In the view of constructivist scholars, international organizations, together with non-state actors and epistemic communities, play an important role in shaping and framing normative beliefs of state actors, as well as serve for the internalization of new norms (Finnemore and Sikkink 1998).

Environmental migration is a fairly new concept, and arguably the concept exhibits a certain degree of fuzziness: to start with, a clear-cut definition is missing, stemming from the fact that causal linkages between migration and environmental degradation as a consequence of climate change are hard to establish, and individual migration decisions are also driven by other factors. Environmental migration combines and merges environmental and migration related issues that so far have been dealt with separately in international policy making and norm setting (Dun and Gemenne 2008). Moreover, environmental migration actually lies between the two regimes'complexes of migration and climate change, making coherent norm implementation and application all the more difficult. Norm entrepreneurs – meaning those interested in changing existing or developing new social norms – that advocate environmental migration come from different institutional backgrounds and have diverse understandings of its meaning and scope. Most of all, advocates of environmental migration have often diverging agendas in mind when pushing the concept: some view the issue from a humanitarian angle and call for increased international legal protection of environmental migrants; others make a case for deepened environmental protection and climate change mitigation efforts; again others view environmental migration mainly as a security issue, calling for tighter migration controls (see Mayer 2014). The purpose of this present chapter is to review the institutional framework surrounding environmental migration with a view to the question of how international governmental organizations treat the concept.

International migration is an issue area which by its nature should demand international cooperation if joint problem solving were the common aim of policy makers of destination and origin countries alike. States have, however, so far refrained from really cooperating on a global scale, leaving migration issues, including environmental migration, being dealt with by more or less weakly linked institutions without hierarchical rules, and a highly fragmented international regulatory framework (GCIM 2005: 66). The lack of a coherent and comprehensive international migration regulatory framework is all the more astonishing given that by the end of 2013, there were 232 million international migrants, i.e., foreign born or foreign citizens, with almost 59 per cent of these living in developed regions (UN 2013: 1). At the same time, 51.2 million people were forcibly displaced, 6 million more than in 2012. Refugees account for 16.7 million people worldwide, asylum seekers for 1.1 million people, and internally displaced, people forced to flee to other parts of their own country, account for 33.3 million people (UNHCR 2014: 5). The numbers show that the largest number of international migrants are outside their place of origin due to reasons other than forcible displacement, on the other hand, the number of forcibly displaced people is the highest since the end of World War II, mostly due to recent conflicts in Syria, but also the Central African Republic, Colombia and South Sudan. The distinction between voluntary and forced movements of people is important as it has different repercussions for international legal protection (Kälin and Schrepfer 2012: 29). We, however, have a much less clearer picture when it comes to estimating the extent to which migration is actually environmentally induced. Indeed, projections on future environmentally-induced migration patterns vary so greatly that the only reliable proposition we can make is to point to the need for better and more detailed data on the causes, extent and consequences of environmental migration (Brown 2008). Further complications arise from the complex process of isolating environmental drivers from other migration causes, which is most often a combination of different factors.

The causes of environmental migration are most often associated with the effects of anthropogenic climate change. Again, international collaboration is crucial for mitigating climate change impacts, and as a truly global commons problem, effective outcomes will not be achieved if individual actors advance their interests independently of others. Collective action with regard to climate change mitigation and adaptation faces several problems: the actors involved hold diverse perceptions of the costs and benefits of collective action; sources of emission are unevenly distributed; the impacts of climate change are uncertain and distant in space and time; and mitigation costs vary across regions and actors. Although the United Nations Framework Convention on Climate Change (UNFCCC) is specifically designed to serve as a universal and comprehensive regulatory framework for the diverse aspects of climate change, it rather functions as an umbrella and forum, in which states discuss and negotiate (de Coninck and Bäckstrand 2011). Increasingly other institutions at global, regional, national and local levels have emerged, together with public–private initiatives and transnational networks. From a functional point of view, problems and issues associated with regulating climate change are so diverse 'that a single institutional response is exceptionally difficult to organize' (Keohane and Victor 2010: 14).

Two important international policy processes are likely to shape the international development framework over the next decade(s): the negotiations of a post-2015 sustainable development agenda, replacing the Millennium Development Goals (MDGs) after 2015, and negotiations of a new climate change agreement, replacing the Kyoto Protocol whose commitment period will end in 2020. Both policy processes are likely to have considerable impact on the future of the environmental migration concept, in terms of its definition, its content and its application in practice. Thus, the post-2015 Sustainable Development Goal (SDG) agenda, as well as the climate change regime negotiations offer the opportunity to observe a possible norm cascade of environmental migration emerging, meaning the formation, diffusion and internalization of new international norms. The chapter is structured as follows: firstly, theories of international relations, namely realism, institutionalism and constructivism are discussed with a view to their explanations and interpretations of the rise and effects of international organizations. Next, the discussions of the post-2015 SDG agenda and the climate change negotiations are analysed to assess the extent that environmental migration has become an emerging norm in these policy processes and regime complexes. It follows an explanation for the institutional fragmentation with regard to environmental migration, and an analysis of the possible prospect of a norm cascade taking place in the before mentioned policy arenas. Eventually, this can guide pundits of environmental migration to better understand the institutional context in which discussions of the concept take place.

Do they make a difference? Theoretical views on the role of international organizations

Putting the environmental migration concept into practice relates closely with general problems of global governance, such as the under-provision of key policy areas with global public goods, contrasted to the inordinate proliferation of standards and regulations, and the fragmentation and dispersion of regulatory systems over different organizations and regimes (Habermas 1998; Held 1999). International relations scholars have long discussed the effects of international institutions and international collaboration on state preferences and behaviour. The three main schools of thought – realism, liberal institutionalism and constructivism – have also been described as power-, interest- and knowledge-based approaches to explaining the evolution and function of international institutions (Hasenclever *et al.* 1997). The three schools hold different interpretations of how and why new issues, such as environmental migration, emerge on the international agenda, and which role and function international organizations have to this effect. Thus, international relations theories are useful tools for understanding when and why international organizations take up and discuss new topics, if and how they bring these forward, and why in certain cases international collaboration on new subjects remains weak and fragmented.

Realism is a power-based theory, which seeks to explain the establishment of international organizations in an anarchical and non-hierarchical world with the distribution of state power and material interests. States are unitary and rational actors that subordinate international organizations and international norm setting to their sovereignty, power and interests (Mearsheimer 1994/1995; Waltz 1979). Hegemonic stability theory, a refinement of realist approaches, stipulates that hegemons who hold a preponderance of power are crucial actors for establishing and maintaining international regimes that further their interests in specific issue areas in order to maintain a stable order. The hegemonic power enforces rules and regulations, but regimes decline when power is more equally distributed among its members (Gilpin 1987; Krasner 1976; Snidal 1985). According to realists, international regimes and organizations reflect the overall distribution of power and capabilities in the international system – regulatory outcomes merely reflect the interests and preferences of the most powerful actors. Thus, environmental migration will play a prominent role on the agenda of international organizations, if the topic converges with the interests and preferences of the most powerful states, who will also decide on the institutional location of where to discuss and negotiate the issue.

Liberal institutionalism is an interest-based theory that stresses the importance of international institutions as arenas of joint problem solving of collective action problems. International organizations serve a functional need of states to provide global public goods in an increasingly interdependent world. In contrast to realist accounts, institutionalism argues that power alone is not decisive, but that rules, norms and institutions affect the behaviour of states. Institutions are not necessarily understood as organizations with buildings, administrations or budget; they rather refer to customs and practices aimed at achieving common goals. Even powerful states seek collaboration due to reasons of efficiency and legitimacy (Abbott and Snidal 1998; Keohane 1984; Young 1997). Typical obstacles to international cooperation for solving collective action problems include actor insecurity over the commitment of other actors, the unequal distribution of costs and benefits of cooperation and the attractiveness of free-riding. International regimes instead allow norm-based cooperation in specific issue areas by providing information through monitoring, and by defining defection and prescribing sanctions for defection, thereby reducing the fear that states are being exploited by others. International institutions reduce regulatory ambiguities and transaction costs. The likelihood of future cooperation is increased by creating iteration and thus reducing the costs of future agreements through institutionalized cooperation (Axelrod 1984; Keohane and Nye 1977; Oye 1986). Although most migration flows (still) take place internally, one can nevertheless consider environmental migration as an international phenomenon, given that the main causes of environmental degradation, for instance through climate change, are found beyond the borders of affected countries. As an international phenomenon, environmental migration lends itself to an institutionalized solution in which states seek to find common rules and regulations within an international organization or regime for solving this particular collective action problem. The effectiveness of any international institution is closely linked to its design (Koremenos *et al.* 2001). For instance, increased membership expands the breadth of an agreement, however, increased numbers of actors also reduce efficiency in terms of finding an agreement in the first place. More regime members are likely to increase the possibility of diverging preferences, so that any agreement is likely to be shallow, reflecting the lowest common denominator. On the other hand, a broad scope of issues covered may even facilitate cooperation by providing opportunities for issue linkages (Martin 1994).

Recently the institutionalist school has been developed further, now addressing the issue of regime complexes, which is not a hierarchical, integrated and comprehensive regulatory regime but rather a loose set of coupled regimes and institutional efforts that exist as regime complexes (Keohane and Victor 2010). Institutionalists speak of international regime complexity when nested, partially overlapping and parallel international regimes exist that are not hierarchically ordered. The lack of any overarching hierarchy makes it difficult to resolve the question of whether a particular issue should be authoritatively dealt with (Alter and Meunier 2009). Institutions serve to create rule-based rather than power-based outcomes because 'in general, greater institutionalization implies that institutional rules govern more of the behaviour of important actors' (Goldstein *et al.* 2001: 3). In the case of environmental migration, we see that the issue is spread over a range of different governmental and non-governmental international and regional organizations. Deliberations on environmental migration take place between two already existing regime complexes, one on climate change and the other one on migration, adding to the overall complexity of addressing environmental migration.

Constructivism is a knowledge-based theory that stresses the evolution of norms, discourses, identity, knowledge and values, and emphasizes the role of non-state actors, scientific (epistemic) communities and civil society (Haas 1990). Constructivists consider international norms as intersubjective conceptions of appropriate behaviour that shape international cooperation, with norm entrepreneurs (Finnemore and Sikkink 1998) transforming the interests and preferences of governments by setting into motion a norm cascade, understood as a shift towards the adoption and acceptance of new norms (Sunstein 1996). Institutions are systems of norms, being collective standards of appropriate behaviour on the basis of given identities. Institutions are ideas that alter behaviour of actors through socialization and learning – following a logic of appropriateness. 'Players' in international relations not only exchange moves and information on preferences, they have the possibility to communicate and argue over validity claims (Risse 2000). In this view the evolution of international regimes, treaties and organizations cannot be only explained by power capabilities or state interests but by normative and discursive shifts, where scientific knowledge plays a pivotal role in framing uncertainty and presenting new scientific evidence for policy makers.

> The vast majority of states today see themselves as part of a 'society of states' whose norms they adhere to not because of on-going self-interested calculations that it is good for them as individual states, but because they have internalized and identify with them.
>
> (Wendt 1999: 242)

In the constructivist view, norm entrepreneurs – state and non-state actors alike – are engaged in a normative discourse on the validity of the environmental migration concept. The discourse is not only shaped by scientific evidence and knowledge but also by identities prescribing what is considered appropriate behaviour. Eventually, a norm cascade is set into motion, and states accept and internalize the concept of environmental migration as a common standard of behaviour.

Environmental migration and its institutional context

In this section the institutional framework surrounding environmental migration will be reviewed with a view to the question of how international governmental organizations treat the concept. Mayer (2014) distinguished four different normative enterprises with regard to environmental migration, each of which are advocated by different norm entrepreneurs. Environmental migration as an issue of international assistance is promoted by United Nations (UN) agencies (e.g., United Nations Development Programme, UNDP), international development agencies (World Bank, Asian Development Bank) and various non-governmental organizations (NGOs) (CARE International, Christian Aid). The protection of forced migrants is promoted by academics as well as the United Nations High Commissioner for Refugees (UNHCR) and the International Organization for Migration (IOM). Environmental migration viewed in the context of arguments about environmental sustainability is promoted by academics, environmental NGOs and some international institutions such as the United Nations Environment Programme (UNEP) or the UNFCCC. The last normative enterprise views environmental migration as a security issue, and is promoted by think tanks, international institutions, namely the UN Security Council, researchers, as well as industrial lobbies.

Out of the plethora of different institutional locations for deliberating on environmental migration, two have been chosen for the purpose of this chapter: the first are the negotiations of a post-2015 sustainable development agenda to replace the MDGs; the second is the negotiation of a new climate change agreement under the auspices of the UNFCCC to replace the Kyoto Protocol after its second commitment period ends in 2020. These processes have been selected because both will shape the international development framework over the next decade(s). Although not a normative, but rather an operational instrument, the MDGs have already had considerable influence on national and international development policy agendas, whether or not one considers the achievements of the MDGs so far to be a success story (Clemens *et al.* 2007; Fukuda-Parr *et al.* 2013). Whatever form the new SDGs will take, and which specific goals and targets will be included, it is likely that they will shape the work of international institutions within and outside the UN system. The same holds true for negotiations of a new climate change agreement, given the overall importance climate change plays on international policy agendas already. Given the prominence of both policy processes, it is worthwhile analysing the extent to which they address environmental migration, in terms of its definition, its content and its application in practice. In this sense, the post-2015 SDG agenda and the climate change regime negotiations offer the opportunity to observe a possible norm cascade of environmental migration emerging.

The post-2015 Sustainable Development Goals

Considerable work has been undertaken within the UN and its system over the past years in elaborating a new international development agenda, serving as the successor of the MDGs, whose target date is 2015. The outcome of the negotiations of the so-called post-2015 SDGs will determine the development priorities of the international community, and will also influence the way development cooperation is structured by addressing questions of development effectiveness, financing and accountability. Although it is still open as to which specific outcomes, concrete targets and indicators will be included in the SDGs, preliminary observations on the general direction of the negotiations can nevertheless be drawn on the basis of published negotiation documents.

The SDG process started in 2012 with the Rio+20 Conference and in early 2013 an Open Working Group (OWG) of the UN General Assembly commenced its work, presenting its report in July 2014 (UN 2014a). By the end of 2014 the UN Secretary-General presented a synthesis report on principles, goals and targets of possible SDGs.[1] Whereas the early phase of the SDG process has seen considerable input from non-state actors (gathered around so called major groups), as well as from other UN entities, the second phase is characterized by increased member state influence. With its universal membership, developing countries have considerable influence in UN decision making, albeit only in the form of UN General Assembly declarations, the most likely form of the new SDGs. However, as the implementation of the SDGs will be linked to more general questions of development cooperation, such as aid effectiveness and financing, it is the donor community, thus developed countries, that will play the key role. In its report, the OWG proposed a set of 17 different SDGs, each accompanied by a set of targets and indicators but with varying degrees of measurability and specificity. In comparison to the MDGs, which encompassed eight goals, the SDGs are much broader in scope. According to the OWG the SDGs 'seek to complete the unfinished business of the MDGs and respond to new challenges', with targets 'defined as aspirational global targets, with each Government setting its own national targets guided by the global level of ambition, but taking into account national circumstances' (UN 2014a: para. 18). However, the list of proposed SDGs is tentative, and the specific outcomes will depend on the ability of groups of like-minded states to articulate and negotiate their preferences for the post-2015 development agenda.

With regard to the concept of environmental migration, two specific goals of the proposed SDGs are of interest. One is goal 13, which reads 'Take urgent action to combat climate change and its impacts', accompanied by an asterisk stating 'Acknowledging that the UNFCCC is the primary international, intergovernmental forum for negotiating the global response to climate change'. The climate change goal is accompanied by five different targets; three of these (13.1 to 13.3) refer in a rather general manner to strengthening resilience, integrating climate change in national policies and improving education and capacity on climate change mitigation and adaptation. Target 13.a makes reference to the commitment undertaken by developed-country parties to the UNFCCC to the goal of jointly mobilizing US$100 billion annually by 2020 to address the needs of developing countries. A last target, also in a very general manner, calls for promoting mechanisms for raising the capacity for effective climate change-related planning and management in the least developed countries, focusing on women, youth and local and marginalized communities. Thus, the climate change SDG 13 is seemingly situated in an unsuitable location to integrate environmental migration as a concept. The goal and its targets are formulated in such a general manner, that almost anything could be placed under this heading – environmental migration could, for instance, fall under mitigation and adaptation measures. In any case, this would still leave the interpretation and application of the concept in practice in the hands of national policy makers, without any international guidance.

Migration as an overall topic is not included in a stand-alone goal within the set of proposed SDGs. It is however, mentioned under goal 10 'Reduce inequality within and among countries', which consists of ten different targets relating to socio-economic inequalities, again with varying degrees of specificity and clarity. Target 10.7 calls to 'Facilitate orderly, safe, regular and responsible migration and mobility of people, including through the implementation of planned and well-managed migration policies'. No mention is made of any international framework, not to speak of international cooperation. Thus, again, the focus for implementing target 10.7 would be left to national policy makers, however, without any measurable benchmark provided. In addition, the target clearly emphasizes regular migration, supposedly as opposed to unregulated, dangerous, or irregular migration. However, for the majority of migrants worldwide – voluntary or forced – regular migration channels rarely exist, if at all, leaving them with irregular migration channels as their only option. Thus, the context of target 10.7 also does not seem suitable for addressing environmental migration, due to the fuzziness and lack of clarity, its clear focus on national policy making and the lack of any measurable specific target against which actions could be monitored. Actually, one could say that target 10.c is a non-target, as states could easily subsume the current status quo under it, without having to engage in any specific policy measures aimed at facilitating environmental migration. Further, specific is target 10.c, which proposes to reduce by 2030, 'to less than 3 per cent the transaction costs of migrant remittances and eliminate remittance corridors with costs higher than 5 per cent'. This very specific proposal actually has its roots in an initiative brought forward by Australia and Canada to the G20 to create an innovative financing mechanism to reduce the cost of migrants' remittances (G20 2014). Although such an initiative would actually reduce profits for remittance sending institutions, almost all of which are based in developed countries, considerable additional financial resources could be leveraged, which would add to ODA in developing countries. Therefore, it is actually not unlikely that target 10.c will make it into the final set of SDGs as developed countries could with little regulatory effort achieve this target. However, the link to environmental migration is again rather weak at best, as costs of remittances typically play a role at the end of the migration process, when the migrant has safely arrived at the country of destination and has found a job.

Overall, the post-2015 SDG framework in its present form is very vague and unspecific both on climate change and migration. It is thus a rather unlikely institutional location, in which deliberations of environmental migration issues will play more than a marginal role in the forthcoming negotiations of the final set of SDGs. Interestingly, none of the major groups and stakeholders proposed any significant changes to the proposed set of SDGs – environmental migration seems to have been a non-issue, and even just the issue of migration alone was left more or less in its current form (UN 2014b). On the other hand, the proposed SDGs are broader in scope regarding included issues than are the MDGs, whose eight targets do not make any specific reference to migration or climate change.[2]

Climate change

Climate change will remain high on the international agenda. As well as the Kyoto Protocol, parties to the UNFCCC have agreed to further commitments, which are included in the Bali Action Plan (2007), the Copenhagen Accord (2009), the Cancún agreements (2010), and the Durban Platform for Enhanced Action (2012). In 2011, parties adopted the 'Durban Platform for Enhanced Action', agreeing to 'develop a protocol, another legal instrument or an agreed outcome with legal force under the Convention applicable to all Parties' (UNFCCC 2012). The new treaty is to be adopted at the twenty-first Conference of Parties (COP21) in Paris in late 2015, with its implementation starting after 2020. The climate change negotiation process was accompanied by presentations of the Assessment Reports of the Intergovernmental Panel on Climate Change (IPCC), the expert body providing the scientific evidence on climate change guiding the negotiation process. The IPCC synthesis report/approved summary for policy makers states that 'climate change is projected to increase displacement of people (medium evidence, high agreement)' and that:

> populations that lack the resources for planned migration experience higher exposure to extreme weather events, particularly in developing countries with low income. Climate change can indirectly increase risks of violent conflicts by amplifying well-documented drivers of these conflicts such as poverty and economic shocks (medium confidence).
>
> (IPCC 2014)

Thus, although it is acknowledged that climate change is likely to impact migration patterns in the future, the degree of these impacts are not quantified, meaning neither alarmist nor sceptics (Mayer 2014) in the debate about environmental migration are confirmed.

The first time environmental migration played a role in the negotiations was in November 2010 in Cancún (COP16). The outcome document of the Ad-hoc Working Group on Long-term Cooperative Action under the Convention invites states to take '[m]easures to enhance understanding, coordination and cooperation with regard to climate change induced displacement, migration and planned relocation, where appropriate, at the national, regional and international levels' (UNFCCC 2010). Parties also adopted the Cancún Adaptation Framework (CAF) for enhancing action on adaptation, including through international cooperation. The implementation of the framework mainly relies on information sharing on adaptation measures taken, capacity building for formulating national adaptation programmes of actions and plans, and providing finance, technology and capacity-building to implement adaptation projects at local, national, sub-regional and regional levels. For that purpose the Adaptation Committee was established, and (insufficient) funding provided (UNFCCC 2013). Apart from the Cancún Adaptation Framework, environmental migration has not played so far a significant role in the negotiations of a new climate change agreement. Thus, the topic falls under soft governance functions performed by the UNFCCC – regulatory developments addressing the topic are not yet in sight. Activities are restricted to information sharing, awareness raising and capacity-building, information provision, and financing projects on climate change adaptation and mitigation. In addition, these activities unfold in the context of national adaptation plans and actions (UNFCCC 2014b), addressed in least developed countries (LDCs), which may or may not include environmental migration issues.

This section has shown that in none of the institutional frameworks reviewed, environmental migration plays more than a marginal role. In the case of the post-2015 SDG agenda, migration is mentioned in such vague and ambiguous terms, that any meaningful action to fulfil the related target can be ruled out. The same holds true for climate change-related goals and targets mentioned in the proposed SDGs. Environmental migration, however, has also only played a marginal role in the climate change negotiations, here only in terms of soft modes of governance, leaving strict control over the issue in the hands of states. Despite progress achieved at the COP20 in Lima in December 2014 (UNFCCC 2014a), it still remains unclear whether there will be an agreement (and most of all in what form) at the end of the climate change negotiation process. In case there is no agreement, the question after COP21 will be whether negotiations are to continue or not. In case the answer is no, those states in favour of an agreement might opt for a more pluri-national and/or regional approach. The question would be to what extent such regional approaches would be based on the provisions of the UNFCCC and its accompanying Kyoto Protocol. In case there is an agreement, existing mitigation and adaptation measures as set forth in the Kyoto Protocol are likely to be intensified, possibly with more funding available. The findings of this section raise the question why the environmental migration concept is treated so marginally in both the SDGs and the climate change negotiations. The next part will address this question by applying international relations theories to the discussions of the environmental migration concept.

Explaining institutional fragmentation of environmental migration

Why is international collaboration on the topic of (environmental) migration so fragmented? And where organizations have picked up the topic, why are soft governance functions predominant? According to realists, international institutions reflect the interests of dominant states and do not influence the behaviour and preferences of sovereign states. International organizations are not independent from state power but rather further the interests of the most powerful states. Following the realist perspective, migration policies remain in the firm hands of national policy making, even in politically highly integrated institutions like the European Union. Realists also claim that international organizations remain neutral on genuinely new topics, particularly in an institutional context that requires consensus. Environmental migration is a new topic: negotiating any regulatory framework within the context of the post-2015 agenda or the climate change negotiations, that both require consensus for reaching agreements, is already difficult without the inclusion of new concepts. The negotiations already include a wide range of contentious topics, and any inclusion of additional issues would make reaching an agreement less likely. Even if a different institutional location were sought to include environmental migration in its regulatory framework, for instance a revision of the 1951 Geneva Convention, or adopting a whole new Protocol would be almost equally difficult. Powerful states, which are destination countries for many migrants, would most likely postpone or delay such negotiations. Even if an agreement were reached, ratification of such an instrument by powerful, destination countries would be more than unlikely. Thus, from a realist perspective it is not surprising at all that environmental migration plays hardly any role in the post-2015 and climate change negotiations.

Realists, moreover, argue that international organizations lack teeth in enforcement and regulatory powers because states are not willing to give up core governance functions. And indeed, in the field of migration most international organizations are mainly engaged in soft governance functions such as information sharing, studies, workshops, and capacity building, and to a much lesser extent in the deliberation and adoption of new norms and regulations. International hard law (Snidal and Abbott 2000) in the field of migration is confined to the Geneva Convention on the protection of refugees, adopted in the aftermath of World War II and its massive migration movements, and the International Labour Organization (ILO) Conventions Nos. 97 and 143 on Migrant Workers. The Geneva Convention was almost universally accepted and set forth minimum standards for the treatment of refugees and asylum seekers, thus forced migrants. The ILO instruments set minimum standards for migrant workers, but are much less accepted as the rather low ratification records for both Conventions show.[3] It is however questionable, whether the scope of application of this hard law on international migration includes environmental migrants at all. Thus, in areas that touch upon national security and sovereignty, such as migration, states are not willing to give up power and delegate it to international institutions. A similar situation exists regarding climate change where the most contentious issues in the negotiations are the degree and scope of legal obligations of member states. From a realist perspective, the scarcity of deep and broad agreements on international migration and climate change, gives reason to doubt that a regulatory framework on environmental migration will be adopted. Many arguments brought forward by proponents of the environmental migration concept, particularly those emphasizing the humanitarian assistance and environmental sustainability are idealistic and conflict with hard interests of powerful states, who seem to favour a securitization of the issue. Conflicting positions and preferences, however, tend to maintain the status quo in the post-2015 and climate change negotiations, given the difficulties in finding a common ground and collaborating on a common agenda.

The core argument of the institutionalist perspective is the functional need for coordination in jointly solving collective action problems. Addressing climate change is a truly collective action problem, in which costs and benefits of cooperation are unequally distributed and free-riding is attractive. The situation is further complicated by the 'common but differentiated responsibilities and respective capabilities' approach, set forth in Article 3 of the UNFCCC, according to which the obligations and costs of reducing current emissions are placed on developed countries given their historical responsibility for current levels of greenhouse gases in the atmosphere. An international climate change agreement that is effective requires almost universal participation – at least of major greenhouse gas emitting states. The inclusion of developing countries and those in transition in reduction obligations is, however, a highly conflictive issue in the negotiations. Agreeing on legally binding and institutionalized commitments is even more ambitious with a large membership, and consensual decision making. Although the two largest emitters – the US and China – have shown a willingness to compromise at COP20 in Lima, it is far from clear to what extent they will accept a legally binding agreement that imposes deep reduction commitments. The most likely scenario, following the rational design logic of institutionalism, given the broad membership base, is either a legally binding agreement with shallow commitments, or an agreement with deep reduction commitments that will not be legally binding, thus soft law.

With regard to migration, the costs and benefits of collaboration between migrant sending and receiving countries are unevenly distributed, and it is particularly countries of destination which prefer international non-collaboration over collaboration, confirming the institutionalist assumption that the larger distributional implications are, the higher bargaining costs become, making the adoption of an agreement less likely (Koremenos *et al.* 2001). The Geneva Conventions are an exception in this regard as their main principle – non-refoulement, i.e., the prohibition on repatriating victims of persecution to their persecutors, or to places where their lives or freedom would be threatened – is generally recognized as a peremptory norm (ius cogens) of international law, from which no derogation is permitted, whether or not states have ratified the respective instrument in question. Otherwise, international collaboration on migration remains shallow, and is fragmented and dispersed over different institutions, without a coherent, coordinated institutional response leading to inconsistencies in framing and treatment (Raustiala and Victor 2004). From an institutionalist perspective, it is evident that governing a complex and hybrid issue like environmental migration which lies between the migration and climate change regime complexes is a particular challenge. Governance functions in a potential environmental migration regime complex would need to address questions of asylum, humanitarian and border policies, the facilitation of migration as an adaptation strategy, but also questions of internal relocation and resettlement. These aspects all point to different methods of addressing the concept, reflecting the diverging framing approaches described by Mayer (2014). Negotiating and agreeing on a regime complex that governs such diverging aspects of environmental migration in a coherent and efficient manner is an enormous challenge. Thus, following an institutionalist view it is most likely that environmental migration will be dealt with in different institutional locations between the migration and climate change regime complexes, for instance the UNHCR, IOM or the ILO among others.

Constructivists consider international norms as intersubjective conceptions of appropriate behaviour that shape international cooperation. For COST action members, for instance, 'contributing to social justice and to the heightened perception of questions of social (in)equality in "climate migration" should be the leading normative direction of its activities' (www.climatemigration.eu/). The constructivist view focuses on the evolution of norms through discourses, and emphasizes the role of non-state actors, epistemic communities and civil society as norm entrepreneurs, setting in motion a norm cascade that finally leads to norm internalization. Setting into motion a norm cascade with regard to environmental migration, however, faces several difficulties. First of all, following Mayer (2014), norm entrepreneurs of environmental migration are diverse in terms of their concrete understanding of environmental migration, their institutional background, but also with regard to the specific objectives these actors aim to achieve by pushing the concept further. Environmental migration is promoted by several different UN agencies, international development agencies, various NGOs, academics and think tanks. Thus, the diversity of these norm entrepreneurs makes it difficult to set into motion a norm cascade, as the motivations and understandings of the issue diverge. Thus with regard to environmental migration we find a situation in which several norm entrepreneurs hold different views and preferences on the concept of environmental migration, its content, purpose and objectives. The most likely scenario from a constructivist perspective is that norm entrepreneurs engage in less institutionalized forums to deliberate the concept further until it eventually emerges into a soft law instrument, after having convinced a group of like-minded states. Paragraph 14f of the CAF already points in that direction, as do, for example, deliberations taking place in the context of the Nansen Initiative, launched in late 2012 by the governments of Switzerland and Norway, addressing the development of a protection agenda for people displaced across international borders by natural hazards, including the effects of climate change (www.nanseninitiative.org/). As the evidence base for the concept of environmental migration is still weak, actors are still in the process of arguing over the validity of the concept, preferably in a non-hierarchical setting.

Conclusion

Environmental migration is an issue area that is new on the international agenda, although research on and analysis of the topic is increasing. However, a range of uncertainties remain, for instance with regard to the probable extent of the phenomenon, but also with regard to the question of how much of this migration will be internal, and how much international – which will be crucial for the further international normative and governance development. Given these uncertainties, the direction the concept will take in the years to come is not clear. Genuine regulatory developments on environmental migration within and across different international institutions seem for the time being unrealistic. Neither the SDGs nor the climate change negotiation processes have addressed environmental migration more than very indirectly. Explanations for this vary according to the theoretical stand one takes. Realists would argue that powerful states simply are not interested in pushing the concept further, unless it is framed in a manner that addresses their security concerns. Institutionalists in contrast would point to the distributional problems between migration sending and receiving countries, aggravating an institutional solution to effectively addressing environmental migration. Constructivist approaches could be viewed as the most 'realistic' as they would point to the need for further deliberations and arguing over the validity of the concept, on the basis of sound scientific evidence. All this leaves the question open of what would really be in the real and genuine interest of environmental migrants.

Notes

1 See   http://sustainabledevelopment.un.org/content/documents/5527SR_advance%20 unedited_final.pdf [Accessed 16 March 2015].
2 See www.un.org/millenniumgoals/global.shtml [Accessed 16 March 2015].
3 As of the end of 2014, 49 states had ratified C97, and C143 by only 23, see www.ilo. org/dyn/normlex/en/f?p=NORMLEXPUB:11300:0::NO::P11300_INSTRUMENT_ ID:312242 [Accessed 16 March 2015] and www.ilo.org/dyn/normlex/en/f?p=NORML EXPUB:11300:0::NO:11300:P11300_INSTRUMENT_ID:312288:NO [Accessed 16 March 2015].

References

Abbott, K.W. and Snidal, D. (1998) Why states act through formal international organizations. *Journal of Conflict Resolution*. 42(1): 3–32.
Alter, K.J. and Meunier, S. (2009) The politics of international regime complexity. *Perspectives on Politics*. 7(1): 13–24.
Axelrod, R.M. (1984) *The evolution of cooperation*. New York: Basic Books.
Axelrod, R. and Keohane, R.O. (1985) Achieving cooperation under anarchy: strategies and institutions. *World Politics*. 38(1): 226–54.
Brown, O. (2008) The numbers game. *Forced Migration Review*. (31): 8–10.
Clemens, M.A., Kenny, C.J. and Moss, T.J. (2007) The trouble with the MDGs: confronting expectations of aid and development success. *World Development*. 35(5): 735–51.
de Coninck, H. and Bäckstrand, K. (2011) An international relations perspective on the global politics of carbon dioxide capture and storage. *Global Environmental Change*. 21(2): 368–78.
Dun, O. and Gemenne, F. (2008) Defining environmental migration. *Forced Migration Review*. (31): 10–11.
Finnemore, M. and Sikkink, K. (1998) International norm dynamics and political change. *International Organization*. 52(4): 887–917.
Fukuda-Parr, S., Greenstein, J. and Stewart, D. (2013) How should MDG success and failure be judged: faster progress or achieving the targets? *World Development*. 41: 19–30.

36   *Lars Thomann*

G20 (2014) *Policy note: growth and development* [online]. Available: https://g20.org/wp-content/uploads/2014/12/policy-note-growth-and-development.pdf [Accessed 18 March 2015].

Gilpin, R. (1987) *The political economy of international relations*. Princeton: Princeton University Press.

Global Commission on International Migration (GCIM) (2005) *Migration in an interconnected world: new directions for action*. Geneva: GCIM.

Goldstein, J., Kahler, M., Keohane, R. and Slaughter, A.-M. eds. (2001) *Legalization and world politics*. Cambridge: MIT Press.

Haas, E.B. (1990) *When knowledge is power: three models of change in international organizations*. Berkeley: University of California Press.

Habermas, J. (1998) Die postnationale Konstellation und die Zukunft der Demokratie. *Blätter für deutsche und internationale Politik*. 7(98): 804–17.

Hasenclever, A., Mayer, P. and Rittberger, V. (1997) *Theories of international regimes*. Cambridge: Cambridge University Press.

Held, D. (1999) *Global transformations: politics, economics and culture*. Stanford: Stanford University Press.

Intergovernmental Panel on Climate Change (IPCC) (2014) Climate change 2014: synthesis report – summary for policymakers [online]. Available: www.ipcc.ch/pdf/assessment-report/ar5/syr/AR5_SYR_FINAL_SPM.pdf [Accessed 18 March 2015].

Kälin, W. and Schrepfer, N. (2012) Protecting people crossing borders in the context of climate change: normative gaps and possible approaches. *Legal and Protection Policy Research Series* [online]. Available: www.unhcr.org/4f33f1729.html [Accessed 27 February 2015].

Keohane, R.O. (1984) *After hegemony: cooperation and discord in the world political economy*. Princeton: Princeton University Press.

Keohane, R.O. and Nye, J.S. (1977) *Power and interdependence: world politics in transition*. Boston: Little, Brown.

Keohane, R.O. and Victor, D. (2010) *The regime complex for climate change*. Discussion Paper 10–33. Cambridge: Harvard Project on International Climate Agreements.

Koremenos, B., Lipson, C. and Snidal, D. (2001) The rational design of international institutions. *International Organization*. 55(4): 761–99.

Krasner, S.D. (1976) State power and the structure of international trade. *World Politics*. 28(3): 317–47.

Martin, L.L. (1994) Heterogeneity, linkage and commons problems. *Journal of Theoretical Politics*. 6(4): 473–93.

Mayer, B. (2014) 'Environmental migration' as advocacy: is it going to work? *Refuge: Canada's Journal on Refugees*. 29(2): 27–41.

Mearsheimer, J.J. (1994/1995) The false promise of international institutions. *International Security*. 19(3): 5–49.

Oye, K.A. (1985) Explaining cooperation under anarchy: hypotheses and strategies. *World Politics*. 38(1): 1–24.

Oye, K.A. ed. (1986) *Cooperation under anarchy*. Princeton: Princeton University Press.

Raustiala, K. and Victor, D.G. (2004) The regime complex for plant genetic resources. *International Organization*. 58(2): 277–309.

Risse, T. (2000) 'Let's argue!': communicative action in world politics. *International Organization*. 54(1): 1–39.

Rittberger, V., Zangl, B. and Kruck, A. (2013) *Internationale Organisationen*. 4th edn. Wiesbaden: Springer.

Snidal, D. (1985) The limits of hegemonic stability theory. *International Organization.* 39(4): 579–614.

Snidal, D. and Abbott, K. (2000) Hard and soft law in international relations. *International Organization.* 54(3): 421–56.

Sunstein, C.R. (1996) Social norms and social roles. *Columbia Law Review.* 96(4): 903–68.

United Nations (UN) (2013) *International migration report.* New York: United Nations Department of Economic and Social Affairs.

United Nations (UN) (2014a) *Report of the Open Working Group of the General Assembly on Sustainable Development Goals* [online]. UN Doc. A/68/970. Available: www.un.org/ga/search/view_doc.asp?symbol=A/68/970 [Accessed 18 March].

United Nations (UN) (2014b) *Final compilation of amendments to goals and targets by major groups and other stakeholders including citizen's responses to MY world 6 priorities* [online]. Available: https://sustainabledevelopment.un.org/content/documents/4438mgscompil ationowg13.pdf [Accessed 18 March 2015].

United Nations Framework Convention on Climate Change (UNFCCC) (2010) *Report of the conference of the parties on its sixteenth session, held in Cancún from 29 November to 10 December 2010* [online]. FCCC/CP/2010/7/Add.1. Available: http://unfccc.int/resource/docs/2010/cop16/eng/07a01.pdf#page=2 [Accessed 18 March 2015].

United Nations Framework Convention on Climate Change (UNFCCC) (2012) *Report of the conference of the parties serving as the meeting of the parties to the Kyoto Protocol on its seventh session, held in Durban from 28 November to 11 December 2011* [online]. FCCC/KP/CMP/2011/10/Add.1. Available: http://unfccc.int/resource/docs/2011/cmp7/eng/10a01.pdf [Accessed 18 March 2015].

United Nations Framework Convention on Climate Change (UNFCCC) (2013) *Report of the adaptation committee* [online]. FCCC/SB/2013/2. Available: http://unfccc.int/resource/docs/2013/sb/eng/02.pdf [Accessed 18 March 2015].

United Nations Framework Convention on Climate Change (UNFCCC) (2014a) *Lima call for climate action puts world on track to Paris 2015* [online]. Press release, 14 December 2014. Available: http://newsroom.unfccc.int/lima/lima-call-for-climate-action-puts-world-on-track-to-paris-2015/ [Accessed 18 March 2015].

United Nations Framework Convention on Climate Change (UNFCCC) (2014b) Subsidiary body for scientific and technological advice. Good practices in and lessons learned from national adaptation planning [online]. Available: http://unfccc.int/resource/docs/2014/sbsta/eng/misc08.pdf [Accessed 18 March 2015].

United Nations High Commissioner for Refugees (UNHCR) (2014) *Global trends 2013: war's human cost.* Geneva: UNHCR.

Waltz, K. (1979) *Theory of international politics.* New York: McGraw Hill.

Wendt, A. (1999) *Social theory of international politics.* Cambridge: Cambridge University Press.

Young, O.R. (1997) *Global governance: drawing insights from the environmental experience.* Cambridge: MIT Press.

3 Climate change and environment related migration in the European Union policy

An organizational shift towards adaptation and development

Julia Blocher

Introduction

For years scholars and policy makers have been promoting international cooperation on 'global migration governance' as necessary to ensure orderly movements and to provide schemes that would enhance the role of migration in development (Castles 2004). Environment and climate change-induced migration has been considered an 'emerging' issue in European academic and policy discussions for nearly a decade.[1] The increased attention given to this topic in European policy discourses, as well as allocation of resources by the European Union (EU), reflects this trend.

Scholars have also more recently responded to interest in these linkages, and reacted to a largely negative and deterministic public narrative on the effect of environmental change on migration, by arguing human mobility should be a consideration in climate change adaptation strategies. Increasing focus is given to how governments can enhance this potential (Foresight 2011). Publications on the topic have been growing in number since 1990, with noticeable spikes in 2007 and 2011 (Piguet and Laczko 2014: 4–5). These years were crucially important for the change in the framing of climate change and migration issues. The former year corresponds to a notable wave of developments in climate change-related science. In 2007, following the publication of a number of reports that proved influential in security debates (Haldén 2007; WGBU 2007), the discussion on environmental security became increasingly focused on the security impacts of climate change (Trombetta 2008: 138). The latter year, 2011, follows the first inclusion of migration and displacement in a UNFCCC negotiating text for the Cancún Adaptation Framework. Interest in these linkages was piqued as stakeholders, and especially developing countries, explored avenues through which to direct adaptation funding. The inclusion of the concept in a number of strategic documents and reports (discussed below), particularly in the years 2010 and 2011, evidences the development of EU-level policy on climate security.

Interest in this topic in the international community is an ongoing trend, evidenced by continued, if modest, investments into related research and policy dialogues; slowly advancing discussions among Commissioners and concerned international and non-governmental organizations (NGOs) active in policy advocacy; state-driven processes such as the Nansen Initiative and Global Migration Group; and policy think-tanks of diverse foci.[2] Calls for a policy apparatus to ensure that future affected people will be able to enjoy the full range of freedoms, as well as to prepare for the eventual population movements, is likely to remain on European political agendas for years to come. However, it is unclear if a recent focus on the role of migration in development as a strategy to adapt to climate change, and environmental changes more generally, signifies a change in the institutionalization of migration cooperation.

This chapter focuses on the EU for a number of reasons. Chiefly, it serves as the most developed example of regionalized or supranational governance and is in a unique position to drive state cooperation on environment and climate change-induced migration issues. This is relevant for migration policy because the EU can endorse a common migration and asylum policy. In comparison to individual states, the policy actions of regional organizations have significant power and reach, which affect neighbouring and non-member states (Geddes and Somerville 2012: 1015). The EU uses its own legal, institutional and political processes to promote political agreements among states, which then become essentially binding on member states, prospective member states and cooperative partners with which they share historical ties (Geddes and Somerville 2012: 1018). In addition, the EU has a long history of enacting and implementing asylum and migration policies while being an active participant in a number of international bodies and partnerships to discuss migration policies, supporting the governance agenda of the International Organization for Migration (IOM), the Global Forum on Migration and Development, their member states, and their civil society and non-governmental partners. Finally, one could point to the EU's already powerful role in developing international migration governance through its support of regional and national mobility dialogues.

The chapter will be structured as follows. Tackling the research questions will first require tying together conceptual threads, specifically those used to analyse drivers of change in intergovernmental organizations as complex systems: organization studies, as applied through the lens of new institutionalism. Second, an overview of the relevant organizations and actors within the EU will be provided, along with their treatment of environment and migration concerns to-date. A number of institutional developments are addressed. Of note is the buttressing of organizational groups concerned with these questions and the development, albeit slowly, of a strategic discussion on migration leading to the EU's revised 'Global Approach to Migration and Mobility' (GAMM), characterized by the EU as its overarching framework for external migration and asylum policy (EU Council 2012a). Consideration is given to practical action in terms of implementation of existing instruments and budget allocations to the issue of environmental migration.

The questions this assessment seeks to explore are: In regards to the development of the nebulous policy area concerned with the linkages between environment and migration, has an institutional change occurred in the EU? As a corollary to this, to what extent has the EU built a cooperative and comprehensive migration policy framework that accommodates a common approach to addressing the linkages between environment and migration?

This chapter is based on desk research based mainly on EU-released documents and grey literature as well as personal communications with policy experts working within and with the European Commission. A secondary goal is to provide a comprehensive overview of the significant moments in which environment and climate change factors in migration have entered into EU policy discussions to-date, a task which has not yet been comprehensively attempted. However, it would not be possible in the scale and scope of this chapter to go into detail on all the difficulties of EU policy formation and implementation that may touch on environmental factors, and there are other works that begin to do so admirably (cf. Castles 2004; Geddes and Somerville 2012, 2013). Nor does this chapter seek to provide legal arguments for the inclusion of environmental factors in the existing shared protection system (see Lülf in this volume). This chapter focuses conceptually on planned or voluntary types of migration rather than displacement, although an explicit distinction is unnecessary in the discussion that follows. It explores how environmental factors in migratory processes have been articulated and implemented in EU frameworks, communications and instruments. I argue that the institutional place of environmental migration has shifted away from its previous footing in asylum issues and 'climate security' to one of inclusion in technical and financial support for climate change adaptation and development cooperation. As will be demonstrated, soft instruments or governance modes on environment, migration and development that are being developed have greater potential for an EU-wide approach to migration linked to environmental change than 'hard' commitments in the migration and asylum regimes.

Theoretical framework

Underlying the development of the indistinct policy area concerned with the linkages between environment and migration is a standardization and spreading of ideas and views, which are later translated into organizational strategies and practice.

To address the research question, the discussion below incorporates concepts developed in organization studies through a neo-institutional lens to develop a policy mobilization and change perspective. One benefit of this approach is that it avoids the many theoretical pitfalls that arise in attempting to apply neoliberal and realist theories in international relations (see Thomann in this volume), which struggle to explain EU behaviour. Few theories can begin to account for the 'Europeanization' of a policy area. New institutionalist arguments have been applied for many years to companies and organizations to understand their behaviour (e.g., DiMaggio and Powell 1983, 1991), and have more recently begun to include NGOs, international organizations, and regional intergovernmental organizations such as the EU (cf. Ellis 2010).

While much early neo-institutionalist thought sought to explain how institutional effects exerted constraints on organizations and led to conformity as well as path dependency (cf. Clemens and Cook 1999; Meyer and Rowan 1977), later work sought to explain innovation and change in organizations (cf. Scott *et al.* 2000). Institutionalization was re-hewn as a political process, shaped by the relative positions between actors, disparate interests and pressures on different levels of a system.[3] The central unit of analysis for many authors was the organizational field, the interlocking structures that delineate an area of institutional life. Fields are a community of disparate agents that engage in common activities and share distinctive characteristics (Wooten and Hoffman 2008: 131), may operate in distinct or multiple fields (Fligstein and Stone Sweet 2002), and span across formal organizational structures. Fields may also be defined by a coalition sharing common interpretations of what are conceived to be main issues. Fields are dynamic and form around issues considered to be important to the interests and objectives of a constellation of actors or organizations (Hoffman 1999). Fields are also dynamic; they are areas of contestation where constituents defend their interests and set the course for future strategies (Seo and Creed 2002).

My analysis takes an intra-organizational approach to understand these coalitions in the EU and their shared meanings gathered around their central issue. The institutional position of EU policy relating to environment, climate change and migration is investigated, and ultimately, the likely path of this emerging policy area. Baker and Faulkner (2005) argue the shape of fields may be deduced by examining the character and extent of organizations' involvement in particular interest areas. Thus the composition of organizations and the types of fields observed can help to deduce an organization's overall interests and commitments (Baker and Faulkner 2005: 532–5). Actions taken by key actors and interactions among them must be assessed along with their contents and quality.

In the unique case of the EU, the level of analysis must exist at multiple levels because the organizational environment of each unit contains numerous institutional influences, due to the unique political make up of the union and institutional influences that cut across formal structures. A number of different actors at multiple levels and scales are relevant. A multi-level approach is needed to resolve the tensions between micro- and macro-level approaches, as suggested by Baum (2005). New and changing actors must also be taken into account, as EU structures are created and reformed. Taking the analysis at the intra-organizational level, organizational fields cut across organizational units and departments. The context or institutional 'environment' is composed of pressures from divisions and sub-organs that make up the larger whole of the organization. This is coherent with 'traditional' international organization theories that take the organization itself, and bodies within them, as the unit of analysis (Ness and Brechin 1988). These approaches view intergovernmental organizations like the EU as complex systems with their own forms and processes, which have the ability to forge their own path by using its institutional abilities to achieve its interests.

As with many other studies into organizational fields, this exploration emphasizes outcomes rather than mechanisms. These outcomes will be represented by relevant communications, reports and working documents as well as press statements. The use of specific terms and concepts relating to each field's central issue are highlighted in these products and placed on a timeline of events. The key discussions, meetings, funding commitments and structural changes on this timeline reflect interactions between key actors and actions to address environment, climate change and migration issues. The importance and shape of fields, as described above, in addition to distinguishing them from merely loose constellations of actors, can also be deduced at moments that test its shared meanings and main issue. For this reason, the discussion below gives particular attention to times in which structural changes have occurred; points at which the fields described were tested and subsequently dissolved or were re-established (an approach put forward by Reay and Hinings 2005).

The emergence of environment, climate change and migration in the EU

Movement of people is a constituent element of European economic and political integration, holding important implications for building a common 'European' identity and polity. When compared to other regional organizations, the EU boasts the most comprehensive common free movement policies while playing an active role in enhancing international cooperation on migration.

Despite this, migration and asylum policies in general have lagged behind other policy areas (Popp 2014). It was a lengthy and contentious process for migration policies to achieve their current anchorage in EU institutions. This late development is to a large degree due to reluctance to enter areas of 'high politics' and diverging national interests (Geddes and Somerville 2012). Of note is the fact that the EU model for migration enshrined in agreements in the early 1990s was based on free movement of *European* citizens moving from one member state to another. Entry and integration of migrants from outside the EU was left to bilateral discussions. Progress on internal and external migration policies has been tampered by disaccord between member states who tend to favour reverting to the 'lowest common denominator' standards of the most restrictive approaches to migration and asylum and those who favour more open approaches (Castles 2004).

Objectives to addressing citizens from outside of the EU were ushered in by the 1997 Treaty of Amsterdam. The treaty set out a plan to introduce joint policies for 25 states, by the target date of May 2004. These covered management of migration flows, common rules and standards for asylum, partnership with countries of origin and integration of third-country nationals. Though the Amsterdam treaty communitarized these policies, it does not amount to a comprehensive migration policy.

Within a few years, however, it was evident that adoption of a common migration and asylum policy was not feasible (cf. Castles 2004). A number of states chose to opt out of common asylum and migration policy as it progressed since the Amsterdam treaty came into force in 1999; the UK and Ireland are not part of the Schengen area, and Denmark can opt out of post-Amsterdam treaty developments. An uneven migration governance system and national interests hindered progress towards a common external approach.

Momentum, albeit uneven, continued forward. A key moment was marked by an informal Heads of State of Government meeting in October 2005, convened to discuss the impact of globalization on the European economy. Diverging from the agenda, substantial discussion on the issue of undocumented migration and internal security was reportedly a high point of the day (UK Press Office 2005). The result was the Communication of 30 November 2005 entitled 'Global approach to migration: Priority actions focusing on Africa and the Mediterranean'. Among a number of follow-up communications, it was presented in December 2005 to the Justice and Home Affairs (JHA) Council and endorsed by the Council within a few months (EU Council 2006).

In parallel, the issue of environmental migration was mainly addressed within the frame of asylum and refugee issues. Communalization of this policy area and competencies were in their nascent stages. The first significant mention of the implications for protection was at the EU Council in 1999 (McAdam 2012). A verdict was necessary on whether people moving as a result of environmental factors – natural hazard-induced disasters, in particular – could avail themselves of subsidiary protection. Consensus did not appear achievable. Debates on environmental factors as possible grounds for protection were politically unpopular among a number of Western member nations, and considered by many as a matter to be left to the prerogative of states.

For example, a key strategic document on climate change in the context of development cooperation produced by the Commission does not consider the issue of migrants or displaced people arriving in the EU, stating only that conflicts and food insecurity are potential outcomes of mass migration within partner countries lagging in development (EC 2003: 11).

The security field

A notable shift occurred from 2004 to 2009. The first mention of the links between environmental change and migration was made in a green paper: 'Adapting to Climate Change in Europe' (EC 2007). The paper was outward-facing and intended to lay the ground for the Commission's action plans. The green paper contained a clear indication that the EU's Common Foreign and Security Policy had an important role to play in dealing with the effects of climate change, including migration. The document refers to 'enhancing the EU's capacity to prevent and deal with conflicts such as border disputes and tensions over access to natural resources and natural disasters accentuated by climate change as well as their potential consequences such as forced migration and internal displacements of persons' (EC 2007: 20–1).

The paper prompted the Council to invite the High Representative of the Union for Foreign Affairs and Security Policy (HRUFASP) and the Commission to jointly assess the potential security implications of climate change from an EU perspective. This resulted in the 'Joint Paper on Climate Change and International Security' (CCIS) in 2008, sometimes referred to as the 'Solana Report'.

The paper described what was characterized as strategic thinking into how climate change may cross over into other governance areas, including migration (EC 2008a). The report discusses the issue of climate change as one of increasing migratory pressures, alluding to the mass flight of millions of potential migrants to EU borders and suggesting that 'environmentally-triggered additional migratory stress' (EC 2008a: 10) should accelerate the development of a comprehensive European migration policy. The issue of climate-induced mass migration propagated within military circles as an issue of climate security (cf. Center for Naval Analyses Corporation 2007; US Department of Defense 2010: 85), is evident in the report (cf. Randall in this volume). The report framed climate change as a 'threat multiplier' and migration trigger and its dividends in human displacements as a threat to security: 'Climate change is best viewed as a threat multiplier that exacerbates existing trends, tensions and instability. The core challenge is that climate change threatens to overburden states and regions which are already fragile and conflict-prone. The risks include political and security risks that directly affect European interests' (EC 2008a: 2). The role of migration as a positive adaptation strategy is not given consideration. The EU Council welcomed the report and requested a follow up, which was given by the High Representative at the end of December. Meanwhile, the issue of climate change and security was given higher priority within the HRUFASP.

In April 2009, the European Commission launched a white paper on 'Adapting to climate change: towards a European framework for Action'. While largely aimed at cross-sectorial issues of climate security and in consolidating the EU approach ahead of the UNFCCC Conference of the Parties (COP) meeting in Copenhagen in 2009, the paper makes a brief reference to security and migration: 'Failure to adapt could have security implications. The effects of climate change on migratory flows should also be reflected in the broader EU reflection on security, development, and migration policies' (EC 2009: 15–16).

Recommendations from the European Commission (EC 2008b) on strengthening a coherent approach to migration were adopted in the Stockholm Program, the EU's five-year plan for internal security policy covering the period 2010–2014 (EU Council 2009). The program calls for greater focus on climate change as a driver of security-relevant migratory flows.

In response to the EU Council's request for 'an analysis of the effects of climate change on international migration, including its potential effects on immigration to the European Union' (EU Council 2009: 3) the Commission committed to release two communications on the subject on the EU's global approach to migration. The first, a communication on the GAMM was presented as a comprehensive revision of the 2005 'Global approach to migration: Priority actions focusing on Africa and the Mediterranean', expanding from its prior focus on borders and migration flows from the Mediterranean (discussed above). The second, on climate change and migration, was postponed; climate change is very briefly mentioned in the GAMM. Eventually, the promised communication was released in 2013 as a Commission Staff Working Document entitled 'Climate change, environmental degradation, and migration', which is effectively a detailed background paper adopted as part of the EU Strategy on adaptation to climate change (EC 2013a). These are discussed further below.

A disparate and relatively amorphous community of actors and units concerned with security emerges from within home affairs and justice portfolios in the Directorates-General (DGs) of the European Commission;[4] the Parliament's committee on civil liberties, justice and home affairs; the JHA; the Committee of the Regions; and a number of EU agencies including, but not limited to, the European Agency for the Management of Operational Cooperation at the External Borders of the Member States of the European Union (FRONTEX) and European Asylum Support Office (EASO). The European Commission should normally drive migration policy development and implementation, as proposing and implementing legislation is its area of responsibility. However, it has been acknowledged by experts on EU policy that the predominance of the Justice and Interior ministers in the JHA Council within migration discussions has had an effect on the character of these discussions as well as the migration agenda that has been advanced (Tamas 2012).

Momentum to include environmental factors into the migration and asylum regime is marked by the number of EU-led communications, reports, and conferences referencing this issue from 2007 to 2011. These efforts have noticeably lagged since. The decrease in interest is at least in part because member states did not consider the issue a priority, except 'to avoid any connection to asylum policy' (Somerville 2011: 7). In addition, a number of urgent political and security crises have since consumed the attention of security actors, including the Syrian refugee crisis and tensions with Russia (Youngs 2014). Since the publication of the GAMM (EC 2011a), discussions on the security concerns associated with migration and climate change have rarely been EU-led.

Relating environment and climate change to asylum and protection took on a more nuanced character. Actors sympathetic to the topic have adopted the more modest approach of including environmental factors into regimes to protect internally displaced people (Youngs 2014), as well as disaster risk reduction and management. As external policies, these issues mainly fall into the remit of the European Commission's Humanitarian Aid and Civil Protection department (ECHO) and the Directorate-General for International Cooperation and Development (DG DEVCO/EuropeAid).

Between 2009 and 2011, environmentally-related migration and conventional asylum-seeking were increasingly treated as entirely separate issues within political debates. Issues relating to the natural environment were removed from the remit of the Home Affairs DG as well as from the policy portfolio for internal migration and asylum issues. This became clear in 2011 when the communication on climate change and migration called for in the Stockholm action plan became little more than a footnote in the broader communication on migration (the GAMM). The choice to de-prioritize the topic may reveal an intention to avoid its possible interference with advancing restrictive immigration and asylum policies (Geddes and Somerville 2012: 1020). As the aim of a 'common immigration policy' (Art. 17) was set out in the Lisbon Treaty in 2009, it simultaneously made a significant blow to the ability of EU actors to develop a common migration policy by reaffirming this policy area lies within the domain of member states (Art. 79[5]). Efforts to integrate environmental causes into the refugee protection regime were gradually abandoned. This observation is reinforced by the purposeful exclusion of environmental factors in the drafting of the EU Qualification Directive in 2011 (see Lülf in this volume). The Home Affairs DG was renamed *Migration and Home Affairs* in 2014, effectively reiterating that, within the current college of commissioners, responsibilities and policy leadership for migration remain entrenched in internal and security-dominated issues of immigration and asylum. The act of making this change is significant in that the alternative would have been to create a portfolio for migration that is separate from issues of internal security, and in which environment and development issues could have featured.

Two instruments of the GAMM can be implemented to assist migration from third countries, both of which are types of bilateral cooperation frameworks: the Mobility Partnerships (MPs) and the Common Agendas for Migration and Mobility (CAMMs). The former are applied to the EU neighbourhood and priority countries through the work of the EU External Action Service and in consultation with the Committee for the Regions.[5] The latter are intended for countries outside of the neighbourhood with which EU states would like to enhance cooperation. At the time of writing, CAMMs have been discussed at separate meetings for Brazil, India and Ethiopia. A review of the current MPs and CAMMs in place[6] reveals that the links between climate change and migration as adaptation, and even development potential, are hardly considered. The focus is mainly on visa liberalization for students and highly skilled workers, and on enhancing remittances potential and avoiding 'brain drain' (EC 2011b). This 'Migration and development' pillar of the GAMM has been interpreted in the MPs that exist, as well as proposed CAMMs, to be on these lines. Today, environmental issues are not systematically included in migration profiles or mobility dialogues, the two main implementing arms of the GAMM.

In addition, the usefulness of the GAMM in promoting a coherent and cooperative approach to climate change adaptation and development, and of migration governance more generally, has been eroded by the voluntary and selective nature of its implementation. This has in turn affected the role of the Commission and the External Action Service in promoting cooperative and migrant-centred policies. When asked what kind of circular migration could feature in MPs, the Deputy Head of International Affairs unit in DG Home, responded: 'it is not for the Commission to decide CAMMs: this is being intensely discussed by the Council (…) Member states are challenged to work on them if there are needs in specific labour markets' (EPC 2012: 4). Without significant efforts on the part of the Commission and the External Action Service to ensure the inclusion of climate change adaptation and resilience building strategies, migration and mobility dialogues are likely to be the product of the interests of individual member states.

For the security community, environmental factors and climate change have apparently lost favour as a contested and central issue. The shared meanings and values therein are centred on protection of borders and exclusionary immigration practices. It could be argued that the removal of environmental factors from a protection regime – supported by states and security actors who feared migration *en masse* of affected peoples, and tacitly supported by scholars and policy actors who argued this was an oversimplification of a complex development issue – enabled security actors to deemphasize the issue in their own discussions and focus on 'traditional' security issues related to more immediate crises in Syria and Crimea, as well as turmoil in Egypt and Libya. 'Climate security', meanwhile, has been relegated to sectorial actors (i.e., those concerned with energy security or economic security). Environment and climate change for this network has essentially been crowded out (Youngs 2014).

The security field itself, however, remains intact. Concerns related to migration across the Mediterranean noted in the second paragraph of the GAMM have taken centre stage (EC 2011a: 2), as the actors concerned with migration and asylum have returned to a focus on reducing irregular flows through the implementing instruments of the GAMM. These are mainly the migration profiles and the 'mobility dialogues', which seek to form cooperation with neighbouring countries on issues such as irregular migration and circular migration of skilled workers.

The climate change adaptation and development field

One may observe that the shift away from including environmental issues in migration and asylum policy development was coupled with a move towards greater promotion of the role of migration in climate change adaptation and development cooperation. The GAMM was released in 2011 as a (non-binding) communication; an expression of an intended policy direction. Council conclusions on the GAMM (EU Council 2012a) were later formally approved by the Council's Committee of Permanent Representatives (COREPER) on 18 April 2012 (EU Council 2012b). The GAMM presents several novelties. It emphasizes the need for a migrant-centred approach, facilitating systems to support the development aspect of migration, and recognizing the role of migration in community adaptation strategies. The GAMM makes brief reference to 'the relationship between migration and climate change' (EC 2011a: 6–7). It instead focuses heavily on 'strengthening the synergies between migration and development' (Pillar three) and suggests 'environmentally induced migration' is a means of adaptation to 'adverse effects of climate change'. It falls short of providing concrete steps to enhance migration opportunities or legal provisions. Pillars one, two and four relate to reducing migratory pressures and irregular migration flows.

Linkages between environment and migration were elsewhere accorded some small, if not overdue, thematic funding. A strategy paper for the Thematic Program 'Cooperation with Third Countries in the areas of Migration and Asylum' for 2011–2013 explicitly commits to working more on the nexus between climate change and migration (EC 2011b). This paper also concretized the place of the issue within the remit of DG DEVCO/EuropeAid, which furthermore disposes of 'non-budget' (attributable, although not yet for migration-specific projects) funds earmarked for resilience building through the European Development Fund.

A Commission Staff Working Document on adaptation to climate change, 'Climate change, environmental degradation, and migration', was published by the Directorate-General for Climate Action (DG CLIMA) as a follow-up to the 2009 Council request (EC 2013a). It is relatively ambitious in its inclusion of human mobility in regards to climate change adaptation. As it acknowledges that most migration and displacement will occur inside developing countries, the focus of much of the 35-page brief is on development potential and mitigating the effects of natural hazards on people in the 'Global South' (EC 2013a).

An additional document, the Communication on Maximizing the Development Impact of Migration of May 2013 (EC 2013b), reiterates the fourth pillar of the GAMM. Intended as a position paper ahead of the High Level Dialogue on Migration. Published by DG DEVCO/EuropeAid the document reiterated the Staff Working Document on climate change and migration, noted above, and concretizes the EU's position on environmental factors as causes of migratory flows within and between developing countries, noting that the inter-linkages between climate change, environmental degradation and mobility require consideration within a development context. It addresses the importance of climate change adaptation and disaster risk reduction in reducing displacement, and the role of migration as a strategy to strengthening adaptation and household resilience. The communication furthermore reinforces a 'dual policy framework', that is, in the GAMM and the EU's (external) development policy elaborated by the 2011 'Agenda for Change', the EU's policy for cooperation and development (EC 2011c). Unlike the other two documents, this communication sets technical and financial support in motion, with a focus on climate-vulnerable developing countries and regions.

Dissimilar to internal security, the JHA Ministers of the EU Council are relatively silent on issues of external migration policies. Instead, the Foreign Affairs Council was particularly active on this issue under the Italian presidency of the EU Council in 2014. Council conclusions adopted for the first time with the GAMM (2011) were reiterated in 2014, while calling on the Commission and the European External Action Service (EEAS) to work to address 'the full range of positive and negative impacts of migration on sustainable and inclusive economic, social and environmental development in countries of origin and destination' (EU Council 2014: 4). Astonishingly, the conclusions also suggest a development approach to refugees and IDPs. In parallel to these conclusions by the EU Council, the HRUFASP and Vice President of the Commission sought to separate mobility issues from an asylum frame by highlighting its 'strong links to development and foreign policy' (EEAS 2014).

What is noticeable is the attempt to integrate security-focused reports previously produced by the EU, highlighted above, with relatively detailed reproductions of the scholarly debates on migration as an adaptive strategy into the recent documents produced by the EC. Indeed, the 2013 Staff Working Document duplicates much of the contents of the 2011 UK Foresight report. The influence of environment, migration and development scholars in the area – including those funded by the EU's research programs – is noticeable. This observation supports the existence of strong links between scholars outside of the EU and policy actors within, who influence and are likely to continue to drive policy formulation and institutional development. Such networks have a role in policy selection, innovation, diffusion, and evolution as a process of learning (Adler and Haas 1992).

The climate resilience field, made up of a constellation of actors concerned with development and climate change adaptation, and led by DG DEVCO/ EuropeAid and DG CLIMA, has already started influencing the Commission. The existence of a coalition of climate resilience actors is evidenced by a number of working documents, held consultations, and developed forums promoting the treatment of migration in terms of development related resilience building. The restructuring of the Commission, when DG CLIMA was separated from DG Environment and its close partnership with DG DEVCO for climate change adaptation projects, funded and implemented around the world, may have also helped to enable this shift. The piecemeal approach that persists for climate change and adaptation recognized in both the Staff Working Document (EC 2013a: 20) and in the 'Agenda for Change' (EC 2011c: 10–11), would seem unlikely to be helped by the introduction of an additional actor in the decision-making process of external-facing policy found in the EEAS and ECHO. However, the EEAS has much control over the financial allocations for and implementation of adaptation efforts in third countries. ECHO has a more targeted remit to deal with natural hazard-induced disasters and displacement, but in so doing contributes to climate change and adaptation and resilience building in general.

Conclusion

A number of authors have suggested that the discussions on environmental factors in human mobility have paralleled those of asylum and immigration. This chapter departs from this view, suggesting instead that the discussions have taken place in two intra-organizational fields; one concerned with climate security and one concerned with climate change adaptation and development. The timeline and detail given above goes some way to tracing concepts and issues of environment, climate change and migration as they developed within two main networks of actors. The story of the development of the indistinct policy area in the EU concerned with the linkages between environment and migration is one of a spreading and contesting of ideas and views in these two organizational fields, which also led to the translation of these ideas to organizational strategies and practice. Outcomes and content of the key points of development for both are represented by the key documents that emerged.

Until recent years, a security field has not only dominated the issue of climate change, environment and migration in the EU, it has been the only voice on the issue. The dominance of security actors in the years leading up to 2011 is clear from the framing of the issue in numerous outcomes. The key actors in the security field can be sketched out by analysing the source and content of publicly available documents, policy discussions, and structural changes within the EU, which all relate climate change and migration to internal affairs; this also allows an intra-organizational field to be identified. The central issue remained the integral security of the EU and its member states – not migration or climate change impacts. Given the popularity of the CAMMs and MPs among certain member states, as well as the historical momentum noted above, it is probable that an ongoing institutionalization of migration governance in the EU will continue. However, these two policy instruments serve to reinforce exclusive and restrictive immigration and asylum systems. At best, these instruments are voluntary and non-binding declarations of cooperation between priority countries and participating EU member states in the interest of mutual benefit on labour migration and development issues. At worst, these are political exchanges between EU states and individual countries, increasing visa liberalization – for students and skilled workers in particular – in exchange for cooperation on combating undocumented migration flows and human smuggling into the EU.

As for the constellation of actors involved in climate change adaptation and development, their interest in migration corresponds to the period in which the GAMM emerged, which also parallels the shift in academic and policy interest in adaptation and in the lead-up to the post-2015 agenda. Relating back to our definition of organizational fields, a distinct separation between climate change actors and development actors is difficult to draw. It further cuts across EU bodies and incorporates external scholars and partners. The shape and extended reach of a unified field, which one may identify as the climate resilience field, is discernable from the outcome documents discussed above, and its ability to remain intact despite restructuring and reform.

Overall, these findings suggest that an effective institutional change has begun to occur in the EU in regards to environment, climate change and migration, or even within migration governance in general. The process of institutionalization of security issues within the EU is manifest, and so it can indeed be possible for issues of common concerns to take this path. Strategic documents since 2011 indicate the environment, climate change, and migration policy area is progressing within the development and climate change adaptation framework. As of yet, however, the outcome has thus far been a weak and unsystematic inclusion of these factors in the practical instruments of the GAMM, the MPs and the CAMMs. Furthermore, migration issues play a small, if not negligible, role in the climate change adaptation and development portfolios implemented by DG CLIMA, DG DEVCO and the EEAS. However, addressing it through the avenue of development and climate change adaptation is a more likely avenue than through the EU's national interest-dominated migration policies and programs appears. In addition, it is a realizable task. The EU is a proven force for mainstreaming policy issues and setting norms to which member states, neighbours and aid recipients adhere. DG CLIMA, DG DEVCO, ECHO and EEAS form a strong coalition to support climate resilience. The climate change DG can influence the direction of climate change adaptation strategic plans and funds, while DG DEVCO implements development cooperation projects chosen as a result, ECHO implements disaster and aid projects chosen, and EEAS bridges cooperation with the nation in which projects are carried out. Not to be forgotten, ECHO programs have directly and indirectly contributed to building resilience of communities vulnerable to climate change and environmental change.

Despite recent national debates on migration and asylum that seem to drive many European countries towards more restrictive approaches, areas for progress on addressing linkages between environment and migration in third countries can be made within existing structures. This includes further implementing development strategies within mobility partnerships and in the range of tools used under the European Neighborhood Policy. Thematic funds for adaptation and development cooperation should be augmented, in particular, the Thematic Program for cooperation with developing countries in the areas of migration and asylum. Specific provisions to address drivers of migration and sensitivity to already mobile populations could be mainstreamed into many adaptation and development funds and projects, as many drivers are already implicitly treated by projects run by DG DEVCO and DG CLIMA.

Yet, treating the causes of environment and climate-related migration through adaptation and development programs does not necessarily imply policies to enhance migration opportunities and protection for climate-affected peoples will be developed. An exclusive focus on the former may be at the expense of handicapping progress on global migration governance supported by some academics, states and international agencies (they can be found, for example, participating in the state-led UN Global Forum on Migration and Development as well as the agency-led UN Global Migration Group). Available resources for reforming global migration systems, both human and capital resources, are finite and currently divided between these two approaches. Bilateral and multilateral migration agreements, if they continue on their current trajectory unimpeded, are likely to remain state-led and piecemeal. However, development of, and adherence to, EU governance on this issue would already be a significant change to the currently fragmented system and create a forward momentum. A next step would be to make concrete strategies and dedicated funding for projects to strengthen climate resilience in the implementation of the GAMM, to fulfil its stated goal of advancing less exclusive and more migrant-centred approaches to migration. Environment and climate change sensitive modules could be systematically included in migration profiles and mobility dialogues. For example, specific migrant categories and policies ensuring protection for people from climate-prone and natural hazard-affected areas could be promoted at the European level. Examples of bilateral and multilateral facilitated labour migration schemes[7] and temporary protection mechanisms for people from areas affected by natural hazards[8] could be expanded upon.

While a more optimistic outlook would expect that ongoing discussions and especially the momentum building within the post-2015 development agenda could enable a more significant institutional evolution towards a cooperative and comprehensive migration policy framework that accommodates a concrete and systematic approach to addressing the linkages between environment and climate change related migration, the end outcome remains uncertain. It may be too soon to draw conclusions on whether, in practical terms, EU instruments as they are currently implemented indirectly have a positive effect on the ability of people to use migration as a strategy to adapt to livelihood-damaging climate change and environmental changes more generally, or, as the case may be, adapt *in situ* to changing environmental conditions. More evaluations and targeted research will be needed to advance the best course going forward.

Notes

1 Separate terms are sometimes used with the implied distinction between a rapid movement of people resulting from 'climate events' (displacement) and a less abrupt movement brought on by environmental degradation (migration). The former 'type' offers the attractive possibility of linking with the anthropogenic causes of climate change.
2 Notably, in the past decade, a number of active policy advocates traditionally concerned with other matters have raised the status of environmental and climate change induced population movements in their work. Humanitarian organizations such as the Norwegian Refugee Council and its Internal Displacement Monitoring Centre, the United Nations High Commissioner for Refugees (UNHCR), and Refugees International have all dedicated resources to internal and cross-border disaster displacement. Environmental organizations like Greenpeace and Earth Policy Institute regularly engage. Finally, a number of security organizations and think-tanks have developed their positions: the Center for Naval Analyses (CNA) Corporation, a US security research entity, raised the alarm with its 2007 report; the North Atlantic Treaty Organization (NATO) included 'climate security' in its 2010 Strategic Concept; the US Department of Defense took up the issue in its 2010 Quadrennial review.
3 Some micro-level approaches focus on the role of individual and entrepreneurial actors, arguing institutions cannot be conceived as entirely external (and constraining) effects on an organization. Change has also been hypothesized as a result of institutional contradictions which lead to collective action (Seo and Creed 2002) and the manipulation of knowledge by epistemic communities (Adler and Haas 1992).
4 Migration and Home Affairs deals with issues related to internal security, including immigration and asylum. The DG for Climate Action (DG CLIM, now DG CLIMA) established in February 2010 took on the remit of leading climate change mitigation and EU emissions trading schemes from DG Environment. Its establishment, as a separate entity from DG Environment, alongside DG Energy, served a dual purpose of signifying the EU's engagement in climate negotiations and freeing the EU's well-established energy and environmental policy areas from contention. Development and Cooperation (DG DEVCO/EuropeAid) leads international cooperation and development policy, including the deliverance of aid.
5 Priority is given to members in the Africa–EU partnership and Rabat process; the Prague process and Eastern Partnership; Latin American and Caribbean States (EU-CELAC); countries included in the Budapest process; and 'strategic partners' Russia, India, China, South Africa, and Nigeria.
6 So far, and in varying stages of domestication: Cape Verde, Moldova, Georgia, Armenia, Morocco, Azerbaijan, Tunisia, and Jordan.

7 See New Zealand's Pacific Access Category for Pacific Islanders (New Zealand Government 2015).
8 For example, Finland's Aliens Act (Finnish Ministry of the Interior 2004: ch. 6, s. 88a[1]), Sweden's Aliens Act (Swedish Ministry of Justice 2005: ch. 4, s. 2a) and the United States' Temporary Protection Status and Deferred Enforced Departure (USCIS 2015). However, all three pre-suppose the affected individual is already on the territory of the protecting state when the request for protection is issued, and thus are unlikely to be helpful for people *in situ* during extreme weather events or for people affected by slow-onset events.

References

Adler, E. and Haas, P.M. (1992) Conclusion: epistemic communities, world order and the creation of a reflective research program. *International Organisation.* 46(1): 367–90.
Baker, W.E. and Faulkner, R.R. (2005) Interorganizational networks. In *The Blackwell companion to organizations,* ed. J.A.C. Baum. Malden: Blackwell Publishing.
Baum, J.A.C. (2005) An introduction. In *The Blackwell companion to organizations,* ed. J.A.C. Baum. Malden: Blackwell Publishing.
Castles, S. (2004) The factors that make and unmake migration policies. *International Migration Review.* 38(3): 852–84.
Center for Naval Analyses Corporation (2007) *National security and the threat of climate change* [online]. Available: www.cna.org/reports/climate [Accessed 12 December 2014].
Clemens, E.S. and Cook, J.M. (1999) Politics and institutionalism: explaining durability and change. *Annual Review of Sociology.* 25: 441–66.
Council of the European Union (EU Council) (2006) *Presidency conclusions of the Brussels European Council* [online]. 15914/1/05, Rev. 1, 15/16 December 2006. Available: www.consilium.europa.eu/ueDocs/cms_Data/docs/pressData/en/ec/87642.pdf [Accessed 12 December 2014].
Council of the European Council (EU Council) (2009) *The Stockholm programme: an open and secure Europe serving and protecting the citizens* [online]. Doc. 17024/09. Available: http://register.consilium.europa.eu/doc/srv?l=EN&f=ST%2017024%202009%20INIT [Accessed 12 December 2014].
Council of the European Council (EU Council) (2012a) *Conclusions on the global approach to migration and mobility* [online]. 9417/12, 3 May 2012. Available: http://register.consilium.europa.eu/pdf/en/12/st09/st09417.en12.pdf [Accessed 12 June 2014].
Council of the European Council (EU Council) (2012b) *Transcript of the 3168th meeting of the Council of the European Union* [online]. 25 May 2012. Available: www.eumonitor.eu/9353000/1/j4nvgs5kjg27kof_j9vvik7m1c3gyxp/vizv41uu8oxa/f=/10171_12.pdf [Accessed 12 December 2014].
Council of the European Council (EU Council) (2014) *Council conclusions on migration in EU development cooperation* [online]. Foreign Affairs (Development) Council, 12 December 2014. Available: www.consilium.europa.eu/uedocs/cms_data/docs/pressdata/EN/foraff/146182.pdf [Accessed 12 December 2014].
DiMaggio, P.J. and Powell, W.W. (1983) The iron cage revisited institutional isomorphism and collective rationality in organizational fields. *American Sociological Review.* 48: 147–60.
DiMaggio, P.J. and Powell, W. (1991) Introduction. In *The new institutionalism in organization analysis,* eds. P.J. DiMaggio and W.W. Powell. Chicago: University of Chicago Press: 1–38.

Ellis, D.C. (2010) The organizational turn in international organization theory. *Journal of International Organization Studies.* 1(1): 11–28.

European Commission (EC) (2003) *Communication from the Commission to the Council and the European Parliament: climate change in the context of development cooperation* [online]. 11 March 2003. Available: http://eur-lex.europa.eu/legal-content/EN/TXT/?uri=CELEX:52003DC0085 [Accessed 12 December 2014].

European Commission (EC) (2007) *Adapting to climate change* [online]. Doc. 354, 29 June 2007. Available: http://europa.eu/legislation_summaries/environment/tackling_climate_change/l28193_en.htm [Accessed 10 July 2014].

European Commission (EC) (2008a) *Climate change and international security: paper from the High Representative and the European Commission to the European Council* [online]. 14 March 2008. Available: www.consilium.europa.eu/ueDocs/cms_Data/docs/pressdata/EN/reports/99387.pdf [Accessed 10 July 2014].

European Commission (EC) (2008b) *Strengthening the global approach to migration* [online]. 8 October 2008. Available: http://europa.eu/legislation_summaries/justice_freedom_security/free_movement_of_persons_asylum_immigration/jl0008_en.htm [Accessed 10 July 2014].

European Commission (EC) (2009) *Adapting to climate change: towards a European framework for action* [online]. 1 April 2009. Available: http://eur-lex.europa.eu/LexUriServ/LexUriServ.do?uri=CELEX:52009DC0147:EN:NOT [Accessed 10 July 2014].

European Commission (EC) (2011a) *Global approach to migration and mobility* [online]. 18 November 2011. Available: http://ec.europa.eu/dgs/home-affairs/what-we-do/policies/international-affairs/global-approach-to-migration/index_en.htm [Accessed 10 July 2014].

European Commission (EC) (2011b) *With third countries in the areas of migration and asylum, 2011–2013 multi-annual strategy paper* [online]. Available: https://ec.europa.eu/europeaid/thematic-programme-cooperation-third-countries-areas-migration-and-asylum-2011-2013-multi-annual_en [Accessed 12 December 2014].

European Commission (EC) (2011c) *Increasing the impact of EU development policy: an agenda for change* [online]. 13 October 2011. Available: http://eur-lex.europa.eu/legal-content/EN/TXT/PDF/?uri=CELEX%3A52011DC0637&qid=1412922281378&from=EN [Accessed 12 December 2014].

European Commission (EC) (2013a) *Climate change, environmental degradation, and migration: an EU strategy on adaptation to climate change* [online]. 16 April 2013. Available: ec.europa.eu/clima/policies/adaptation/what/docs/swd_2013_138_en.pdf [Accessed 10 July 2014].

European Commission (EC) (2013b) *Maximizing the development impact of migration: the EU contribution for the UN high-level dialogue and next steps towards broadening the development-migration nexus* [online]. 21 May 2013. Available: http://ec.europa.eu/europeaid/sites/devco/files/communication-maximising-the-development-impact-of-migration_en_11.pdf [Accessed 12 December 2014].

European External Action Service (EEAS) (2014) *Remarks by High Representative Federica Mogherini following the Foreign Affairs Council in format of development* [online]. 12 December 2014. Available: http://eeas.europa.eu/statements-eeas/2014/141214_02_en.htm [Accessed 12 December 2014].

European Policy Centre (EPC) (2012) *Mobility partnerships: an effective tool for EU external migration policy? Policy Dialogue* [online]. 12 June 2012. Available: www.kbs-frb.be/

uploadedFiles/2012-KBS-FRB/05%29_Pictures,_documents_and_external_sites/12%29_Report/EPC_MobilityPartnerships.pdf [Accessed 14 March 2015].

Finnish Ministry of the Interior (2004) *Aliens Act (301/2004, amendments up to 1152/2010 included)* [online]. Available: www.finlex.fi/en/laki/kaannokset/2004/en20040301.pdf [Accessed 14 March 2015].

Fligstein, N. and Stone Sweet, A. (2002) Of polities and markets: an institutionalist account of European integration. *American Journal of Sociology*. 107: 1206–43.

Foresight (2011) *Migration and global environmental change: final project report*. London: The Government Office for Science.

Geddes, A. and Somerville, W. (2012) Migration and environmental change in international governance: the case of the European Union. *Environment and Planning C: Government and Policy*. 30(6): 1015–28.

Geddes, A. and Somerville, W. (2013) Migration and environmental change: assessing the developing European approach. In *Policy Brief Series*. (2). Brussels: Migration Policy Institute Europe.

German Advisory Council on Global Change (WGBU) (2007) *World in transition: climate change as a security risk*. Flagship report. London: Earthscan.

Haldén, P. (2007) *The geopolitics of climate change: challenges to the international system*. Stockholm: FOI Swedish Defence Research Agency.

Hoffman, A.J. (1999) Institutional evolution and change: environmentalism and the US chemical industry. *Academy of Management Journal*. 42(4): 351–71.

McAdam, J. (2012) *Climate change, forced migration, and international law*. Oxford: Oxford University Press.

Meyer, J.W. and Rowan, B. (1977) Institutionalized organizations: formal structure as myth and ceremony. *American Journal of Sociology*. 83: 340–63.

Ness, G.D. and Brechin, S.R. (1988) Bridging the gap: international organizations as organizations. *International Organization*. 42(2): 245–73.

New Zealand Government (2015) *Pacific access category* [online]. Available: www.immigration.govt.nz/migrant/stream/live/pacificaccess/ [Accessed 8 April 2015].

Piguet, E. and Laczko, F. (2014) Regional perspectives on migration, the environment and climate change. In *People on the move in a changing climate*, eds. E. Piguet and F. Laczko. Dordrecht: Springer.

Popp, K. (2014) Regional policy perspectives. In *People on the move in a changing climate*, eds. E. Piguet and F. Laczko. Dordrecht: Springer.

Reay, T. and Hinings, C.R. (2005) The recomposition of an organizational field: health care in Alberta. *Organization Studies*. 26(3): 351–84.

Scott, W.R., Reuf, M., Mendel, P.J. and Caronna, C. (2000) *Institutional change and health care organizations: from professional dominance to managed care*. Chicago: University of Chicago Press.

Seo, M.G. and Creed, D. (2002) Institutional contradictions, praxis, and institutional change: a dialectical perspective. *The Academy of Management Review*. 27(2): 222–47.

Somerville, W. (2011) The politics and policies of environmental migration. In *Improving the governance of international migration: the Transatlantic Council on Migration*, eds. Bertelsmann Stiftung and Migration Policy Institute. Berlin: Bertelsmann Stiftung.

Swedish Ministry of Justice (2005) *Aliens Act (2005: 716)* [online]. Available: www.government.se/sb/d/5805/a/66122 [Accessed 14 March 2015].

Tamas, K. (2012) How comprehensive is the EU's global approach to migration? In *Migration policy practice: a bimonthly review by and for policymakers worldwide*, eds. A. Solon and F. Laczko. Geneva: IOM.

Trombetta, J. (2008) Environmental security and climate change: analysing the discourse. *Cambridge Review of International Affairs*. 21(4): 585–602.

UK Press Office (2005) *Press conference at EU informal summit Hampton Court, 27 October* [online]. Available: www.le.ac.uk/eg/hvdc/Link%20pages/News%20Items/Press%20 conference_PM_%20Hampton%20Court.doc [Accessed 14 March 2015].

US Citizenship and Immigration Services (USCIS) (2015) *Temporary protected status* [online]. Available: www.uscis.gov/humanitarian/temporary-protected-status-deferred-enforced-departure/temporary-protected-status [Accessed 14 March 2015].

US Department of Defense (2010) *Quadrennial defense review report*. Washington: Department of Defense.

Wooten, M.E. and Hoffman, A. (2008) Organizational fields: past, present and future of a core construct. In *Sage handbook of organizational institutionalism*, eds. R. Greenwood, C. Oliver, R. Suddaby and K. Sahlin. London: Sage Publications.

Youngs, R. (2014) *Climate change and European security*. Oxford: Routledge.

Part 2
The role of courts

4 European courts as pacemakers for defining and potentially expanding protection for environmental migrants in Europe

Charlotte Lülf

Introduction

Severe changes in the environment have always caused movements within or across state borders, with persons attempting to circumvent or adapt to the new living conditions. While some disciplines have discussed human mobility and climate change for decades, this issue has only recently arrived in legal debates. Although various branches of general public international law cover areas such as refugees, migrants or environmental matters, they do not establish a comprehensive regime for the protection of people fleeing natural disasters and currently one can observe barely any legal initiatives on the international plane. In 2007, the Intergovernmental Panel on Climate Change (IPCC) stressed that the future increase of droughts, intense tropical cyclone activity and extreme high sea levels will cause an increase in population movement (Pachauri and Reisinger 2007: 53).[1]

> A growing number of people flee because of multiple causes of injustice, exclusion, environmental degradation, competition for scarce resources and economic hardship caused by dysfunctional states. Some leave voluntarily, some flee because there is no other choice.
>
> (Council of Europe 2008)

This multi-causality leading to their flight hampers the development of a distinct legal branch for people fleeing natural disasters or severe effects of environmental change. The traditional distinction of voluntary and involuntary movement of people is increasingly challenged and, although environmental factors have been recognized as a driver of voluntary human mobility, there is now a growing awareness of its involuntary character, not simply as driver but as a coercive cause that makes flight the only survival strategy (European Commission 2013: 138). Not only is the traditional distinction between voluntary and involuntary migration called into question but also the question of natural and man-made disasters. Considering recent debates and research on environmental disasters and climate change, it is increasingly acknowledged that these are also 'of our own making' (Kolmannskog and Myrstad 2009: 320). What does that imply for the application of existing regulations?

While experts have estimated that a majority of environmental migrants are likely to flee neighbouring countries or regions, Europe will also need to prepare for reception requests and ensure legal certainty when asylum and protection applications under these grounds arise. This chapter aims at providing an overview of the existing regulations and the ongoing debate for the protection of environmental migrants in Europe.[2] With the lack of explicit legal protection and the political reluctance of the European member states to extend their commitment through new laws, the existing regulations must be assessed for their applicability to climate change and environmental disasters. This chapter will assess the role of the European judiciary, as currently the most active legal actor in this area: Europe possesses a multi-layered architecture comprised of the national courts and the European Court of Human Rights (ECtHR) and the Court of Justice of the European Union (ECJ). The two supranational courts play a unique role in the application of laws in Europe, as the ECtHR interprets and applies regional human rights law and the ECJ gives authoritative guidance to the European Union (EU) and its member states.

Falling outside the scope of the 1951 Convention on Refugees and its 1967 Protocol, environmental migrants have to be addressed through other instruments of asylum and human rights law. The EU Qualification Directive (QD), in particular, could potentially provide for a protection status. The jurisprudential practice of both regional courts in regards to the QD's scope and its relation to human rights law will be analysed. The jurisprudence on the non-refoulement principle of article 3 of the European Convention on Human Rights (ECHR), can be interpreted as applying to environmentally displaced persons. Whether this broadened scope can be transferred to the application of the QD must be assessed separately. The chapter evaluates the role of the judiciary in defining, redefining and potentially expanding protection. Finally, it turns to the question of whether one can already identify the evolution of a protection framework for environmental migrants through European human rights and/or European asylum law.

Legal protection for environmental migrants in Europe

The European asylum system and its instruments

The EU, with its distinct legal architecture, offers a very specific regional approach to asylum law and asylum policies. Since the establishment of the EU, the protection grounds complementary to the Refugee Convention have differed widely between the EU member states. This, however, changed with the development of a Common European Asylum System, established by the Tampere and The Hague programmes. Departing from the traditional guarding of national sovereign prerogatives, the idea of designing one single space of protection for refugees and people in need of complementary protection was drafted: 'In the longer term, Community rules should lead to a common asylum procedure and a uniform status for those who are granted asylum valid throughout the union' (European Parliament 1999: 15).

Five main first generation legal instruments provide the legal structure for the asylum acquis, the Temporary Protection Directive (TPD) 20/07/01, the Reception Condition Directive 27/01/03, the Dublin Regulation 10/02/03, the QD 29/04/04 and the Asylum Procedure Directive 01/12/05 (European Commission & DG Justice, Freedom and Security 2009: 3). The Hague Programme, as the second stage in the process, required the Commission to evaluate these first phase instruments and submit second phase instruments by the end of 2010. These second phase instruments were, following the Policy Plan on Asylum of June 2008 and the European Pact on Immigration and Asylum of October 2008, supposed to raise protection standards, adopt uniform provisions and ensure consistent application. The instruments have all been subject to amendments and changes, and since 2011 the second generation of these instruments are being transposed and implemented (European Commission & DG Migration and Home Affairs 2014).

In particular two instruments must be analysed for their potential protection character concerning people fleeing natural disasters: the TPD and the QD. Following the armed conflict in the Former Yugoslavia and its massive consequences for voluntary and involuntary displacement for single European states, the TPD 20/07/01 was adopted in 2001. It is to be implemented in cases of mass-influxes of displaced persons due to an incapacity by the receiving state to process all claims individually (McAdam 2011: 38f.). States discussed including natural disasters within the scope of the TPD during its drafting process, but this was eventually rejected by the majority of states. Furthermore, as the TPD has not been used in practice, either for natural disasters or armed conflict, it will not further be discussed in this chapter. Instead, the QD must be assessed for its potential for people fleeing natural disasters.

Subsidiary protection status

The EU Directive 2004/83/EC and its Recast 2011/95/EC (i.e. the QD) for the first time established a secondary protection status. As a legislative act under the first EU pillar, the QD was drafted to extend a harmonized minimum standard of protection EU-wide and consequently replace the net of deviating domestic legislation and the discretion of governments. As codified in article 1:

> The purpose of this Directive is to lay down standards for the qualification of third-country nationals or stateless persons as beneficiaries of international protection, for a uniform status for refugees or for persons eligible for subsidiary protection, and for the content of the protection-granted.

In comparison to the TPD, the QD was designed to address individual claims and grant individual protection, originally designed for non-Europeans that were not eligible for protection under the 1951 Convention (European Commission

2001a: 510). It was, however, not intended 'as a radical overhaul of protection' but as a harmonizing codification of the existing and observed state practice. The primacy of the 1951 Convention was not to be questioned but was paralleled by a complementary status (McAdam 2007: 56).

Looking at recent figures, the 28 member states of the EU registered 398,200 asylum claims in 2013, a 32 per cent increase on 2012 (301,000). EU states together accounted for 82 per cent of all new asylum claims submitted in Europe (UNHCR 2014: 2, 8). Current numbers indicate that 15.1 per cent of the first instance decisions on asylum in Europe granted refugee status, while 13.8 per cent granted subsidiary protection (10.8 per cent in 2012). The proportional dissemination of refugee and subsidiary protection status varies strongly within the different EU member states. While Sweden granted subsidiary protection in 35 per cent of its decisions, the Netherlands 22.2 per cent, Italy 22.0 per cent, other countries such as the United Kingdom (UK) (0.3 per cent), Greece (1.3 per cent) or France (2.5 per cent) only rarely consider subsidiary protection (BAMF 2014). Notwithstanding the domestic variations, the QD and its subsidiary protection status has become an important instrument for non-Convention refugee claims and consequently a clear and consistent interpretation of its terms and scope is indispensable.

The QD itself does not offer a definition of subsidiary protection but it does establish criteria to identify beneficiaries of subsidiary protection. Under article 2(f) and (g), third country nationals and stateless persons are eligible if they face a risk of suffering serious harm as a result of their refoulement. Serious harm is defined in article 15 as:

a   the death penalty or execution,
b   torture or inhumane and degrading treatment or punishment of the applicant in the country of origin,
c   serious threat to a civilian's life by reason of indiscriminate violence in situations of international or internal armed conflict.

The status of subsidiary protection offers a range of different rights to asylum-seekers, although not completely congruent to refugee status. To benefit from these rights, people must fulfil the eligibility criteria as referred to above. However, on matters of environmental disasters or climate change, articles 2 and 15 are completely silent. Interestingly, however, the idea of subsidiary protection for people fleeing environmental disasters was already discussed during the drafting processes of the QD, as evidenced in the Discussion Paper of the European Commission of 1999 (European Parliament 1999: 6; McAdam 2012: 103).

The original proposal of the QD defined, next to paragraph (a) and (b) in article 15(c) eligibility as 'a result of systemic or generalized violations of their human rights'. Serious violations of human rights often occur during times of natural disasters and not necessarily only during times of armed conflict. Among others Piotrowicz and Van Eck argued one could interpret that systematic or generalized violations of human rights would entail violations during or due to times of natural disasters and therefore as a situation establish protection under article 15 (Messineo 2011: 10).

Furthermore, the adoption of an article 15(d) had been proposed concerning 'acts outside the scope of litra a–c (…) entitl[ing] the applicant to protection against refoulement in accordance with the international obligation of Member States' (Council of the European Union 2002: 4). However, the Danish presidency explicitly emphasized that acts and treatment would cover solely man-made disasters not those arising out of natural disasters or situations of famine (Council of the European Union 2002: 2). The final version of the QD was then also further limited. The proposed wider reference to the general field of human rights law was replaced by the limitations of 'situations of international or internal armed conflict' in article 15(c). The proposed article 15(d) was excluded altogether explicitly due to its broad scope: Germany, Belgium, Spain and France held that it was 'too vague and could allow a wide margin of interpretation' (Council of the European Union 2002: 11). Consequently, a narrow reading and exclusion of natural disasters can be considered as the intention of the QD's drafters which would contradict any broadening interpretation of the terms today. On the other hand, if one can prove an evolving character and reinterpretation of the terms, departing from their original meaning, one could argue that the terms and their interpretation have changed their meaning and scope in accordance with contemporary developments.

As an inclusion of a specific reference to environmental displacement in a new regulation is unlikely in the near future, the question must be whether natural disaster can be subsumed under the now codified paragraphs of article 15(a)–(c). Article 15(a) is interpreted as to relate to 'legal, administrative, police and/or judicial measures which either persecutory in themselves or have the appearance of the law and are sufficiently linked to make return to the country of origin untenable' with the most prominent cases being the death penalty or executions (European Commission 2001b: 19). Article 15(c) was defined by the ECJ in its renowned *Elgafajj* judgment as applying solely to indiscriminate violence occurring in situations of armed conflict. Both do not offer an interpretative space to include environmental disasters in their scope of application. Therefore only article 15 paragraph (b) could potentially be applied to this context.

The ECJ has, until now, not decided on article 15(b) matters linked to environmental disasters. One can, nonetheless, turn for guidance to the field of human rights law and the evolving jurisprudence of the ECtHR. The European legislator has established a close link between its Union asylum law regulations of article 15(b) and European human rights law, as article 15(b) mirrors the wording of article 3 ECHR. Therefore one can pose the question of what the exact scope of article 3 is and whether it might include protection for environmental migrants? In a second step, the relationship between the QD and the European Convention must be considered to evaluate whether one can transfer evolving case law concerning article 3 ECHR to the interpretation of article 15(b) QD.

Regional human rights law

The effects of climate change and environmental disasters affect infrastructure, social welfare, healthcare and general living standards in the respective areas. It severely affects the enjoyment of human rights such as the right to life, rights to adequate food, freedom from hunger, or the right to adequate housing. However, violations of human rights by their countries of origin will not simultaneously entail positive obligations on destination countries, i.e., European states. Although, states might legally not be obliged to balance poor living conditions in countries of origin, one can question if they have the right to return people to these respective countries and thus the fundamental principle of human rights law comes to the fore: the principle of non-refoulement. Non-refoulement as a term refers to a principle that is defined in a number of international and regional treaties and customary law.[3] 'The' principle, however, differs, depending on the various legal sources in which it is enshrined, and thus differs also in its scope, its wider content, the group of beneficiaries and the addressees of its obligatory nature (Messineo 2011: 4).

   Under European human rights law, the principle of non-refoulement is most prominently encompassed in the European Convention. Although, as the House of Lords held in its *R. v. Special Adjudicator* case, all human rights potentially entail a non-refoulement obligation in theory, by balancing these obligations against national immigration laws, not all violations of a human right will be disproportionate and establish a prohibition on return (Kacaj v. Secretary of State of the Home Affairs Department 2002: 26). The most prominent articles containing non-refoulement obligations that have been repeatedly acknowledged are article 2, '*Everyone's right to life shall be protected by law*' and article 3, '*No one shall be subjected to torture or to inhuman or degrading treatment or punishment*'. The principle of non-refoulement is considered to be an inherent part of both articles – 'If article 3 may be engaged it is difficult to follow why, as a matter of logic, article 2 could be peremptorily excluded. There may well be cases where article 3 is not applicable but article 2 may be' (Regina v. Special Adjudicator ex parte Ullah [FC] 2004: 40) – albeit article 2 alone as non-refoulement basis has never been successfully argued in court.[4]

   Article 3 ECHR prohibits the return of anyone to a place where they would face 'real and substantiated' risk of ill-treatment, thus limiting the parties to the convention from expelling aliens from their state territory. Article 3 ECHR has been the subject of many judgments, first and foremost by the ECtHR, addressing the scope and content of the prohibition. The *Soering* and *Cruz Varas v. Sweden* Cases of 1989 and 1991 can be considered as starting points (Mole and Meredith 2010). Much wider in scope than article 3 Convention Against Torture, article 3 ECHR encompasses inhuman or degrading treatment without accepting limitations or establishing exceptions, as strongly reaffirmed by the Court, for instance in *Saadi v. Italy*: 'As the Court has repeatedly held, there can be no derogation from that rule' (Saadi v. Italy 2008: 38). It establishes a non-derogable right and while 'states face immense difficulties in protecting the communities

(...) this must not call into question the absolute nature of article 3' (Saadi v. Italy 2008: 138).

Turning the attention to the question of natural disasters and human rights law, one again has to stress that both prominent non-refoulement provisions in the European Convention do not contain specific reference to natural disasters or climate change. However, they are to be interpreted as applying widely and consequently recent jurisprudence must be analysed to assess whether the prohibition of forcible return to disaster affected countries is debated or applied in the ECtHR's jurisprudence.

Expanding jurisprudence of the European Court of Human Rights

Legal protection for people fleeing environmental disasters has as such never been decided upon by either the ECJ or the ECtHR. Nonetheless, argumentation and interpretations of other judgments could lead to the future protection of environmental migrants. This section will mainly address the evolving case law of the ECtHR concerning article 3.

Article 3 ECHR contains the three hierarchical elements, torture, inhumane and degrading treatment or punishment, which have been considered as distinct but related: 'It is plain that there may be treatment to which all these descriptions apply, for all torture must be inhumane and degrading treatment, and inhumane treatment also degrading' (Addo and Grief 1998: 511). While torture is, by definition,[5] excluded in the context of environmental disasters, inhumane or degrading treatment or punishment can be considered as potentially including situations caused by natural disasters, as those often coincide with violations of human rights of socio-economic character. These could be, for instance, the right to food, housing, healthcare or social welfare. As socio-economic rights have in the human rights framework quite often a less prominent role than is attributed to civil and political rights, the holistic approach argues that also civil and political rights inherently contain socio-economic rights. The norms could therefore be used 'as vehicles for the direct or indirect protection of norms of another treaty dealing with a different category of human rights' (Scott 1989. 771). On several occasions, the court rejected the violation of socio-economic rights as activating the principle of non-refoulement, which would prevent any application in situations of natural disasters. The ECtHR has referred to practical considerations that would limit the preclusion of return to those affected states of origins. In *N. v. UK*, the bench stressed that varying conditions in the repelling state and country of origin could not be balanced by the Court (N. v. United Kingdom 2008: 44). In *F. v. UK* the Court clearly emphasized '[o]n a purely pragmatic basis, it cannot be required that an expelling Contracting State only return an alien to a country which is in full and effective enforcement of all the rights and freedoms set out in the Convention' (F. v. United Kingdom 2004: 12).

There are not many successful cases that establish broad protection from forcible return to countries in which socio-economic rights are at risk. However, on can deduce a potential development from the case law of the ECtHR.

One important development in non-refoulement cases is the detachment from the traditional actors of persecution; these have always been states through their organs. The sources of risk are not confined by the article but have traditionally been aligned with the conduct of state officials and an intentionally inflicted serious harm, such as expulsion to countries where the claimant would fear torture or execution. Judgments, such as *H.L.R. v. France* or *Ahmed v. Austria*, have expanded the interpretation to include acts committed by private individuals (H.L.R. v. France 1997: 32). With regards to climate change and environmental disasters the question of sources of the risk of ill-treatment is decisive and debates on the distinction of man-made versus natural causes can again be referred to. One can in this regard make a distinction in the jurisprudence of the ECtHR. On one hand there have been cases litigated on harm that was naturally occurring, without responsibility of the receiving state; on the other hand, there are cases where actors in the receiving country are considered to be the predominant cause of the risk of ill-treatment (Scott 2014: 413). These two types of assessments of harm can potentially be applied to situations of natural disasters.

Following the traditional distinction of natural disasters as naturally occurring phenomena, not being man-made, the first type of 'purely natural occurring harm' as engaging article 3 protection seems promising. In this type of harm, the state itself can neither be directly nor indirectly made responsible for the harm. The most prominent case of non-refoulement and violations of socio-economic rights in the receiving country, *D. v. UK*, falls into this category and is therefore considered as a potential role model case for environmentally-displaced claimants. This case lays the cornerstone for any argumentation on the prohibition of return to countries where it is feared that socio-economic rights will be violated by naturally occurring harm. The ECtHR stressed that,

> [S]ufficient flexibility to address the application of that Article in other contexts which might arise (…) the source of that risk of proscribed treatment in the receiving country stems from factors which cannot engage either directly or indirectly the responsibility of the public authorities of that country it is not prevented from scrutinising a claim under Article 3.
>
> (D. v. United Kingdom 1997: 49)

The scope of ill-treatment in the country of destination, St Kitts, was analysed as to whether it would include lack of medical care (D. v. United Kingdom 1997: 53–4). The ECtHR considered the level and quality of domestic healthcare systems and income and social security in a non-refoulement case evolving an HIV positive claimant. These exceptional circumstances included poor medical conditions in the country of origin, no reliability of whether he would get a hospital bed and therewith also the risk of further infections in case of lack of shelter and proper nutrition or any palliative care. These circumstances were further enhanced by the lack of familiar or social support and the general health and sanitation situation in the country that all would 'subject him to acute mental and physical suffering' (D. v. United Kingdom 1997: 52). However, consideration of a risk of ill-treatment in *D.* and comparable cases, the court established a high threshold of both 'very exceptional' circumstances and 'compelling humanitarian considerations' (D. v. United Kingdom 1997: 54). Until now, *D. v. UK* is the sole judgment in which the court's assessment of the situation considered the threshold of extreme exceptional circumstances to be so high as to constitute a violation of article 3 in case of return.

N. v. UK was a comparable case concerning the return of an HIV/AIDS infected person to Uganda, in which the bench held, in contrast to *D. v. UK*, that the circumstances were not sufficiently exceptional as to entail a violation of article 3. The bench ruled that the return of the applicant, because she was not in the last stages of illness and could find adequate care with her family, was not sufficient to amount to a breach of article 3: 'The fact that the applicant's circumstances, including his life expectancy, would be significantly reduced if he were to be removed from the Contracting State is not sufficient in itself to give rise to breach of article 3' (N. v. United Kingdom 2008: 42). They explicitly referred to the limited protection of socio-economic rights as it was 'essentially directed to protect civil and political rights' (N. v. United Kingdom 2008: 44) and 'Advances in medical science, together with social and economic differences between countries, entail that the level of treatment available in the Contracting state and the country of origin may vary considerably. (…) Article 3 does not place an obligation on the Contracting state to alleviate such disparities through the provision' (N. v. United Kingdom 2008: 44). The dissenting judges heavily criticized the neglect of socio-economic rights protection in favour of civil and political considerations (N. v. United Kingdom 2008: Joint Dissenting Opinion: 4).

Similarly in 2011, the court delivered its judgment in *Yoh-Ekale Mwanje v. Belgium* concerning the detention of an HIV woman from Cameroon, and although her article 3 complaint was dismissed, six out of seven judges called for the Grand Chamber to revise its ruling in *N. v. UK*. The extreme severity of the threshold was not considered consistent with the object and purpose of article 3, establishing a fundamental human right (Yoh-Ekale Mwanje v. Belgium 2012: Partly Concurring Opinion: 6). In a later case, *Bensaid v. UK*, a comparable threshold to that of *D. v. UK* was again not reached. This case examined the refoulement of a schizophrenic application and its return to Algeria. In reference to *D. v. UK*, the judgment states the circumstances were 'less certain and more speculative'. However, also in this case the separate opinion stressed that there was 'considerable hesitation' and 'powerful and compelling humanitarian considerations in the present case which would justify and merit reconsideration by the national authorities of the decisions to remove the applicant to Algeria' (Bensaid v. United Kingdom 2001: Separate Opinion). These cases can be discussed as first steps in expanding the scope of article 3 and could be applied to situations of natural disasters where the affected state has insufficient resources to care for the basic needs of the affected persons.

Considering more recent case law of the ECtHR, the types of naturally occurring harm have been widely replaced by article 3 situations, in which the court considered the humanitarian situation in the receiving country but linked

to the conduct of human actors – not to an occurring natural harm. In M.S.S. *v.*
Belgium and Greece, the ECtHR considered article 3 as encompassing the denial
of basic socio-economic rights in refoulement cases. Here it was even more
important as the court assessed the principle within the EU context, reflecting on
the transfer of an asylum seeker under Dublin II. The bench held that asylum
seekers, due to their special vulnerabilities, were in need of special protection.
The bench, furthermore, considered the living conditions of the applicant in
Greece, characterized by extreme poverty, being unable to cater for the most
basic needs such as food hygiene and a place to live as a violation of article 3
(M.S.S. v. Belgium and Greece 2011: 251).

In *Sufi and Elmi*, the Court again considered the humanitarian situation, and
further evolved the MSS assessment concerning refugees and IDP camps in
Somalia and Kenya. The Court evaluated the living conditions in the refugee
camps to be so inadequate that a return would breach article 3. Although
extending again the assessment to the living conditions in the country of origin
to encompass poor living conditions, the Court tied the source of the ill-treatment
to human conduct: With regards to the actors, multiple actors were seen as
causing or contributing to the humanitarian crisis, including, among others, the
Ethiopian forces and the non-state armed group, Al-Shabab.

> If the dire humanitarian conditions in Somalia were solely or even
> predominantly attributable to poverty or to the state's lack of resources to
> deal with a naturally occurring phenomenon, such as a drought, the test in
> *N. v. the United Kingdom* may well have been considered to be the appropriate
> one. However, it is clear that while drought has contributed to the
> humanitarian crisis, the crisis is predominantly due to the direct and indirect
> actions of the parties to the conflict.
>
> (Sufi and Elmi v. United Kingdom 2011: 281)

This argumentation is established as the predominant cause test (Scott 2014:
415). The Court held that droughts would not generally cause a violation of
article 3, but if the predominant cause is the action of the parties to the conflict,
then it is not necessary to apply the exceptionally high threshold test. For the
predominant cause test, the humanitarian situation, however, would need to be
characterized by an inability to cater for the most basic needs, vulnerability to
ill-treatment and the prospects of improving the situation in the near future. In
Sufi and Elmi, the Court found these criteria fulfilled, as there was only limited
access to food and water, the IDPs were with regards to access to shelter, at the
risk of being exploited by landlords, as well as vulnerable with regards to violent
crime, exploitation, abuse and forcible recruitment in the camps and without
much prospect of improvement within a reasonable time frame (Sufi and Elmi v.
United Kingdom 2011: 291). However, the existing case law does not clarify
whether all mentioned three criteria must be proven cumulatively in order to
apply this lower threshold (Scott 2014: 416).

What can be observed in these judgments discussed above is a strong reluctance to find violations of article 3 for socio-economic matters, as the threshold of the exceptional circumstances for cases of purely naturally occurring harm is almost never reached. The second test that can be applied is including the humanitarian situation in the receiving country, setting lower than 'exceptional' standards. However, in these types of cases, the root cause for the situation precluding return must be predominantly found in human conduct. A multi-causality of the causes and actors involved is herein already acknowledged. McAdams underlined, in concrete applications, the multi-causality of harm would work in favour of the applicant and 'the combination of environmental, social, economic and political factors, which draw on human-made as well as natural vulnerabilities, may better substantiate an Article 2 or 3 claim' (McAdam 2011: 21).

Relation of Article 3 ECHR and Article 15 Qualification Directive

Article 3 ECHR has been subject to a number of cases broadening the traditional scope of its application. Article 15 establishing subsidiary protection under European asylum law has until now not been considered in judgments on natural disasters. In particular for asylum seekers the relation between article 3 ECHR and article 15 QD is of utmost importance. Article 3 grants non-refoulement protection while article 15 and the QD establish a protection status comparable to that granted by the 1951 Refugee Convention. This status entails rights to residence permits, travel documents, social welfare, healthcare or access to employment. If the evolving case law of article 3 can be transferred to article 15, people fleeing natural disasters might, in the future, be considered eligible for subsidiary protection.

Recital 25 of the QD refers to the ECHR and article 3 by underlining that the criteria of eligibility should be drawn from international obligations under human rights law. And as article 15(b) mirrors article 3 in the exact wording, one can strongly argue for a common development and application of the case law, by the ECtHR as well as the ECJ. The identical character has been furthermore acknowledged in the case law: article 15(b) 'corresponds, in essence' to article 3 ECHR and if anything than article 15 would go beyond article 3 due to its subparagraph (c) (Elgafaji v. Staatssecretaris van Justitie 2009: 28–9). In *Sufi and Elmi*, the ECtHR upheld a comparable protection: 'based on the ECJ's interpretation in *Elgafaji*, the Court is not persuaded that article 3 of the Convention, as interpreted in *NA* [N.A. v. United Kingdom 2008], does not offer comparable protection to that afforded under the Directive' (Sufi and Elmi v. United Kingdom 2011: 226).

If one would want to argue for a different interpretation due to the QD being Union Law and article 3 being human rights law, one can also refer to article 4 of the Charter of Fundamental Rights: article 15(b) as well as article 3 ECHR is again exactly mirrored by article 4 Charter. In *N.S.* of 2011, the Court rejected a different scope of protection granted by article 3 ECHR and article 4 Charter. (N.S. and others v. Secretary of State for Home Affairs Department 2011: 94, 106). The Court of Justice stated in *Salahadin Abdulla* and *Bolbol*:

Directive 2004/83 must for that reason be interpreted (…) in a manner consistent with (…) other relevant to in point 1 of the first paragraph of Article 63 EC, now Article 78(1) TFEU. As is apparent from recital 10 to that directive, Directive 2004/83 must also be interpreted in a manner consistent with the fundamental rights and the principles recognized in particular, by the Charter of Fundamental Rights of the European Union.
(Nawras Bolbol v. Bevándorlási és Állampolgársági Hivatal 2010: 36–8)

The reference to article 78(1) TFEU again refers to the consistent application, albeit different jurisdiction:

1. The Union shall develop a common policy on asylum, subsidiary protection and temporary protection with a view to offering appropriate status to any third-country national requiring international protection and ensuring compliance with the principle of non-refoulement. This policy must be in accordance with the Geneva Convention of 28 July 1951 and the Protocol of 31 January 1967 relating to the status of refugees, and other relevant treaties.

Although the above supports a close link and coherent interpretation of both fields of law, the autonomy of Union law and consequently the autonomy of CJEU jurisprudence from European Human Rights Law and cases of the ECtHR is nonetheless often stressed. Further, Advocate General Melozzi reiterated this point on the relation between article 3 ECHR and article 15(c) QD:

[T]he real point of the debate (…) concerns, in actual fact, the scope of the protection which must be afforded to applicants for asylum on the basis of Community law (…) the answer to that question cannot be inferred from Article 3 of the ECHR but must be sought principally through the prism of Article 15 c) of the Directive.
(Elgafaji v. Staatssecretaris van Justitie 2009: 17, 19)

Furthermore he said 'Community provisions, irrespective of which provisions are concerned, are given an independent interpretation which cannot therefore vary to and/or be dependent on developments in the case law of the European Court of Human Rights' (Elgafaji v. Staatssecretaris van Justitie 2009: 19). An in-depth concretization of the relationship and its influence on the jurisprudence is still debated by scholars. However, a further obstacle to the transfer of the broader interpretation of the ECtHR to the QD for protection for persons fleeing natural disasters remains. With regards to the two types of harm discussed, the QD itself rejects an application of its terms to purely naturally occurring harm. Article 6 QD explicitly addressed *Actors of persecution or serious harm* and exhaustively refers to: a) the state; b) parties or organizations controlling the state or a substantial part of the territory; c) non-state actors, if it can be demonstrated that the actors mentioned in point a) and b) including international organizations, are unable or unwilling to provide protection against persecution or serious harm as defined in article 7. The QD, in comparison to the silent article 3 ECHR, thus restricts its application to serious harm resulting from human conduct and would solely encompass the humanitarian situations if predominantly caused by states, parties or organizations with territorial control or non-state actors, cases such as the mentioned *Sufi and Elmi*, rather than the medical cases, *D. v. UK* or *N. v. UK*.

The *internal flight alternative* is another criterion restricting the application of the QD. Article 8 QD stresses that,

> As part of the assessment of the application for international protection, Member States may determine that an applicant is not in need of international protection if in a part of the country of origin, he or she (…) b) has access to protection against persecution or serious harm as defined in Article 7.

In the determination of whether or not other parts of a country would provide for an internal protection alternative, the burden of proof lies with the member states. Problematic is the fact that the assessment of such internal protection is individually made, combining general circumstances in the country as well as personal circumstances of the applicant. This leads to varying assessments by the courts of the member states as well as among the member states (UNHCR 2011: 79ff.). In cases of natural disasters these would most likely become applicable as one can imagine most events to have territorially restricted consequences and will offer sufficient possibility of seeking refuge in other non-effected areas of the country – and thus precluding the application of the QD and its subsidiary protection status.

Conclusion

In all cases the characterization of a violation of a socio-economic right, for instance access to healthcare, as included in inhumane or degrading treatment, was only considered under the most extreme circumstances. It has been argued by the ECtHR that the lack of respective services or resources in the country of origin will only by itself amount to a violation of article 3 if survival would be assessed as impossible after return. The ECtHR has precluded return because of an article 3 violation in only one case. The assessed cases mostly concern the lack of adequate medical care, social welfare, living conditions, but have so far not considered situations of natural disasters. In more recent judgments, the court furthermore chose to link the humanitarian situation to the conduct of state or non-state actors instead of assessing a purely naturally occurring harm with an exceptionally high threshold. One can therefore witness a general evolvement of the case law concerning socio-economic rights in the scope of article 3, however, while potentially opening the interpretation to include events of natural disasters, the threshold is either set so high as to exclude application in mostly all cases, or focuses on human involvement in the ill-treatment.

The Court of Justice has not ruled on matters of environmental displacement in regards to Union Asylum Law and therefore the possibility of transferring the interpretation of ECHR provisions to the QD provisions was considered. Although the EUs general incentive is to establish a coherent and harmonized interpretation of both fields of law, the autonomy of Union law is still very much put in focus. Furthermore, with regards to purely naturally occurring disasters, the Qualifications application is restricted as it explicitly foresees human actors of persecution. Against this background, subsidiary protection cases could only be positively assessed in rare cases if some form of human involvement can be proven and internal protection is not given. Currently, a request for preliminary ruling from the Labour Appelate Court of Brussels was lodged on 31 October 2013 (Case C-562/13). The question relates to the interpretation of the QD article 15 (b), when the person seeking asylum 'suffers from an illness which is of such kind as to entail a real risk of his life or physical integrity or a real risk of inhuman or degrading treatment where there is no adequate treatment for that illness in his country of origin'. This judgment will be an opportunity to clarify obligations concerning socio-economic rights violations in Union Law.

All the analysed judgments in themselves must be considered as theoretically progressive concerning socio-economic rights (Kolmannskog and Myrstad 2009: 321). Nonetheless, one cannot identify a framework for the protection of people fleeing natural disasters. Protection has only in the most exceptional circumstances been established for single individuals. The analysis reveals that article 3 protection against non-refoulement might be further expanded to cover wider ranges of socio-economic rights violations and development. However, subsidiary protection for people fleeing natural disasters under the given instruments of asylum law of the EU cannot be considered realistic for the future.

Notes

1   Already in 1990, the IPCC noted that 'the greatest single impact of climate change might be on human migration' (IPCC 1990: 20).
2   As a supranational entity, the EU is characterized by a unique legal structure that establishes a different framework of rights and duties for European citizens. Therefore, intra-European movements due to environmental events will not be discussed as these are covered through different branches of union law. For more information, see European Commission 2013: 11.
3   It is among others contained in the Refugee Convention, the Convention against Torture, the International Covenant on Civil and Political Rights and both the European Charter and European Convention on Human Rights.
4   Only in the *Baader v. Sweden* Case, the ECtHR found a violation of article 2 but also in conjunction with article 3, (App. No. 13284/04, ECtHR, 8 November 2005). The Court denied a similar argumentation of interpreting specific non-refoulement obligations in the articles 8 and 9 as they would naturally be included in any violation of article 3. Interestingly, it has been addressed by the ECtHR itself to recognize other Convention Rights, articles 2, 5, 6, as implicitly establishing non-refoulement obligations. This was among others established in Othman (Abu Qatada) v. United Kingdom 2012: para. 260.
5   In reference to article 1 of the United Nations Convention against Torture: 'The term torture means any act by which severe pain or suffering, whether physical or mental, is intentionally inflicted on a person, for such purposes as obtaining from him or a third

person information or a confession, punishing him for an act he or a third person has committed or is suspected of having committed (…)'.

References

Addo, M.K. and Grief, N. (1998) Does article 3 of the European Convention on Human Rights enshrine absolute rights. *European Journal of International Law.* 9: 510–24.

Bensaid v. United Kingdom (2001) App. No. 44599/98, 6 February 2001.

Bundesamt für Migration und Flüchtlinge (BAMF) (2014) Das Bundesamt in Zahlen 2013: Asyl, Migration und Integration. *Bundesamt für Migration und Flüchtlinge* [online]. Available: www.bamf.de [Accessed 28 November 2014].

Council of Europe (2008) *Environmentally-induced migration and displacement: a 21st century challenge,* Doc. 1178523 [online]. Available: www.refworld.org [Accessed 2 October 2014].

Council of the European Union (2002) *Presidency note to the Strategic Committee on Immigration, Frontiers and Asylum,* LIMITE ASYLILE 43, 12148/02 [online]. Available: https://www.eerstekamer.nl [Accessed 28 October 2014].

D. v. United Kingdom (1997) App. No. 30240/96, 2 May 1997.

Elgafaji v. Staatssecretaris van Justitie (2009) Case C-465/07, 17 February 2009.

European Commission (2001a) *Explanatory Memorandum to the proposal of the Commission on a qualification directive* [online]. Available: www.refworld.org [Accessed 11 October 2014].

European Commission (2001b) *Proposal for a Council Directive on minimum standards for the qualification and status of third country nationals and stateless persons as refugees or as persons who otherwise need international protection* [online]. Available www.refworld.org [Accessed 29 September 2014].

European Commission (2013) *Staff working paper: climate change, environmental degradation, and migration, communication from the Commission to the European Parliament.* Brussels: European Commission.

European Commission and DG Justice, Freedom and Security (2009) *Acquis of the European Union* [online]. Available: http://ec.europa.eu [Accessed 2 October 2014].

European Commission and DG Migration and Home Affairs (2014) *Common European asylum system* [online]. Available: http://ec.europa.eu [Accessed 2 October 2014].

European Parliament (1999) *Presidency conclusions: Tampere European Council of 14–15 October 1999* [online]. Available: www.europarl.europa.eu [Accessed 2 October 2014].

F. v. United Kingdom (2004) App. No. 17341/03, 22 June 2004.

H.L.R. v. France (1997) App. No. 24573/94, 9 April 1997.

Intergovernmental Panel on Climate Change (IPCC) (1990) *First assessment report.* Cambridge: Cambridge University Press.

Kacaj v. Secretary of State of the Home Affairs Department (2002) EWCA Civ 314.

Kolmannskog, V. and Myrstad, F. (2009) Environmental displacement in European Asylum Law. *European Journal of Migration and Law.* 11(4): 313–26.

McAdam, J. (2007) *Complementary protection in International Refugee Law.* Oxford: Oxford University Press.

McAdam, J. (2011) *Climate change displacement and International Law: complementary protection standards* [online]. Available: www.unhcr.org [Accessed 29 September 2014].

McAdam, J. (2012) *Climate change, forced migration, and International Law.* Oxford: Oxford University Press.

Messineo, F. (2011) Non-refoulement obligations in Public International Law: towards a new protection status? In *Research Companion to Migration Theory and Policy*, ed. S. Juss. London: Ashgate.

Mole, N. and Meredith, C. (2010) Asylum and the European Convention on Human Rights. *Human Rights Files*. (9): 19–80.

M.S.S. v. Belgium and Greece (2011) App. No. 30696/09, 21 January 2011.

N. v. United Kingdom (2008) App. No. 26565/05, 27 May 2008.

N.A. v. United Kingdom (2008) App. No. 25904/07, 06 August 2008.

Nawras Bolbol v. Bevándorlási és Állampolgársági Hivatal (2010) Case C 31/09.

N.S. and others v. Secretary of State for Home Affairs Department (2011) C-411/10 and C-493/10.

Othman (Abu Qatada) v. United Kingdom (2012) App. No 8139/09, 17 November 2012.

Pachauri, R.K. and Reisinger, A. eds. (2007) *Climate change 2007: synthesis report, contribution of Working Groups I, II and III to the fourth assessment report of the Intergovernmental Panel on Climate Change*. Geneva: Intergovernmental Panel on Climate Change.

Regina v. Special Adjudicator ex parte Ullah (FC) (2004) UKHL 26, 17 June 2004.

Saadi v. Italy (2008) Appl. No. 37201/06, 28 February 2008.

Scott, C. (1989) Interdependence and permeability of human rights norms: towards a partial fusion of the International Covenants on Human Rights. *Osgoode Hall Law Journal*. 27(3): 769–878.

Scott, M. (2014) Natural disasters, climate change and non-refoulement: what scope for resisting expulsion under articles 3 and 8 of the European Convention on Human Rights? *International Journal on Refugee Law*. 26(3): 404–32.

Sufi and Elmi v. United Kingdom (2011) App. No. 8319/07 and 11449/07, 28 June 2011.

United Nations High Commissioner on Refugees (UNHCR) (2011) *Safe and last? Law and practice in selected EU member states with respect to asylum seekers fleeing indiscriminate violence: a UNHCR research project* [online]. Available: www.unhcr.org/4e2d7f029. html [Accessed 29 September 2014].

United Nations High Commissioner on Refugees (UNHCR) (2014) *UNHCR asylum trends 2013: levels and trends in industrialized countries* [online]. Available: www.unhcr. ch [Accessed 29 September 2014].

Yoh-Ekale Mwanje v. Belgium (2012) App. No. 10486/10, 20 December 2012.

5 Complementary protection

The role of courts in expanding protection to 'environmental refugees' in domestic asylum regimes

Thea Coventry

Introduction

While humans have always used migration as a survival strategy in response to environmental degradation (IOM 2007: 1), climate change will lead to increased numbers of displaced persons, both within nation states and across national borders (UNHCR 2009b: 4). The existing international refugee law framework, centring on the 1951 Convention relating to the Status of Refugees ('1951 Refugee Convention'), does not adequately provide for persons displaced because of natural disasters or environmental degradation. However, some states, including EU member states, Hong Kong, Mexico, Canada, the United States, New Zealand and Australia,[1] have recently expanded their protection regimes, awarding protection or relief from deportation to asylum seekers falling outside of the 1951 Refugee Convention protection grounds (Mandal 2005: xiii). Persons can access asylum when a country's international *non-refoulement* obligations are triggered under international human rights law, particularly the human rights conventions (CAT 1984; ICCPR 1966). This chapter assesses the role of judges and tribunal members in three common law states in expanding complementary regimes to persons displaced because of natural disasters or the slow-onset impacts of climate change. These countries have been chosen as they have similar legal systems and tribunal-based review mechanisms for asylum claims. The case law from Australia, New Zealand and Canada, while nascent, reveals that statutory provisions restricting complementary protection to individually targeted rather than general human rights violations curtails the ability of judicial actors to extend protection grounds.

International asylum law

The 1951 Refugee Convention and its amending protocol of 1967, which is the cornerstone international instrument in refugee law, requires states to grant asylum to persons having a well-founded fear of persecution due to their race, religion, nationality, membership of a particular social group or political opinion (Refugee Convention 1951). Given the Convention was drafted in response to

World War II mass displacement (Kolmannskog 2012: 1075), it reflects the political and geographic nature of the refugee problem at the time, and does not envisage protection extending to displacement from environmental degradation. However, while refugee law is informed by the broad object and purpose of the Convention and amending protocol, it remains a dynamic body of law and has proved sufficiently flexible to-date to respond to social changes, such as gender-based persecution, which was not originally considered by its drafters (Kolmannskog 2012: 1075; UNHCR 2001). Despite this, the following analysis reveals only limited space within existing international and European asylum law for climate change displaced persons.

1951 Refugee Convention

'Refugee' as a legal term is defined by article 1 of the 1951 Refugee Convention, read in conjunction with the 1967 Protocol. A refugee is considered as a person who:

> Owing to well-founded fear of being persecuted for reasons of race, religion, nationality, membership of a particular social group or political opinion, is outside the country of his or her nationality and is unable, or owing to such fear, is unwilling to avail himself or herself of the protection of that country; or who, not having a nationality and being outside the country of his former habitual residence as a result of such events, is unable or, owing to such fear, is unwilling to return to it.
>
> (art. 1)

The definition contains several elements, which make its application to environmentally displaced persons problematic. Firstly, a person applying for refugee protection must have crossed an international border; secondly, they must be unable to access protection of his or her own country; and finally, they need to have been persecuted for reasons of race, religion, nationality, membership of a particular social group or political opinion.

Most climate change and environmentally-induced migration will fail to meet this definition for the following reasons. It is anticipated that most climate change induced movement will be internal and gradual rather than traversing an international border (UNHCR 2009a: 4). While some cross-border displacement is likely to occur, it is unlikely to be in overwhelming numbers or in the form of 'flight' from persecution. Further, as McAdam discusses, classifying 'climate change' as 'persecution' is problematic, firstly because a sufficiently serious violation of a human right must be demonstrated and secondly, a 'persecutor' needs to be established (McAdam 2011a: 12–13). Extensive human rights violations, and other kinds of serious harm, can however meet the threshold seriousness to constitute persecution through accumulation, although the violations would not amount to persecution when assessed individually (UNHCR 2011: 3). However, while the 'persecution' element could conceivably be met in situations of extreme human rights violations, establishing a persecutor is more complex under international law. While identifying a 'persecutor' might be possible in cases of man-made disaster, such as a nuclear power plant meltdown, the 'persecutor' for climate change would be the industrialized countries who have failed to meet obligations to cut greenhouse emissions under international conventions (Kälin and Schepfer 2012: 8–9). A subsequent connection between the state's failure to cut emissions and the harm causing the person to migrate subsequently needs to be proven. McAdam highlights this 'reverses the refugee paradigm' as the person fleeing 'persecution' is now seeking protection in the country actually causing the harm (McAdam 2011a: 12).

This analysis was recently supported in a New Zealand High Court Case, where Justice Priestly rejected an application by a Kiribati man for refugee protection under the 1951 Refugee Convention on the grounds of 'passive persecution' from climate change-related degradation of the Kiribati atolls (Teitiota v. Ministry of Business, Innovation and Employment 2013). While the presiding judge was sympathetic to the man's plight, he held this would not entitle him to protection under the 1951 Refugee Convention because New Zealand defines persecution as the 'sustained or systemic violation of basic human rights demonstrative of a failure of state protection' (Teitiota v. Ministry of Business, Innovation and Employment 2013: [53]). The Court further rejected the argument that the 'international community' is the persecutor through contributing to climate change, as there is no evidence of intentional persecution on the part of the international community in releasing carbon emissions (Teitiota v. Ministry of Business, Innovation and Employment 2013: [55]).

Finally, the persecution needs to be on account of the person's race, religion, nationality, membership of a particular social group or political opinion, which given the indiscriminate nature of environmental degradation is unlikely to be present (Mandal 2005: 9). However, the United Nations High Commissioner for Refugees (UNHCR) has noted that situations might arise where a victim of a natural disaster flees their country of origin because their Government has consciously withheld assistance to punish or marginalize them on one of the refugee definition's five persecution grounds (UNHCR 2009a: 7). Such persons could be legitimately classified as refugees under international law. Because of the legal complexities described above the UNHCR criticizes the use of the terms 'environmental refugee' or 'climate refugee'. While noting certain groups of migrants who are in need of humanitarian assistance, fall outside the scope of international protection, the UNHCR warns against amending the 1951 Refugee Convention to include those displaced across borders because of long-term climate change or sudden natural disasters. The UNHCR is concerned that expanding the definition will provoke state parties to request a renegotiation of the Convention, which could result in a lowering of protection standards and state obligations for Convention refugees globally (UNHCR 2009a: 9).

Non-refoulement and complementary protection

In contrast to the highly-restricted refugee definition, complementary protection schemes are more likely to afford, at least, a theoretical protection space to cross-border environmentally displaced persons. Mandal notes the phrase 'complementary protection' derives from the practices that have developed in industrialized states to provide protection or relief from deportation for asylum seekers falling outside the scope of the 1951 Refugee Convention (Mandal 2005: ix, 2). Complementary protection is not a legal term, but a catch-all generic phrase for the additional protection schemes implemented by states in addition to the 1951 Refugee Convention, such as 'subsidiary protection', 'humanitarian protection' and 'temporary asylum', and as such it is not defined in any international treaty or instrument (UNHCR 2000: [2]). To date the European Union, the United States, Canada, Mexico, Australia, New Zealand and Hong Kong have all introduced complementary protection schemes into their domestic legal or administrative frameworks, but with broadly differing criteria to determine the scope of the protection (Dicker and Mansfield 2012; Loper 2010). Eligibility for protection ranges from international law *non-refoulement* obligations, purely compassionate reasons to practical obstacles to removal (UNHCR 2000: [4]). Further, a state's complementary protection obligations depend on the international conventions to which it is a party (aside from general Customary International Law obligations). These obligations include the right not to be arbitrarily deprived of law in article 6 and of the prohibition of torture and cruel, inhuman or degrading treatment or punishment under article 7 of the International Covenant on Civil and Political Rights (ICCPR), and the prohibitions on *refoulement* in the Convention against Torture and Other Cruel, Inhuman or Degrading Treatment or Punishment.

A fundamental difference between the 1951 Refugee Convention and complementary protection is that complementary protection assesses the potential harm to the person seeking asylum should they be removed from the state, rather than the nature of persecution they might suffer. The *non-refoulement* obligations can be activated where there are substantial grounds for believing that the person will suffer significant harm on return, with significant harm generally understood to be arbitrary deprivation of his or her life, death penalty, torture, cruel, inhuman or degrading treatment or punishment (Department of Immigration and Border Protection [Australia] 2014). While climate change obviously does not constitute an independent human rights violation its environmental effects could violate particular human rights giving rise to protection claims. Consequently, the UNHCR suggested that return of persons who have fled natural or ecological disasters to their country of origin could, in exceptional circumstances 'reach a level of severity amounting to inhuman treatment', thus activating *non-refoulement* obligations (UNHCR 2005: 6).

Despite the current restrictive global policies towards asylum, there is some indication from state practice and European Court of Human Rights (ECtHR) judgments that existing universal and regional standards on complementary protection could offer protection to persons forcibly displaced because of climate change or environmental events across national borders (McAdam 2011a: 15). The 1972 Declaration of the United Nations Conference on the Human Environment (Stockholm Declaration) recognized 'a fundamental right to freedom, equality and adequate conditions of life, in an environment of a quality that permits a life of dignity and well-being' (Stockholm Declaration 1972), and although the United Nations human rights treaty bodies have not recognized an actual 'right to a healthy environment' they have clearly recognized the intrinsic link between the *realization* of many human rights and the environment, such as the right to life, to health, food, water and housing (Human Rights Council 2009).[2] Despite the Office of the High Commissioner for Human Rights describing the range of rights potentially affected by the impacts of climate change, only a few could give rise to a *non-refoulement* protection obligation. These are the right to life (or arbitrary deprivation of life) and the right not to be subjected to torture or cruel, inhuman or degrading treatment or punishment as they contain absolute prohibitions, meaning the state cannot justify returning a person in any circumstances, on *refoulement*. However, while socio-economic harms may activate the *non-refoulement* principle they do not constitute an unqualified ban on the state returning the person and can be balanced against other state interests. Thus, as Leighton notes, because legal standards have not yet adequately caught up with the scientific predictions on the effects of climate change, predictions about the application of human rights law remains somewhat speculative (Leighton 2010: 2).

Common law systems

Within common law systems members of the judiciary have the capacity to 'make new law', either by specifying how statute applies to a particular situation, clarifying the law or by using common law principles to create law where no statutory law exists. Modern common law systems are generally uncodified – the law being created through a mix of individual and free standing legislative instruments and judicial precedent (the subsequently binding interpretations of statute and case-based decisions of judges). Thus, judges play an incredibly significant role in creating and shaping the law. In contrast, civil law is codified, with the legal codes being constantly updated with new legislated topics. Judges, in civil law systems, have a more limited role in investigating the case and applying the code (Robbins Collection 2014). The debate concerning the role of judges in creating new law is broad and extensive, and well beyond the subject of this chapter, but their ability to legitimately adapt existing law to new situations remains.[3]

The complementary protection regimes in Canada, New Zealand and Australia are all relatively recent (2002, 2009 and 2011 respectively), and only a limited number of cases have sought protection due to environmental degradation. The United States of America is not considered in this chapter as its complementary protection scheme is limited only to the Torture Convention *non-refoulement* obligations. In all three states, assessment of complementary protection claims are processed at the same time as Refugee Convention claims and unsuccessful applicants may seek merits review through immigration or refugee tribunals. In the three case study countries, applicants may seek review 'on the facts' of the original decision by a government official rejecting their asylum claim. The applicant may then present their situation before the tribunal member, who hears the arguments from both parties, including fresh evidence not heard during the original application. This differs from judicial review, where predominantly only errors of law made by the original decision maker can be assessed by the court judges. Conventionally, tribunal decisions are not binding on subsequent judicial decision makers, and do not 'create' law or set precedents as judges in courts can. However, their decisions do guide subsequent decisions made by other tribunal members on similar facts. Thus, they can have a quasi-precedential role. Further, tribunal members make decisions independent from official governmental policies, and can send strong alternative messages about their country's asylum responsibilities, thus often sending ripples through the public sphere beyond the applicant's actual case.[4] Only a limited number of cases, to-date, have considered complementary protection because of environmental degradation, hence the small case analysis presented here.

In both the Australian and Canadian legislation, persons are excluded from accessing complementary protection when the harm suffered or threatened would be faced by the population of the country of origin generally. This is particularly relevant for environmental degradation as it does not 'target' individuals but affects whole countries or regions. A similar provision was removed from the New Zealand legislation before it was enacted on the grounds that it 'failed to meet New Zealand's international obligations', and would exclude 'indiscriminate or generalized risk of violence' (New Zealand Human Rights Commission 2007: [11.5]–[11.6]). The removal was recommended to bring it into line with the European Council Qualification Directive 2004/83/EC (Council of the European Union 2004), '(…) an applicant must demonstrate that there is a real chance that, if returned to his or her country of origin the applicant would face serious harm' (McAdam 2011b: 711).

The removal of this exclusionary ground allowed New Zealand Tribunal members from the Immigration and Protection Tribunal to consider generalized dangers arising from climate change when considering protection applications. As discussed in detail below, both the Tribunal members and the High Court took the opportunity presented by two ultimately unsuccessful applications to extend the possible grounds of complementary protection. In doing so they relied heavily on ECtHR decisions considering article 3 of the ECtHR, Human Rights Committee comments, and academic discussions by key experts on climate change and migration. In contrast, Canada has not seen any cases seeking complementary protection on environmental grounds, and the Australian case law is extremely limited. Thus, to what extent other common law judicial actors (including judges, tribunal members or mediators) will use European decisions to inform decision-making, and take an expansive approach to their complementary protection regimes remains to be seen.

Table 5.1

Country/ Body	Non-Refoulement	Legislation/ Instrument	Prohibited Reasons	International Protocols
European Union (Excluding Denmark)	Non-refoulement	Qualification Directive 2004/83/EC – arts. 2(f) and 15	Death penalty or execution, torture, inhuman or degrading treatment or punishment, serious and individual threat to life because of indiscriminate violence in situations of international or internal armed conflict	CAT ICCPR
Australia	Grant of protection visa	Migration Amendment (Complementary Protection) Act 2011	Arbitrary deprivation of life, death penalty, torture; subjected to cruel or inhuman treatment or punishment; or degrading treatment or punishment	ICCPR CAT
Canada	Refugee Protection Conferred	Immigration and Refugee Protection Act SC 2001, c. 27, s. 97	Torture, risk to life or risk of cruel and unusual treatment or punishment (uses exceptions to define scope)	CAT ICCPR
Hong Kong	Developing non-refoulement, not accepted by government	Basic Law 1991 Bill of Rights Ordinance Case law: Secretary for Security v. Sakthevel Prabakar; C. v. Director of Immigration	Torture, cruel, inhuman or degrading treatment or punishment	CAT
			Refugee status determined by UNHCR	
Mexico	Non-refoulement	Decree on the Law on Refugees and Complementary Protection (amending General Population Act) s. 2(IV)	Torture or cruel, inhuman or degrading punishment	CAT ICCPR
New Zealand	Cannot be deported	Immigration Act 2009 ss. 130, 131	Torture, cruel treatment (meaning cruel, inhuman or degrading treatment or punishment)	CAT ICCPR
United States	Withholding of removal	Immigration and Nationality Act 1952 8 CFR ss. 208.16, 208.17	Torture	CAT

Source: Author

Australia

The federal government introduced the Protection (Class XA)(subclass 866) visa for complementary protection into Australia's migration regime in March 2012. In Australia, complementary protection describes protection for persons outside the scope of the Refugee Convention, where there exists a *real risk* that the person would suffer *significant harm* as a necessary and foreseeable consequence of being deported (Migration Amendment (Complementary Protection) Act 2011 [Australia]: s. 36(2)). The non-*refoulement* obligations are only triggered by the ICCPR and its optional death penalty protocol, and the Torture Convention. Flowing from these Conventions, significant harm is restricted to arbitrary deprivation of life, death penalty, torture, cruel or inhuman treatment or punishment or degrading treatment or punishment (Migration Act 1958 [Australia]: s. 36(2A)). However, the conventions are not directly referred to in the legislation and an alternative definition for 'significant harm' is provided.

Prior to the introduction of the Complementary Protection Visa, one tribunal case considered a refugee application by a Kiribati man on the grounds that climate change was rendering his village uninhabitable. The member was invited by the Applicant's representative to creatively interpret Australia's migration laws to accommodate climate change refugees, by considering climate change a form of persecution, and heavily affected persons from the Kiribati Islands as a 'particular social group' (0907346 [2009] RRTA [New Zealand]: [22]). While not rejecting that the applicant might fall into the particular social group of persons 'fleeing their home country for environmental reasons', the Tribunal member found there was no 'agent of persecution' or discriminatory element aimed at the man because he belonged to such a social group. Specifically in regard to climate change the Tribunal member stated:

> There is simply no basis for concluding that countries which can be said to have been historically high emitters of carbon dioxide or other greenhouse gases have any element of motivation to have any impact on residents of low lying countries such as Kiribati, either for their race, religion, nationality, membership of any particular social group or political opinion.
>
> (0907346 [2009] RRTA [New Zealand]: [51])

Unlike Refugee Convention protection, persons seeking complementary protection are not required to prove persecution on the grounds of race, religion, nationality, or membership of a particular social group or political opinion. However, few cases have considered the effects of environmental degradation since 2012. In *SZSFX v. Minister for Immigration and Border Protection* (2013) the judge stated at [32]:

> I do not find persuasive the applicant's contention that being exposed to pollution can of itself amount to 'degrading treatment' for the purposes of s 36(2)(aa) of the Migration Act. The mere fact that someone happens to

live in a polluted environment cannot of itself, in my view, found a claim to complementary protection.

Given the government's unwillingness to address the sources of local pollution, and the social repercussions the applicant and her husband experienced following protests and complaints, the judges complete exclusion of pollution from 'degrading treatment', seems out of step with the trend in the ECtHR, to include inability to access healthcare, shelter, social security or protection (in addition to a severity threshold) as degrading treatment (see M.S.S. v. Belgium and Greece 2011; Sufi v. United Kingdom 2011). The judge further noted that the 'real risk' of significant harm needs to be felt by the applicant personally not the population generally. This provision acts to limit applications under complementary protection on climate change or environmental grounds (Migration Act 1958 [Australia]: s. 32(2B)(c)). The provision has also been criticized as being incongruent with international human rights obligations, which do not require exceptionality of treatment. McAdam notes the exclusion could also permit deportation in cases with risk of genocide, starvation or indiscriminate violence (McAdam 2011b: 712). While the one judicial review case to date rejected environmental pollution as a ground for complementary protection, there is still space within Australia's common law system for the higher courts to find the current complementary protection regime does not comply with Australia's human rights obligations, and expand the definition of 'degrading treatment'.

New Zealand

New Zealand introduced complementary protection into its Immigration Act in 2009. Sections 130 and 131 provide that a person must be recognized as a protected person in New Zealand if there are substantial grounds for believing that the person would be in danger of being subjected to torture (section 130) or arbitrary deprivation of life or cruel treatment (section 131) if deported from New Zealand. Unlike the Australian provisions, the New Zealand provisions directly refer to, and incorporate the definitions of, the Convention Against Torture and the Convention on Civil and Political Rights, and do not exclude protection when the risk is a general one in the person's country of origin (Immigration Act 2009 [New Zealand]: ss. 130–131; see also McAdam 2009). The New Zealand legislation also preserves a humanitarian jurisdiction for cases where harm falling outside the scope of sections 130 and 131 can still be considered (Immigration Act 2009 [New Zealand]: ss. 206208).

Prior to the amendment of the Immigration Act 2009 several claimants in related cases from Tuvalu argued environmental factors including inundation, salinization of fresh water and coastal erosion, meant they should be considered as refugees. While expressing sympathy for their plight the claims were dismissed by the member on the basis that environmental problems on Tuvalu indiscriminately applied to all Tuvaluans, and were not directed against a Convention ground (Refugee Appeal Nos. 72185, 72186, 72189–95, 72179–81,

72313, 72314, 72315, 72316 (2000) [New Zealand]). Since sections 130 and 131 were introduced, three cases have directly considered climate change as a ground for protection.

In 2013 a Kiribati island man applied for refugee and complementary protection asylum in New Zealand. Following rejection of his application he appealed to the New Zealand Immigration and Protection Tribunal. His application was on the grounds that the Kiribati atolls would become inhabitable due to ocean inundation and environmental degradation (Teitiota v. Ministry of Business, Innovation and Employment 2013: [16]). His subsequent appeal of the primary Tribunal decision was rejected, and a further request for leave to appear before the New Zealand High Court was rejected at first instance and again on appeal (AF (Kiribati) 800413 2013; Teitiota v. Ministry of Business, Innovation and Employment 2013; Teitiota v. Ministry of Business, Innovation and Employment 2014). In 2014, a Tuvaluan family also applied for asylum on the grounds they would be in danger of arbitrary deprivation of life, or of being subjected to cruel treatment if returned to Tuvalu because of the effects of climate change. The issue here was whether the Government of Tuvalu was failing to take steps within its power to protect the applicants' lives from climate change (AC (Tuvalu) 800517–520 2014: [3]–[4]).

In *AF (Kiribati)* the Tribunal member rejected previous judicial authority that natural disasters can never lead to Convention protection, and highlighted 'pathways' that could lead to protection, such as following environmentally-related conflicts, or where environmental degradation is used as a weapon of oppression (AF (Kiribati) 800413 2013: [51]–[60]). This analysis was endorsed by the High Court on appeal. The Tribunal had previously found that human rights violations, such as real risk of starvation following discriminatory denial of food following drought, could also amount to 'being persecuted' in the Refugee Convention context (Refugee Appeal No. 74665 2004: [89]). The Tribunal members noted that the 'right to life' found in section 131 had not been statutorily defined, and thus allowed guidance from European cases, academic commentary and Human Rights Committee Comments. To this end, the Tribunal accepted that the prohibition on arbitrary deprivation of life found in article 6 ICCPR must 'take into account the positive obligation to fulfil the right to life by taking programmatic steps to prove for the basic necessities of life', including failure to respond to natural hazards. Drawing on the ECtHR case law (Budayeva and others v. Russia 2008; Öneryiliz v. Turkey 2004), the Tribunal thus reasoned that failure to protect life from natural hazard related risks could constitute an 'omission' to prevent arbitrary deprivation of life (AF (Kiribati) 800413 2013: [87]). However, the appellant failed on this ground as the risk was not sufficiently 'imminent' and the Kiribati Government had been both internationally active about its plight, and taken regulatory steps domestically in relation to the risks. Thus, no 'omission' could be made out (AF (Kiribati) 800413 2013: [88]). The appellant's fear of risk to life, such as drowning in a storm surge, remained at the level of conjecture. However, this discussion acknowledges that where climate change or environmental degradation poses a documented threat to life (i.e., drownings have occurred), combined with state failure to respond to risks, protection could be granted. This analysis was again supported by the High Court.

In the Tuvaluan case, the Tribunal member reiterated that analysis needs to focus on state protection from qualifying harm (being deprivation of life and cruel treatment), and whether the risk of harm reaches the 'in danger' threshold (AC (Tuvalu) 800517–520 2014: [57]). The fact that the danger arises from the negative effects of climate change or natural disaster did not exclude it from the scope of section 131. Thus, for 'slow-onset disasters', the existing negative impacts of climate change needed to be considered alongside anticipated consequences, which consequently shapes the specific content of the 'state's duty to protect'. Progressing even further than the 2013 case, the Tribunal member held that the 'growing recognition of the existence of positive duties on states under international human rights law in the context of natural disasters' provides 'a protection-oriented contour law around which claims for recognition as a protected person under section 131 of the Act may in principle wrap' (AC (Tuvalu) 800517–520 2014: [68]). Further, historical failure by the state to provide protection against known environmental hazards can inform risk of future failure when considering section 131. Thus, while the member acknowledged the 'significant evidential and legal' hurdles, he ultimately found that natural disasters, including climate change, 'provide a context in which a claim for recognition as a protected person under the Act may be properly grounded' (AC (Tuvalu) 800517–520 2014: [70]).

The Tribunal tempered this finding, however, by expressly rejecting, in the New Zealand context, the modified approach developed by the ECtHR to article 3 of the European Convention on Human Rights, which includes foreseeable suffering following deportation to be equated to 'treatment', and noting that the positive obligations on Tuvalu to provide protection from natural disasters cannot extend to mitigating the underlying environmental drivers of global climate change (AC (Tuvalu) 800517–520 2014: [75], [77]–[82]). The Tribunal member saw this limitation to the New Zealand provisions being upheld by the retention of the 'humanitarian protection' provision in section 207, the explicit exclusion of the state of the healthcare system of the origin country as a considering factor in section 131, and the unsettled nature of the ECtHR case law. However, where a state is not in a position to provide humanitarian assistance following a natural disaster, and arbitrarily prevents foreign humanitarian assistance to be deployed, the 'cruel treatment' provision of section 131 can be activated.

While the appellants in both the 2013 and 2014 cases were unsuccessful on the facts, the Tribunal members and the High Court used the cases as an opportunity to extend the possibility of complementary protection to natural disasters resulting from climate change. In doing so, the members and judges relied extensively on European cases, UN human rights body analysis and assessments by field experts, in their detailed findings to supplement the scanty New Zealand case law, and provide factual evidence. While carefully constructed, these cases demonstrate the willingness of the New Zealand judiciary to see themselves as actors able to expand and modify New Zealand's laws to the changing needs of asylum seekers.

Canada

Canada consolidated its refugee protection in 2002 by shifting its complementary protection regime into the same review process as for Convention refugee applicants (Dicker and Mansfield 2012: 5). The Immigration and Refugee Protection Act 2002 now enables the Immigration and Refugee Board to assess both grounds for protection. However, similar to the Australian legislation, applications for protection under section 97(1)(b) where removing a person to their country of former habitual residence would subject them to 'a risk to their life or a risk of cruel and unusual treatment or punishment' are excluded where the 'risk is faced generally by individuals in or from that country' and a reasonable internal flight alternative exists (Immigration and Refugee Protection Act 2001: s. 97(1)(b)). Despite considerably more case law than exists in Australia and New Zealand, no cases have been brought on environmental or climate change grounds.

Only one case in Canada has centred on environmental concerns, but that concerned death threats following environmental activism by a Mexican applicant, rather than an appeal on environmental degradation grounds (X (Re) 2011). The Canadian act does not provide a definition of risk to life, or cruel and unusual treatment or punishment, allowing decision makers to consider international, or other regional or national jurisprudence in determining the extent of the terms (Dicker and Mansfield 2012: 15). However, similar to the Australian legislation the particularity of risk requirement will likely curtail the ability of judicial actors from assessing environmental grounds for asylum claims, as the effects are likely to be generally felt. It is surprising that no Canadian cases have been brought on environmental grounds given the complementary protection legislation was introduced several years before the Australian and New Zealand legislation. However, this is probably due to Australia and New Zealand's geographic location in the pacific region, where the island nations are particularly affected by climate change, in comparison to Canada's relatively isolated position in the far north.

Conclusion

Despite the static nature of its foundational treaty, international refugee law as a whole is sufficiently dynamic to adapt to the changing reality of displacement and protection needs. Complementary protection, as opposed to the Refugee Convention grounds, demonstrates the potential to be adapted to include at least the most extreme cases of persons displaced because of climate change or environmental degradation. The two New Zealand Immigration and Protection Tribunal cases demonstrate the key role the judiciary and merits review members can play in ensuring asylum law remains progressive and adaptable to changing global conditions. While the two cases failed on their facts, the Tribunal members etched out a space for future applications where the risk of harm reaches a sufficient danger threshold and whether origin states are unwilling or unable to provide adequate relief. However, a dynamic and adaptive international refugee law also relies on state governments ensuring their legislation remains in compliance with developing international human rights law, rather than enacting restrictive 'protection regimes' that offer no significantly greater protection than that already available under existing Refugee Convention provisions.

Notes

1 The United Kingdom, as the other common law system with a complementary protection regime, was not analysed as it is a European Union member state, which is assessed in the chapter by Charlotte Lülf in this volume.
2 The Human Rights Council (HRC) notes the following rights will be particularly effected by climate change:
   • Right to water: International Covenant on Economic, Social and Cultural Rights (ICESCR) – glacier and mountain water melt will negatively affect supplies of fresh water, as well as drought and flooding.
   • Right to highest attainable level of health: ICESCR and referred to in five other core international human rights treaties.
   • Right to adequate housing: ICESCR – sea level rise and storm surges will effect coastal settlements, sinking states and low-lying mega deltas.
   • Right to Self-determination: ICESCR and ICCPR.
3 For a concise account of judicial activism, see the discussion by the current Chief Justice of the High Court of Australia (French 2009).
4 The New Zealand *Teitiota* Case was originally misrepresented by the media and created a political and academic debate on the meaning and consequences of the decision.

References

0907346 [2009] RRTA 1168 [New Zealand].

AC (Tuvalu) 800517–520 [2014] NZIPT [New Zealand].

AF (Kiribati) 800413 [2013] NZIPT [New Zealand].

Budayeva and others v. Russia (2008) ECHR. Application No. 15339/02.

Convention Against Torture and Other Cruel, Inhuman or Degrading Treatment or Punishment (CAT), opened for signature 10 December 1984, 1465 UNTS 85 (entered into force 26 June 1987).

Convention Relating to the Status of Refugees (Refugee Convention) 1951, opened for signature 28 July 1951, 189 UNTS 137 (entered into force 22 April 1954).

Council of the European Union (2004) *Council Directive 2004/83/EC of 29 April 2004 on Minimum Standards for the Qualification and Status of Third Country Nationals or Stateless Persons as Refugees or as Persons Who Otherwise Need International Protection and the Content of the Protection Granted*. OJ L. 304/12–304/23, 30 September 2004. 2004/83/EC.

Declaration of the United Nations Conference on the Human Environment (Stockholm Declaration) 1972 11 ILM 1417 (1972) UN Doc. No. A/Conf.48/14/Rev. 1.

Department of Immigration and Border Protection (Australia) (2014) *Fact sheet 61a: Complementary protection*. National Communications Branch.

Dicker, N. and Mansfield, J. (2012) *Filling the protection gap: Current trends in complementary protection in Canada, Mexico and Australia*. New Issues in Refugee Research. (238). Geneva: UNHCR.

French, R.S. (2009) Judicial activism: The boundaries of the judicial role. *LawAsia Conference 2009*.

Human Rights Council (2009) *Report of the United Nations High Commissioner for Human Rights on the relationship between climate change and human rights: summary*. 10th sess., agenda item 2. UN Doc. No. A/HRC/10/61.

Immigration Act 2009 [New Zealand].

Immigration and Refugee Protection Act 2001 [Canada].

International Covenant on Civil and Political Rights (ICCPR), opened for signature 16 December 1966, 999 UNTS 171 (entered into force 23 March 1976).

International Covenant on Economic, Social and Cultural Rights (ICESCR), opened for signature 16 December 1966, 993 UNTS 3 (entered into force 3 January 1976).

International Organization for Migration (IOM) (2007) *Discussion note: Migration and the environment*. 94th sess. UN Doc. No. MC/INF/288.

Kälin, W. and Schepfer, N. (2012) *Protecting people crossing borders in the context of climate change: Normative gaps and possible approaches*. Legal and Protection Policy Research Series. Geneva: UNHCR.

Kolmannskog, V. (2012) Climate change, environmental displacement and international law. *Journal of International Development*. 24: 1071–81.

Leighton, M. (2010) *Climate change and migration: Key issues for legal protection of migrants and displaced persons*. Washington, D.C.: German Marshall Fund of the United States.

Loper, K. (2010) Human rights, *non-refoulement* and the protection of refugees in Hong Kong. *International Journal of Refugee Law*. 22(3): 404–39.

Mandal, R. (2005) *Protection mechanisms outside of the 1951 Convention*. Legal and Protection Policy Research Series. Geneva: UNHCR.

McAdam, J. (2009) Status anxiety: Complementary protection and the rights of non-Convention refugees. *New Zealand Law Review*. 239–56.

McAdam, J. (2011a) *Climate change displacement and international law: Complementary protection standards*. Legal and Protection Policy Research Series. Geneva: UNHCR.

McAdam, J. (2011b) Australian complementary protection: A step-by-step approach. *Sydney Law Review*. 33: 687–734.

Migration Act 1958 [Australia].

Migration Amendment (Complementary Protection) Act 2011 [Australia].

M.S.S. v. Belgium and Greece [2011] ECHR. Application No. 30696/09.

New Zealand Human Rights Commission (2007) *Submission to the Transport and Industrial Relations Committee*. Parliament of New Zealand. Immigration Bill.

Öneryiliz v. Turkey [2004] ECHR 657.

Refugee Appeal Nos. 72179–72181/2000 RSAA (31 August 2000) [New Zealand].

Refugee Appeal Nos. 72185–72186/2000 RSAA (10 August 2000) [New Zealand].

Refugee Appeal Nos. 72189–72195/2000 RSAA (17 August 2000) [New Zealand].

Refugee Appeal Nos. 72313–72316/2000 RSAA (19 October 2000) [New Zealand].

Refugee Appeal No. 74665/2004 RSAA (7 July 2004) [New Zealand].

Robbins Collection (2014) *The common law and civil law traditions* [online]. Available: https://www.law.berkeley.edu/library/robbins/CommonLawCivilLawTraditions.html [Accessed: 10 March 2015].

Sufi v. United Kingdom (2011) ECHR. Application Nos. 8319/07 and 11449/07.

SZSFX v. Minister for Immigration and Border Protection [2013] FCCA 1309 [Australia].

Teitiota v. Chief Executive of the Ministry of Business, Innovation and Employment [2013] NZHC 3125 [New Zealand].

Teitiota v. Chief Executive of the Ministry of Business, Innovation and Employment [2014] NZHC 173 [New Zealand].

United Nations High Commissioner for Refugees (UNHCR) (2000) *Complementary forms of protection: Their nature and relationship to the International Refugee Protection Regime* [online]. EC/50/SC/CRP.18. Available: www.unhcr.org/3ae68d140.html [Accessed 10 March 2015].

United Nations High Commissioner for Refugees (UNHCR) (2001) *Global consultations on international protection/third track: Complementary Forms of Protection*. EC/GC/01/18.

United Nations High Commissioner for Refugees (UNHCR) (2005) *Providing International Protection Including Through Complementary Forms of Protection*. EC/55/SC/CRP.16.

United Nations High Commissioner for Refugees (UNHCR) (2009a) *Climate change, natural disasters and human displacement: A UNHCR perspective* [online]. Available: www.unhcr.org/4901e81a4.html [Accessed 10 March 2015].

United Nations High Commissioner for Refugees (UNHCR) (2009b) *Forced displacement in the context of climate change* [online]. Bonn: Submission to the 6th session of Ad Hoc Working Group on Long-Term Cooperative Action under the Convention. Available: www.unhcr.org/4a1e4d8c2.html [10 March 2015].

United Nations High Commissioner for Refugees (UNHCR) (2011) *Expert meeting on complementarities between international refugee law, international criminal law and international human rights law: summary conclusions* [online]. Available: www.unhcr.org/4e16d0a59.pdf [Accessed 10 March 2015].

X (Re) 2011 CanLII 97878 (CA IRB) [Canada].

Part 3

The role of international organizations

6 The United Nations High Commissioner for Refugees' discourse on environmentally displaced persons

A double-edged sword?

Sinja Hantscher

Introduction[1]

During the Munich Security Conference of 2015, António Guterres, the United Nations High Commissioner for Refugees (UNHCR), was invited to talk about 'the refugee catastrophe'. He declared that the international community should no longer close its eyes to the fact that it had to deal with the largest number of people displaced due to conflict since the Second World War.

In a similar vein to the conflict-driven displacement scenarios mentioned by Guterres, the topic of 'refugee catastrophes' caused by environmental and climate changes has attracted significant attention in the last decades among politicians, scientists, non-governmental organization (NGO) representatives and think tanks. The terms 'environmental migrant', 'environmental refugee' or 'climate refugee' are controversially discussed and the lack of a legal framework to address migration processes in the context of environmental change has been repeatedly criticized. Uncertainty about likely future numbers of environmentally displaced persons (EDPs) is one of the most problematic elements for global policy planning.

In response to the vagueness of when, where and how many people will become environmentally displaced, the topic of EDPs was perceived as possibly implying a certain danger and threat; a risk not only for the people fleeing due to environmental changes or natural disasters, but also as a security threat for the destination communities and countries. From a normative standpoint, this environmental displacement-security argument can be criticized as having negative effects on immigration policies and being grist to the mill of nationalistic groups. By framing EDPs as possible attackers on national sovereignty and as burdens on the economy, the threat perception is intensified.

The interest of this chapter is therefore twofold: on the one hand, to add to the research that applies securitization theory to the context of environmental migration. Here, a particular interest lies in filling the research gap of combining two schools of securitization, the *Copenhagen School* and the *Paris School*, and thus following earlier research by scholars such as Bourbeau, Oels and Trombetta. On the other hand, the aim is to acquire greater insight into the involvement of

UNHCR in the context of EDPs and UNHCR's use of security framings when involving itself with EDPs.

The overall research questions that guide this analysis are as follows: To what extent does UNHCR securitize the issue of EDPs, why and with what consequences? In order to approach the questions, this chapter uses a discursive analysis of UNHCR speeches, policy papers and publications on the topic of EDPs. The time frame of the material is between the years 2009 and 2014, thus taking the United Nations Climate Change Conference of 2009 as a starting point.

With this approach, the chapter contributes to the area of research in security studies that is sometimes referred to as being the most dynamic – the securitization research (Bourbeau 2014: 205). Despite this, the opposing schools of *Copenhagen* and *Paris* have only seldom been combined in research. The recent works by scholars such as Trombetta, Oels and Bourbeau show that the joint analysis with the *Copenhagen* and *Paris* schools is productive in the context of migration research.

The chapter follows a similar approach and introduces both schools in the first section to get a more detailed insight into the securitization processes in the context of EDPs. Not only has the combination of the two frameworks been rather unusual as of late – but also the choice of the object of investigation is rather uncommon: UNHCR being a non-state actor and international humanitarian organization. The background of UNHCR's involvement with EDPs is outlined in the second section of this chapter. This is followed by a third section that analyses UNHCR's framing of EDPs with the help of both schools of the securitization theory. In the analysis section, the relevance of the chapter becomes apparent: Firstly, UNHCR, being an international organization (IO), stretches the use of the securitization theory. Thus, the analysis is in line with a widening of securitization research to include a variety of securitizing actors such as state representatives, NGOs, think tanks, the media and, relevant to this chapter, IOs. Secondly, choosing UNHCR as the object of investigation is unusual in the sense that one would not naturally expect a security-driven discourse from a humanitarian organization that receives its mandate and its funds from states and that, consequently, executes its work under the auspices of external agendas.

Understanding the process of securitization

In order to understand the development of the securitization theory, it is helpful to recapitulate the emergence of the concept. The new approaches in security studies started spreading in the 1990s and were meant as a challenge to traditional realist and neorealist theories (Jackson 2006: 300). In this context, the call for a broadening of the concept of security arose (Booth 1991: 317). Further, the military focus of security was criticized as being too narrow which became apparent in the 'pressures of the security dilemma, the growing appreciation of security interdependence, the widespread recognition that the arms race has produced higher levels of destructive power (…) and the realization of the heavy burden on economies of extravagant defense spending' (Booth 1991: 318).

Scholars of security studies acknowledged that territorial threats and military security still existed, but they demanded the inclusion of other issue areas in the security agenda. Threats such as overpopulation, political oppression, economic collapse, ethnic rivalry, disease, terrorism, crime and the destruction of nature were identified as new security challenges (Booth 1991). Additionally, national politics at the domestic level were acknowledged as being security challenges that have a possible international impact.

The current research on securitization mainly relies on two schools of thought, the *Copenhagen School* and the *Paris School* (Bourbeau 2014: 187). This chapter uses these well-established theoretical approaches to analyse the processes of securitization in an environmental context. The schools both aim to identify whether a specific issue is being securitized, by whom and with what effects. The joint analysis with both schools thus allows for a better understanding of discursive practices and the resultant policy implications. The *Copenhagen School* and the *Paris School* tackle the question whether it is advisable to address issues in all kinds of sectors – e.g., the military, environmental, economic, societal and political sectors (Buzan *et al.* 1998) – in security terms. Both schools thus allow for a critical reflection on securitization processes.

Before applying the securitization theory to the issue of EDPs some critical reflection on the theory is necessary. The intention is to weigh the advantages and disadvantages of the chosen approach and to be familiar with the difficulties that arise with the theory. As a positive element, scholars often point out that the securitization theory enables the identification of the topics whose existence is threatened – the referent object – and to determine the actors who implement the securitizing move – the securitizing actors (Jackson 2006: 301). Adding to this, the theory allows the examination of how a securitization process unfolds by shifting the focus to discursive speech acts. Looking at the theory from a more critical stance, some scholars have pointed out that the securitization theory has a predominantly European-centric perspective as it solely reflects European security concerns (Jackson 2006). Also, the theory lacks a gender-sensitive setting and ignores all other political communication besides speech acts (Jackson 2006). Both schools are criticized for lacking clear methodological detail and for being too imprecise to clearly point at securitization when it is present (Corry 2012: 240). Lastly, the role that is given to the state in the framework is quite prominent; here, the state as the securitizing actor is perceived as being overly central (Jackson 2006: 301).

The Copenhagen School

The securitization theory was originally developed by Barry Buzan, Ole Wæver and Jaap de Wilde of the *Copenhagen School*. The *Copenhagen School* redefined security in a broader sense and developed elements to rethink security.

From the perspective of the *Copenhagen School*, securitization describes an extreme form of politicization; a topic that is 'dramatized and presented as an issue of supreme priority, by labeling it as security' (Buzan *et al.* 1998: 26).

Securitization is understood as 'the move that takes politics beyond the established rules of the game and frames the issue either as a special kind of politics or as above politics' (Buzan *et al*. 1998: 23). In case an issue is taken off the security agenda and shifted back to the normal political discourse, the *Copenhagen School* refers to the issue as being desecuritized (Jackson 2006: 301). The scholars of the *Copenhagen School* thus position themselves in favour of politics of deliberation and against securitization (Corry 2012: 236).

Central to the securitization theory are the discursive framings, the so-called speech acts (Buzan *et al*. 1998: 26). In this process, securitization is 'constituted by the intersubjective establishment of an existential threat with a saliency sufficient to have substantial political effects' (Buzan *et al*. 1998: 25). Here, the language of security is used by the securitizing actor in order to articulate an already politicized issue as an existential threat to a referent object. According to the *Copenhagen School*, NGOs, IOs or states can fulfil the role of a securitizing actor (Jackson 2006: 301). Most importantly, to speak of successful securitization, the audience of the speech act has, firstly, to accept the securitized issue as an existential threat and, secondly, to tolerate 'violations of rules that would otherwise have to be obeyed' (Buzan *et al*. 1998: 25).

A successful securitization of EDPs implies that EDPs are framed in national or international security terms, e.g., as threats to national sovereignty, international peace and security; the speech acts need to include traditional security responses, such as the involvement of the military; and the protection of EDPs need to allow for extraordinary measures that are normally perceived as intolerable by the public. As an example, the securitization of the environment might involve 'limiting national sovereignty for the sake of climate protection, restricting individual liberties through rationing carbon emissions, or opposing existing ethical rules e.g., by legitimizing geo-engineering' (Methmann *et al*. 2013: 119). Securitization from a *Copenhagen School* perspective is understood on the basis of a more contextualized securitization as developed by von Lucke, Wellmann and Diez (von Lucke *et al*. 2014: 860). As such, this chapter is based on a definition of securitization that relaxes the strict focus on grammar and speech acts. The articulation of threats that did not arrive at an existential level yet is nevertheless taken into consideration (von Lucke *et al*. 2014). This broadening of the definition is motivated by earlier research on the securitization of climate change that calls for a context-specific approach and specific awareness when it comes to securitization processes in the environmental sector (for more information on the debate of the securitization of climate change, see Brzoska [2009] and Brauch [2012] as proponents and Trombetta (2008) as a critic).

The Paris School

For some scholars, the *Copenhagen School* and the *Paris School* are interpreted as competing standpoints that have such opposite perceptions of security that one might speak of a battleground between the two theories (Bourbeau 2014: 188). Contrary to this, the chapter is in line with research by Bourbeau (2014) and

Trombetta (2014) and hence interprets the *Paris School* as an insightful further development to Barry Buzan, Ole Wæver and Jaap de Wilde's framework. The sociological approach of the *Paris School* essentially extends the discourse argument of the *Copenhagen School* to non-discursive practices. Additionally, the framework takes the institutions into account that embed the speaker of a speech act into his or her surroundings and thus aims at unveiling the power positions and institutional struggles behind a securitizing act.

According to Didier Bigo and Thierry Balzacq, the central contributors to the *Paris School* framework, 'it is possible to securitize certain problems without speech or discourse and the military and the police have known that for a long time. The practical work, discipline and expertise are as important as all forms of discourse' (Bigo 2000: 194). As a continuation of the *Copenhagen School*, the role of practice is added to the existing tools of securitization. Thus, Balzacq points out that 'because securitization is the product of such a complex repertoire of causes, an investigation on a unique factor (for example, a speech act) may fail if other elements exert a significant influence on the process' (Balzacq 2011: 14).

The *Paris School*'s understanding of security helps to tackle the issue of security professionals and security agencies that authoritatively claim to 'identify threats [and] provoke existing fears to promote their own institutional interests' (Trombetta 2014: 137). Here, a securitization act is not dependent on the presence of exceptional measures, rather, the normal governance mechanisms will be raised to the traditional security field with, for example, policing mechanisms or surveillance (Trombetta 2014). In this understanding of security, technical and professional expertise are given higher significance than in the *Copenhagen School* which also leads to a focus on the degrees of institutionalization that might impact the securitization process. Following this line of thought, the 'spectacular speech acts and calling for new or more extensive forms of governance are likely to occur when institutions are limited as in the case of environmental migration' (Trombetta 2014: 138). Especially relevant in the context of this chapter is the *Paris School*'s focus on the structural position of the speaker of the speech act; securitization is the result of power positions. Analysing a speech act with this analytical framework thus allows a better insight to be gained into the institution behind the person who securitizes an issue (Bigo 2002: 74).

Securitizing environmentally displaced persons? An analysis of UNHCR's discourse

UNHCR is the leading global refugee agency with a focus on rights-based and protection concerns (UNHCR 2014: 13). UNHCR shows tendencies to extend its work to people displaced due to disasters and climate change – whether the environmentally displaced had to relocate in their home country or to a foreign country (UNHCR 2014).

The relatively recent involvement of UNHCR over the last decade in this issue area is interesting from an organizational point of view, given that no single international agency has the sole mandate to deal with persons displaced by disasters (UNHCR 2014). UNHCR argues that the terms 'voluntary migration' and 'displacement' need further improvement when applied to natural disasters and the organization identifies different needs of EDPs in terms of material, assistance and protection (UNHCR 2012: 27). Thus, UNHCR pleads for 'greater nuance' (UNHCR 2012) when applying existing legal frameworks to the issue of environmental and climate changes.

The reason for choosing UNHCR as an object of investigation is the interest in the ambivalence of the organization: although displacement due to environmental and climate changes does not fall under the UNHCR's protection framework, the organization seems to move in the direction of further involvement. Particularly since 2010 a tendency towards involvement by the UNHCR in protection situations is recognizable. UNHCR acknowledges that it has 'an interest in such movements of people and an ability to respond to their needs' (UNHCR 2012: 26). Thus, UNHCR is an interesting actor to choose as a case study because the organization is still taking the first steps of involving itself with the issue of EDPs.

So far, the political support for a new binding international instrument that tackles the legal gap of EDPs crossing international borders is nonexistent. A UNHCR statement of 2009 made clear that UNHCR contests the terminology of 'environmental refugees' as the term is not based in international refugee law and UNHCR fears that the terminology might erode the existing legal regime (UNHCR 2009a: 8–9). Nonetheless, UNHCR has taken steps in the direction of involvement in EDP protection. Guterres already approached the issue of climate change-related movement at an Executive Committee meeting in 2007. According to Guterres, climate change forces rising numbers of people to move due to environmental degradation and UNHCR's role will be to 'alert states to these problems and help find answers to the new challenges they represent' (Guterres 2007: 1–2). Due to Guterres' lead on the issue of environmental migration, UNHCR published its first policy paper on the topic in 2008 (UNHCR 2008) and the organization further participated in the Inter-Agency Standing Committee (McAdam 2011: 8).

Thus, one driver behind UNHCR's engagement with EDPs is Guterres' personal conviction (Hall 2011: 111). In 2012, the organization stated that it would be 'prepared to work with states and other actors to develop a guiding framework or instrument to apply to situations of external displacement outside those covered by the 1951 Convention, and in particular to displacement resulting from climate change and natural disasters' (UNHCR 2012: 28). Here, the willingness of UNHCR indicates that the organization plans to strengthen its efforts on the issue areas discussed in this chapter. Also, UNHCR perceives the development towards the implementation of a new international guiding framework on EDPs as central. In the context of this analysis, official UNHCR publications as well as the speeches of the official spokesperson of UNHCR, High Commissioner Guterres, are interpreted as depicting the organization's perspective. Still, it has to be kept in mind that UNHCR is internally divided on whether and to what extent UNHCR should involve itself with EDPs (Hall

2011: 110). By examining current UNHCR framing of EDPs, possible conclusions can be inferred about UNHCR's underlying intentions.

UNHCR's *securitization of EDPs from a* Copenhagen School *perspective*

Firstly, some evidence for the securitization of EDPs was detectable during the *United Nations Climate Change Conference* in 2009. During a press conference, Guterres warned that 'climate change will become the biggest driver of population displacements, both inside and across national borders' (UNHCR 2009b: 1). Here, the people displaced are not securitized but rather the topic of environmental displacement is conferred into an issue that is of concern to the international community in general. The intended audience of Guterres' speech is primarily people living in the 'northern hemisphere' (UNHCR 2009b), and he made clear that this audience should also expect climate-related population movements. Environmental and climate changes should 'not be considered a distant worry' (UNHCR 2009b). Guterres warned the 'northern hemisphere' that, in the year 2008, the number of EDPs reached 36 million (including natural disasters and climate change-related factors) (UNHCR 2009b).

Two aspects of the speech of 2009 quoted above are relevant in the context of the securitization of EDPs by UNHCR. First of all, Guterres used the extremely high number of people who were displaced by natural disasters in 2008 as a warning that the population movements will affect the northern countries earlier than expected. Thus, Guterres expects that solidarity feelings alone will not be enough; the 'northern hemisphere' has to be confronted with a possible high number of people moving in their direction. Also, by explicitly mentioning that EDPs will move 'across national borders' (UNHCR 2009b), the speech entails the framing of the issue in a security or military perspective; EDPs are framed as intruders into a foreign country. Adding to this, Guterres warned the international community that countries might become 'fortresses' (UNHCR 2009b) in the context of population movements due to environmental changes. This highly defensive term also shows the usage of traditional security terms in the context of environmental displacement. Although Guterres used the fortress as a negative example of how the international community, as well as the nation states, might cope with the predicted situation, the term reflects a securitized image of EDPs. By using this wording, Guterres replicates a dangerous framing of population movements due to natural disasters.

Secondly, the securitization tendencies of UNHCR mentioned above intensified after the dissatisfying outcome of the 2009 *Copenhagen Conference*. In 2011, Guterres' briefing of the UN Security Council contained a framing of the issue of EDPs as a security issue. The High Commissioner exclaimed that climate change is 'the defining challenge of our times' (Guterres 2011: 2) and that climate change reinforces the complexity and scale of human displacement. Environmental and climate changes have 'important implications for the maintenance of international peace and security' (Guterres 2011: 2). The High Commissioner also identified climate change as a 'threat to peace and security' (Guterres 2011: 2) and he explicitly noted that although one might think that environmental changes do not fall within the issue areas of the UN Security Council, for UNHCR the topics around environmental displacement are a 'matter of security' (Guterres 2011: 2) and should not be ignored. In this context, the High Commissioner does not directly frame EDPs as a threat to the security of the international community; however, Guterres indirectly lifts the issue of environmental displacement from the political level to a security level. Guterres further acknowledged that there exist differing predictions of the number of EDPs in the future and he stressed that climate change will determine the 'level of human security available to people in different parts of the world' (Guterres 2011: 1). Thus, Guterres concluded that the effects of environmental changes will have implications for 'human' security – a concept of security that is not explicitly addressed by the *Copenhagen School* and thus goes beyond the scope of this chapter.

This securitizing act is also exemplified in the fact that Guterres referred to the study 'Warming increases the risk of civil war in Africa' (Burke *et al.* 2009) of the Berkeley, Stanford, New York and Harvard universities that indicates a strong correlation between climate change and the occurrence of armed conflict (Guterres 2011: 2). Hence, Guterres revives a recent debate that took place in 2007 when the Nobel Peace Prize was awarded to the Intergovernmental Panel on Climate Change (IPCC) and the discussion on the climate change and conflict nexus reached its peak. Without being able to quote scientific quantifications on this linkage, the High Commissioner proclaimed that 'the linkage is clearly there' (Guterres 2011: 1). In order to emphasize his point, he added that in the year 2010 around 40 million people were displaced due to natural disasters. Guterres finished by stating that the help and protection of EDPs is in the 'common interest' (Guterres 2011: 3) of the international community because otherwise 'further breaches of international (…) security are certain to take place' (Guterres 2011: 3). To sum up, speaking for UNHCR, the High Commissioner transported EDPs into high politics and he does this by leaving a securitized mark on the environmentally displaced.

Thirdly, UNHCR uses the quotes and framings of the IPCC in its publications which are made for politicians, researchers and the public. In this context, the wording of the IPCC's March 2014 report comprises the warning that 'climate change can indirectly increase risks of violent conflicts in the form of civil war and inter-group violence by amplifying well-documented drivers of these conflicts such as poverty and economic shocks' (UNHCR 2014: 13). Here, the individual environmental migrant is not explicitly mentioned because the term climate change is used in a general manner in a rather abstract illusionary and inhuman way. Nevertheless, the report confronts the audience with the possible outcomes of climate change, being 'civil war', 'inter-group violence', 'poverty' and 'economic shock'. Presumably to further the topic of EDPs even more in international fora, UNHCR adds the human factor – the environmentally displaced – to the linkage between climate change and conflict. The UNHCR overview further stresses that 'multiple lines of evidence relate climate variability to these forms of conflict'

(UNHCR 2014). Again, the human impact is framed in a conflict-prone manner and the individual person who is environmentally displaced is not mentioned.

Fourthly, the High Commissioner increasingly mentioned security aspects in the context of environmental displacement throughout his leadership and more frequently in the last few years while speaking to the United Nations Security Council (UNHCR 2014: 15). Guterres makes clear that in case the international community does not fulfil a humanitarian imperative when it comes to EDPs, the whereabouts of displaced populations will lead to conditions 'in which further breaches of international (…) security are certain to take place' (UNHCR 2014). Framing the issue of environmental displacement in front of the United Nations Security Council as a negative 'shadow of the future', Guterres intends to generate an appropriate reaction from the UN member states. Here, the aspect of the audience of the securitizing act of the *Copenhagen School* is important. While such a wording might not be necessary during a UNHCR meeting – because everyone working for UNHCR knows about the urgency and importance of EDPs – Guterres intends to arouse awareness in the Security Council.

UNHCR's securitization of EDPs from a Paris School perspective

From the background of the *Paris School*, certain aspects of UNHCR's approach towards EDPs attract attention. Firstly, in 2011, Guterres identified three areas that needed particular attention from UNHCR. One of these issue areas is the *protection gaps* in the international system for protecting displaced people (UNHCR 2010b: 1). According to Guterres, these gaps stem from the inadequate implementation of existing treaties and gaps in the international protection framework (UNHCR 2010b). Here, the process of securitization lies in the institutionalized aspect of the *Paris School* that is detectable in Guterres' argumentation. The High Commissioner did not only wish for greater access to relevant instruments for all parties involved, he also stressed the necessity of expanding the list of displacement problems in the international context (UNHCR 2010b). Natural disasters and climate change are specifically mentioned as examples for which no international solutions exist. In the context of the *Paris School*, the securitization of EDPs is not necessarily done in a speech act; rather, Guterres called for the expansion of the list of displacement problems to include matters such as natural disasters which will ultimately lead to those issues being given more attention and more funds and will be approached on a higher policy level in the UN apparatus.

After introducing the topic of EDPs in UNHCR's Background Papers in 2010, the organization decided to gather expertise on the issue (McAdam 2014: 14). UNHCR organized the *Expert Meeting on Climate Change and Displacement* in 2011 in order to gain in-depth knowledge and expertise on EDPs (McAdam 2014). This step can be interpreted according to the *Paris School* that gives professional expertise higher significance than the *Copenhagen School* and that allows the taking of steps such as expert group formation. Also, normal governance policies are raised to the traditional security field. Although the instalment of an expert meeting does not automatically lead to an issue being raised to the security field, the group of experts nevertheless gains significant influence on how an issue such as environmental migration will be perceived in the future. It has to show whether the different kinds of sub-organizations and working groups develop an own agenda and try to push the issue towards a security approach.

The role of practice in the *Paris School* – as opposed to the *Copenhagen School*'s focus on discourse – becomes clear in another example of UNHCR's strategy towards environmental migration. The *Nansen Conference on Climate Change and Displacement in the 21st Century* took place in Oslo in 2011; over 200 participants from 40 different countries attended the conference. One of the outcomes of the *Nansen Conference* was the acknowledgement that due to a missing overall terminology of environmental migrants, the inaccurate terms of environmental (or climate) refugee are still widely used and the participants of the conference declared the clarification of terms as high priority (Kälin and Schrepfer 2012: 28). At the *Nansen Conference*, the High Commissioner advocated a 'global guiding framework for situations of cross-border displacement resulting from climate change and natural disasters' (UNHCR 2011: 1). Thus, the issue of EDPs is not securitized in the traditional understanding of the *Copenhagen School*; rather, a tendency towards the securitization of the *Paris School* is noticeable. In other words, UNHCR referred to the need of additional policies, treaties and norms to approach the issue of environmental displacement. Even though UNHCR did not function as a co-sponsor of the conference, the organization still acted as a key player in designing the *Nansen Conference* (McAdam 2014: 15). Not only is the name associated with refugee protection – the name giver Fridtjof Nansen was the first High Commissioner for Refugees, the High Commissioner, in 2011, was also the 'only institutional head to speak in the opening plenary session' (McAdam 2014: 16).

In the sixth version of the UNHCR publication, *The State of the World's Refugees*, the organization clearly formulated the steps that need to be taken in order to be able to tackle the issue of EDPs in the long run. According to UNHCR, 'national laws and policies will need to be adapted and strengthened and regional and sub-regional norms will need to be developed so that governments can hold one another accountable for their responses to displacement caused by climate change' (UNHCR 2012: 28). It becomes clear that UNHCR sees a need to further institutionalize the issue of environmental displacement and wants to strengthen the overall involvement on the national level. Nevertheless, the underlying reasons for these steps are just assumptions and it is rather interpretative to assume that demanding more laws and norms is a form of securitizing the issue. Still, the intensity of the matter of environmental displacement is stressed by the UNHCR as *The State of the World's Refugees* includes recommendations for dealing with EDPs.

According to UNHCR, no actor or institution in the international community is solely responsible for addressing the effects of environmental and climate change (UNHCR 2012). Thus, UNHCR called for 'new forms of multilateral cooperation' (UNHCR 2012) and demanded 'global solidarity' (UNHCR 2012: 28). The question arises whether UNHCR – as an organization that is almost entirely financed by direct voluntary contributions (UNHCR 2010c: 1) – paints a rather dramatic picture of EDPs in order to gain more material support for its protection approach. This would imply that UNHCR's tendency to securitize the issue of EDPs not only aims at helping the displaced but is also motivated out of UNHCR's own self-interest. In other words, one can identify a development of UNHCR involvement with the issue of environmental migration: until the early 2000s UNHCR showed no interest in involving itself with environmental migration but since Guterres took office in 2005, the 'institutional considerations about UNHCR's role as the protection agency' (UNHCR 2010a: 3) seems to have played a major role in UNHCR's engagement. In 2014, UNHCR declared that it plays a leading role – in coordination with UNICEF and OHCHR – in overseeing the protection of disaster-generated internally displaced persons (UNHCR 2014: 16). Thus, UNHCR nowadays jointly cooperates with other organizations in affected countries in cases of displacement due to natural disasters.

A discussion of the findings

When comparing international security organizations with humanitarian organizations, it becomes apparent that security organizations might have an underlying intention to securitize non-traditional security issues such as EDPs. As an example, one can think of the changing international arena since the end of the Cold War in which organizations such as NATO needed to guarantee their survival and promote their relevance (Jackson 2006: 306). In this context it does not come as a surprise that non-military security issues (e.g., environmental change) were framed in security terms. As discussed above, some humanitarian organizations seem to react similarly.

This chapter initially addresses the question of whether humanitarian organizations bandwagon with security organizations when it comes to EDPs and what might be their motivation and intention in using traditional security references (e.g., national or military security perspectives) that clearly lie out of their subject area. UNHCR – the humanitarian organization that is used as the case in point for this chapter – shows tendencies to fulfil above-mentioned hypothesis of an organization that adds traditional security framings to its arguments.

UNHCR's original *raison d'être* is not endangered and issues of refugee protection did not cease to exist. Rather, safeguarding the rights and well-being of refugees will continue to be a pressing issue in national and international politics. That said, UNHCR must have other organizational imperatives to sometimes utilize the security speech act in the case of EDPs. The underlying intention might be to respond to the securitizing practices of other humanitarian organizations that evolve in the field of refugee protection. On a positive note, this might guarantee UNHCR's international standing in the struggle for resources and international influence.

From a more practical side, UNHCR's motivation for above-mentioned speech acts might go back to UNHCR's organizational structure and the influence of individuals on the overall agenda of the organization. This chapter shows to what extent High Commissioner Guterres pushed the issue of EDPs by employing some elements of the *Copenhagen School* and *Paris School* frameworks. On the one hand, one can argue that Guterres increased the chances of UNHCR to be heard by *all* relevant actors in the international sphere, namely humanitarian as well as all organizations that work on security issues. This rather positive interpretation would imply that the chances of support for UNHCR's work improved due to Guterres' dominant presence in several international fora. In a similar vein, UNHCR's international role could only benefit from the cooperation with all kinds of other actors and institutions when it comes to aid from the international community or help in funding – even if these have a non-humanitarian background. On the other hand, the theoretical frameworks of the *Copenhagen School* and the *Paris School* fail to address the question of who uses the securitizing act. In other words, the ingrained dynamics of an organization such as UNHCR are hard to break down with the top-down understanding of the securitization theory (the *top* being a securitizing actor who uses the speech act to influence the audience *on the ground*). Thus, the analysis of UNHCR's securitization of EDPs shows that neither of the two schools mentioned above are sufficient to get a better understanding of the underlying motivations of UNHCR in the context of EDPs. The chapter helps to point out that Guterres' speech acts very likely reflect inner-organizational hierarchies, self-interest and personal beliefs that need not automatically reflect the overall UNHCR position towards EDPs.

Conclusion

As a contribution to research on environmental migration, the findings of this chapter have to be interpreted against the background of existing research on the securitization of climate change. This chapter's aim is not to stress that EDPs should be treated as security threats – rather, the chapter's contribution to research on environmental displacement is to show how an IO like UNHCR approaches the protection needs of EDPs from the perspective of security studies. In this context, the chapter is in line with arguments of securitization skeptics and thus questions UNHCR's successful securitization of EDPs.

The framework of the *Copenhagen School* provides an insight into the discursive framing by UNHCR and thus illustrates that UNHCR does not use the securitization grammar according to the strict guidelines of the theory: the audience of UNHCR's speech act – state representatives and the general public – so far did not accept the securitizing of EDPs and there is no public consent for extraordinary measures in the policy field of environmental displacement as expected by the securitization theory.

From the perspective of the *Paris School*, UNHCR's approach towards EDPs shows some securitizing tendencies, for example in the context of UNHCR's request for further legal frameworks, international norms and institutionalized protection mechanisms. UNHCR voices measures, such as new global legal and political frameworks, the need for more solidarity and the common effort of the international community, as solutions to the issue of environmental displacement. Yet, the analysis just shows tendencies towards securitizing EDPs by the UNHCR based on the material used for this chapter.

The theoretical terms used by the *Copenhagen School* and the *Paris School* frameworks are somewhat vague. As described by other scholars in more detail, the definition of what counts as normal politics and as emergency measures are not sufficiently defined by securitization theory (Jackson 2006: 311). Thus, in the case of a possible securitization of EDPs by UNHCR the question of what policies and measures should be seen as normal policy or as emergency mode is answered on a case-by-case basis and it is thus difficult to draw an analogy between different cases.

Summing up, the omnipresent debate on environmentally induced migration can be interpreted as 'a way to promote environmental actions and new forms of governance of migration inspired by solidarity and human security' (Trombetta 2014: 131). Still, some critics argue that the conception of EDPs in the security context also needs to be regarded carefully and should be seen as problematic (Huysmans 2006). Hence, the different securitizing moves in the context of EDPs – even though not yet fully evolved into a securitization process – imply risk practices all the same (Methmann *et al.* 2013: 119). That said, the security discourses in environmental matters – such as environmental displacement – need to be further approached in order to grasp the different competing discourses in the field (Rothe 2012: 243). This will add to a better understanding of the underlying motivation of the leading actors' involvement in the topic of environmentally displaced migration.

Note

1   The author is grateful to Kerstin Rosenow-Williams, François Gemenne, Nina Hall, Sarah Nash and all other participants of the Cost Workshop 'Organizational Perspectives on Environmental Migration' for their valuable feedback and comments.

References

Balzacq, T. (2011) A theory of securitization: origins, core assumptions, and variants. In *Securitization theory: how security problems emerge and dissolve*, ed. T. Balzacq. New York: Routledge.

Bigo, D. (2000) When two become one: internal and external securitization in Europe. In *International relations and the politics of European integration: power, security and community*, eds. M. Kelstrup and M.C. Williams. London: Routledge.

Bigo, D. (2002) Security and immigration: toward a critique of the governmentality of unease. *Alternatives*. 27: 63–92.

Booth, K. (1991) Security and emancipation. *Review of International Studies*. 17(4): 313–16.

Bourbeau, P. (2014) Moving forward together: logics of the securitisation process. *Millennium – Journal of International Studies.* 43(1): 187–206.

Brauch, H.G. (2012) Policy responses to climate change in the Mediterranean and MENA region during the Anthropocene. In *Climate change, human security and violent conflict: challenges for societal stability*, eds. J. Scheffran, M. Brzoska, H.G. Brauch, P.M. Link and J. Schilling. Berlin and New York: Springer.

Brzoska, M. (2009) The securitization of climate change and the power of conception of security. *S+F Sicherheit und Frieden / Security and Peace.* 27(3): 137–45.

Burke, M., Miguel, E., Satyanath, S., Dykema, J. and Lobell, D. (2009) Warming increases the risk of civil war in Africa. *Proceedings of the National Academy of Sciences of the United States of America.* 106(49): 20670–4.

Buzan, B., Wæver, O. and de Wilde, J. (1998) *Security: a new framework for analysis.* London: Lynne Rienner Publishers.

Corry, O. (2012) Securitisation and 'riskification': second-order security and the politics of climate change. *Millennium – Journal of International Studies.* 40(2): 235–58.

Guterres, A. (2007) *Opening statement at the 58th session of the Executive Committee of the High Commissioner's Program* [online]. Available: www.unhcr.org/4700eff54.html [Accessed 8 March 2015].

Guterres, A. (2011) *New challenges to international peace and security and conflict prevention* [online]. United Nations Security Council briefing 'maintenance of international peace and security'. Available: www.unhcr.org/4ee21edc9.html [Accessed 8 March 2015].

Guterres, A. (2015) *Munich security conference 2015: night owl session 'the refugee catastrophe'* [online]. Available: https://www.securityconference.de/en/media-library/video/single/night-owl-session-the-refugee-catastrophe-1/ [Accessed 8 March 2015].

Hall, N. (2011) Climate change and organizational change in UNHCR. In *Climate change and migration: rethinking policies for adaptation and disaster risk reduction*, eds. M. Leighton, X. Shen and K. Warner. Bonn: United Nations University.

Huysmans, J. (2006) *The politics of insecurity.* Abingdon: Routledge.

Jackson, N. (2006) International organizations, security dichotomies and the trafficking of persons and narcotics in Post-Soviet Central Asia: a critique of the securitization framework. *Security Dialogue.* 37(3): 299–317.

Kälin, W. and Schrepfer, N. (2012) *Protecting people crossing borders in the context of climate change: normative gaps and possible approaches* [online]. Available: www.refworld.org/docid/4f38a9422.html [Accessed 8 March 2015].

McAdam, J. (2011) *Climate change displacement and international law: complementary protection standards* [online]. Available: www.unhcr.org/4dff16e99.html [Accessed 8 March 2015].

McAdam, J. (2014) Creating new norms on climate change, natural disasters and displacement: international developments 2010–2013. *Refuge.* 29(2): 11–26.

Methmann, C., Rothe, D. and Stephan, B. (2013) *Interpretive approaches to global climate governance: (de)constructing the greenhouse.* New York: Routledge.

Oels, A. (2012) From 'securitization' of climate change to 'climatization' of the security field: comparing three theoretical perspectives. In *Climate change, human security and violent conflict: challenges for societal stability*, eds. J. Scheffran, M. Brzoska, H.G. Brauch, P.M. Link and J. Schilling. New York: Springer.

Rothe, D. (2012) Security as a weapon: how cataclysm discourses frame international climate negotiations. In *Climate change, human security and violent conflict: challenges for* societal stability, eds. J. Scheffran, M. Brzoska, H.G. Brauch, P.M. Link and J. Schilling. New York: Springer.

Trombetta, M.J. (2008) Environmental security and climate change: analysing the discourse. *Cambridge Review of International Affairs.* 21(4): 585–602.

Trombetta, M.J. (2014) Linking climate-induced migration and security within the EU: insights from the securitization debate. *Critical Studies on Security.* 2(2): 131–47.

United Nations High Commissioner for Refugees (UNHCR) (2008) *Climate change, natural disasters and human displacement: a UNHCR perspective* [online]. Available: www.refworld.org/docid/492bb6b92.html [Accessed 8 March 2015].

United Nations High Commissioner for Refugees (UNHCR) (2009a) *Climate change, natural disasters and human displacement: a UNHCR perspective* [online]. Available: www.unhcr.org/4901e81a4.html [Accessed 8 March 2015].

United Nations High Commissioner for Refugees (UNHCR) (2009b) *Climate change could become the biggest driver of displacement: UNHCR chief* [online]. Available: www.unhcr. org/print/4b2910239.html [Accessed 8 March 2015].

United Nations High Commissioner for Refugees (UNHCR) (2010a) *Earth, wind and fire: a review of UNHCR's role in recent natural disasters* [online]. Available: www.refworld. org/cgi-bin/texis/vtx/rwmain?page=search&docid=4c21ae7f2&skip=0&query=natu ral%20disaster [Accessed 8 March 2015].

United Nations High Commissioner for Refugees (UNHCR) (2010b) *UN chief says global refugee picture changing fast, new approaches needed* [online]. Available: www.unhcr.org/ print/4cff85049.html [Accessed 8 March 2015].

United Nations High Commissioner for Refugees (UNHCR) (2010c) *ExCom: UNHCR chief warns of rise of new semi-permanent global refugee populations* [online]. Available: www.unhcr.org/4ca9a7b06.html [Accessed 8 March 2015].

United Nations High Commissioner for Refugees (UNHCR) (2011) *UNHCR urges states to redefine response to climate-induced displacement* [online]. Available: www.unhcr.org/ print/4decc5276.html [Accessed 8 March 2015].

United Nations High Commissioner for Refugees (UNHCR) (2012) *The state of the world's refugees: in search of solidarity* [online]. Available: www.refworld.org/docid/5100fec32. html [Accessed 8 March 2015].

United Nations High Commissioner for Refugees (UNHCR) (2014) *UNHCR, the environment & climate change: an overview* [online]. Available: www.unhcr.org/ pages/49c3646c10a.html [Accessed 8 March 2015].

von Lucke, F., Wellmann, Z. and Diez, T. (2014) What's at stake in securitising climate change? Towards a differentiated approach. *Geopolitics.* 19(4): 857–84.

7 The role of the International Organization for Migration in the international governance of environmental migration

Dina Ionesco and Mariam Traore Chazalnoël

Introduction

This chapter provides an analysis of the intergovernmental approach to environmental migration from the perspective of the International Organization for Migration (IOM).[1] The objective of this chapter is to firstly, provide a better understanding of IOM's institutional approach on migration, environment and climate change by analysing how these issues have gradually gained prominence within the organization's work agenda to the point that it is now considered to be a critical area for action; and secondly to relate these developments to broader factors for the global governance of environmental migration and IOM's role in this context.

This chapter is divided into four parts: following an introduction which outlines the scope of the chapter, the chapter offers an analysis of the weight of environmental and climatic factors in the international governance of migration, before studying the development of the environmental migration theme on the international agenda. This chapter then examines the emergence and institutionalization of the theme within IOM. The final part presents a few of the challenges faced within and outside of IOM when developing activities at both policy and operational levels on migration, environment and climate before concluding with a summary of the main arguments developed throughout the chapter.

Current IOM activities on migration, environment and climate change include research and advocacy, work on legal protection, capacity building of policy-makers and practitioners, policy dialogue and partnership development. Activities are implemented at central, regional and national levels through a large range of field operations, with a view to reduce the vulnerability of populations to environmental hazards, to provide assistance to people displaced by natural disasters and environmental and climatic changes and to facilitate migration as a possible adaptation strategy.

These elements are analysed from the perspective of IOM's institutional response, taking into consideration IOM's intergovernmental nature and specific migration dedicated mandate, at the service of member states and other beneficiaries, including migrants and their communities.

Migration policy and governance: what space for environmental and climatic factors?

IOM's work on migration, environment and climate change is conducted through the perspective of migration governance. This entails several objectives, such as monitoring the trends that will characterize environmental migration patterns and flows in the coming years and proposing migration management solutions. Several policy and governance implications also need to be addressed, such as anchoring responses in a rights-based approach and developing policy frameworks that are mindful of the complex nature of environmental migration.

Using intergovernmental space to bring new issues on the policy agenda

By early 2015, IOM had 157 members and 11 observer states, as well as a large number of observers from international and non-governmental organizations. IOM was founded in 1951 by the Migration Conference in Brussels, as the 'Provisional Intergovernmental Committee for the Movement of Migrants from Europe'. Originally, the organization's mission was to assist the large number of people on the move following World War Two's massive displacements of populations. As the years went by, the organization's mandate evolved to encompass migration issues at large, in Europe and worldwide. The text of IOM's Constitution was amended in 1987; the amendments, which entered into force in 1989, reflect the changes that revolutionized the world with the end of the Cold War.

The Constitution sets out for IOM a role as a provider of 'migration services', spanning a wide range of activities, from preparation to migration and medical examinations to the integration of migrants. The Constitution also defines IOM's function as

> a forum to States as well as international and other organizations for the exchange of views and experiences, and the promotion of cooperation and coordination of efforts on international migration issues, including studies on such issues in order to develop practical solutions.
>
> (IOM 1953: ch. 1, art. 1, para. 1.e)

This mandate does not confer the organization a normative role, but it noticeably offers prospects to explore new thematic areas of work at the policy level, providing member states with a policy space where innovative and emerging migration governance questions can be discussed. Developing operational responses does not preclude the development of meaningful policy work. On the contrary, the organization's mandate allows for ambitious action to develop policy informed by, and applicable to, operational realities – policies that can be of concrete guidance and use to member states and beneficiaries themselves. This important aspect influences IOM's contributions to the international governance of environmental migration, as analysed in the second part of this chapter.

Bringing environmental and climatic factors into the traditional migration realm

In the current international landscape, IOM is the only intergovernmental agency with a specific migration mandate and working on a broad range of human mobility matters. The organization handles questions related to 'forced migration': internal displacement, refugees' movements, movements in situations of humanitarian emergency in conflicts and natural disasters, human trafficking, border management and so forth. Yet it is also important to note that IOM has pioneered the development of a whole body of work centred on the notion of migration as a positive and useful phenomenon that can benefit countries and communities of origin and destination, as well as the migrants themselves. Areas of work include voluntary migration, labour migration, diaspora contributions, remittances, migration and development.

Unlike international institutions and NGOs with very specific normative mandates that prompt those to work within constricted confines ('refugees', 'displaced' etc.), the broadness of IOM's activities and the flexibility of the mandate conferred by its member states allow the organization to look into issues at policy, conceptual, legal and operational levels that cover the whole spectrum of human mobility – from forced to voluntary and anywhere in the 'grey zone' in between. Developing the thematic portfolio of environmental migration represents therefore a coherent institutional move for an agency that is defined by the breadth and the relative flexibility of its mandate.

One seminal example of IOM's influence in policy setting relates to 'migration and development' – illustrating the ability of the institution to bring new concepts into the traditional migration realm. In the early 1990s, IOM was among the first players to frame migration as a development matter, and to promote targeted action to harness the potential of migrants and diasporas as development actors. The organization started 'learning by doing', developing a wealth of concrete activities that empirically supported the conceptualization of migration as a potentially positive development outcome that should be encouraged by policy action. IOM built on its operational experience to develop a series of important publications and case studies (IOM 1992b, 1992c, 1992d) and convene various expert meetings that were instrumental in shaping international opinions on migration and development.

The process of elaborating policy and formulating recommendations on the basis of practical, field experiences – a practice that can loosely be defined as a 'bottom-up approach' to policy –- as experienced in the migration and development field, is also to an extent at work in the environmental migration debate. Indeed, interest in the migration–environment nexus and the development of work in this thematic area mirrored in many ways the process the organization went through when consolidating and expanding its expertise and credibility in the migration and environment area. More broadly, looking into this policy formulation process also allows discussion of the various ways new global emerging issues can be integrated into existing institutions in order to enrich international dialogues on migration policy developments.

Accounting for change through structural adjustments

Member states have selected migration, environment and climate change themes on a regular basis since 2007 for policy discussion in IOM's Governing Bodies meetings that set IOM's institutional agenda. In December 2014, the Director General, based on the recommendations of the internal review of IOM's structure and accounting for member states' request to give more visibility to the work undertaken on environmental migration, decided to create a new institutional structure within the organization that would be specifically dedicated to work on questions of environmental and climate induced migration. This entity took the administrative form of a Division, entitled 'Migration, Environment and Climate Change Division', hosted by the organization's Headquarters in Geneva, under the Department of Migration Management. This represented an important institutional turning point for IOM, as IOM's 157 member states endorsed this decision during the 105th Council meeting, recognizing the need for such a structural change.

At the broader level, this development was noteworthy in the wider context of the international governance of environmental migration, as IOM became the first intergovernmental agency to create a specific dedicated structure to shape and encourage work on environmentally-induced migration. Beyond its internal significance, this development reflects at large that states have an established and concrete interest in examining environmental migration questions and in finding practical solutions to the challenges that arise.

Building on the institutional mandate on human mobility and natural disasters within the international system

IOM has been working for many years to respond to natural disasters in the field. Following the 2006 United Nations humanitarian reform, IOM was designated to lead the Cluster of the camp coordination and camp management (CCCM) sector for people displaced by natural disasters – while the United Nations High Commissioner for Refugees (UNHCR) assumed the role in cases of conflict, within the framework of the Inter-Agency Standing Committee (IASC). Each state is responsible for taking care of the victims of natural disasters and other emergencies occurring on its territory (see inter alia UNGA 1991). Where national and local capacities have been overwhelmed, IOM has systematically been called upon by states to help assist and protect populations affected by natural disasters.

A core CCCM function is to gather, monitor and disseminate information on population needs and on displacement patterns and dynamics throughout the crisis. The CCCM Cluster represents a repository of knowledge on displacement dynamics, movement intentions, protection needs and the range of obstacles that may impede durable solutions (IOM 2011). One important example of knowledge collection that can be useful for policy formulation is exploitation and analysis of data collected throughout the activities of the CCCM Cluster. When it comes to environmental migration and natural disasters, the wealth of data collected by various partners during the initial phases of an emergency can inform not only the immediate response but also support the development of future policies on the basis of available evidence, especially in cases where natural disasters are recurrent. In that respect, IOM has developed a data collection methodology that has already been applied in many regions of the world to collect information on displacement linked to conflict and natural disasters, the IOM's Displacement Tracking Matrix (DTM) – the third section of this chapter elaborates on the possible applications of the DTM exercise.

The development of an emerging theme: the emergence of environmental migration on the international and institutional agenda

This section of the chapter offers a brief analysis of the increased attention paid at the global level to climate and environmental issues on the one hand and to migration on the other hand; and of how the emergence of these two sets of issues of global importance converged into the development of a new body of work bringing together migration, environment and climate under one conceptual lens.

The emergence of migration, environment and climate change in global policy processes

Since the early 1990s, increasing awareness of the importance of environmental and climate change on the one hand, and of migration on the other hand, is clearly visible within the international policy debate. On the environmental side, after several years of heated and at times conflictual policy debate, it is now acknowledged that climate change and environmental questions are one of the current global issues that needs to be taken into consideration. For this reason, climate change issues are being treated under a dedicated global policy process within the United Nations Framework Convention on Climate Change (UNFCCC); and the climate question is also integrated in all global policy processes of importance, notably the Post-2015 Development Agenda, the 2016 Humanitarian Summit and the 2015 Disaster Risk Reduction World Conference.

In parallel, migration issues are also increasingly visible and debated, notably with regard to questions related to labour migration and to the link between migration and development policies. Although the topic remains politically sensitive, a consensus emerges on the necessity to link the movements of people to wider processes. In that regard, one of IOM's key roles is to ensure that the 'migration lens' is brought to different policy processes, be it development, climate, humanitarian, health or other topics. This means, inter alia, providing conceptual and technical tools to states and other concerned actors to reflect upon the role and relevance of population movements in different policy areas, support for inclusion of migration matters in relevant processes, capacity building activities for policy-makers as well as operational help to implement concrete activities in the field.

Environmental migration: a global emerging theme of a sensitive nature

As mentioned above, both thematic areas – climate on the one hand and migration on the other – developed at their own pace and in their own fora. However, the increased understanding of climate issues as one of the defining challenges of our times has led to the inclusion of environmental and climate change questions in numerous policy debates, including in migration.

It has now been a few years that different actors – notably intergovernmental and non-governmental institutions and the academia – are attempting to link the climate and environmental questions with the human mobility debate. Even if the lack of evidence and relative dearth of quality research hinders a full understanding of the migration, environment and climate change nexus, it has become abundantly clear that a causal link exists between these different phenomena. If a better understanding of environmental issues has been achieved, it remains difficult to precisely evaluate the impact of climate change and the environment on human mobility.

Several seminal works gave credence to the relevance and importance of the migration, environment and climate change nexus. As early as 1990, the first evaluation report of the Intergovernmental Panel on Climate Change (IPCC) stated that:

> [m]igration and resettlement may be the most threatening short-term effects of climate change on human settlements [and that] [a]s similar events have in the past, these changes could initiate large migrations of people, leading over a number of years to severe disruptions of settlement patterns and social instability in some areas.
>
> (IPCC 1990: 103)

The Fourth Assessment Report of the IPCC (2007) noted that new population movements were one of the main consequences of climate change. The 2014 IPCC report looks even more in depth on issues related to the possible impacts of climate change on migration within two chapters; on rural areas and on human security issues and posits that:

> Climate change is projected to increase the displacement of people throughout this century. The risk of displacement increases when populations who lack the resources to migrate experience higher exposure to extreme weather events, in both rural and urban areas, particularly in low-income developing countries. Changes in migration patterns can be responses to both extreme weather events and longer-term climate variability and change, and migration can also be an effective adaptation strategy.
>
> (IPCC 2014: WG2, ch. 12: 20)

Despite a growing awareness of the need to address this issue, both politically and institutionally, the establishment of specific international environmental migration governance instruments poses many challenges, in a context where environmental migration issues are still often understood as 'emerging'. Several structural elements can be put forward to explain the complexity to formalize an international policy and institutional framework for this theme.

First of all, it remains difficult to isolate environmental factors from all other drivers of migration. One of IOM's key messages is to underline the fact that environmental and climate-induced migration are a multi-causal and multi-dimensional phenomena:

> Environmental and climatic factors are both drivers and pull factors, and they are mediated by economic, social, political and demographic aspects. All these different dimensions together define a community and an individual's resilience and vulnerability.
>
> (IOM 2014a: xi)

Secondly, even if consensus has emerged on the need to tackle climate change, finding a global political agreement on the means of action remains a difficult endeavour, as evidenced by the lengthy negotiations taking place to reach a global agreement in Paris in 2015, under the UNFCCC.

In addition, political sensitivities on the issue of international migration governance in general are high. Thus, the problems encountered in the specific context of environmental migration more generally reflect the difficulties observed within the debate on migration issues at large. These include the sensitivities felt at the international level on a topic that belongs to the domain of national sovereignty.

> The migration, environment and climate change nexus poses a 'double sensitivity challenge'. Climate negotiations are politically delicate, even more so when questions of environmental migration are being examined. Migration is also a highly complex topic and sensitivities regarding inter-State collaboration on migration are persistent.
>
> (IOM 2014a: xi)

Migration is not traditionally an area of interstate cooperation and is not governed by a single applicable legal framework – several international legal categories can be applied, such as international humanitarian law, consular law, human rights law, refugee law and trafficking and smuggling law. This constitutes one of the reasons why it is difficult to design global legal frameworks applicable to all aspects of migration issues. These challenges are also relevant to the question of environmental migration (see the chapters by Coventry and by Lülf in this volume).

Reflecting on and fueling international developments

Parallel advances within the international migration debate and the global climate change discussions were instrumental in bringing environmental migration on the intergovernmental agenda, including within IOM. Mirroring international policy developments, the migration, environment and climate change nexus has gradually emerged as both a stand alone area of study and a cross-cutting issue within the organization. It is now considered across IOM's traditional areas of work, such as border management, migration and development, labour migration, migration and health, humanitarian emergency and crisis recovery; but it is also treated as a fully-fledged institutional theme within a dedicated institutional structure, the Division on Migration, Environment and Climate Change.

If the institutional development of IOM on environmental migration took place alongside global developments, it can be argued that IOM's institutional efforts also drove the emergence of the topic on the international policy agenda. Indeed, the interest of the organization in the issue of environmental migration was evident as early as the 1990s, with the publication of a study entitled 'Migration and the Environment' in 1992 (IOM 1992a), followed by three other IOM publications on the same topic (IOM 1996, 1997 and 1998). In so doing, IOM was one of the first entities to establish the link between climate, environment and human mobility and to conceptualize this nexus. Also crucial were the affirmation of environmental migration as a potentially positive phenomenon and the early conceptualization of migration as a potential adaptation strategy to climate change.

In parallel, several hundred operational projects were developed over the decades (IOM 2013, 2014a). It is of course difficult to highlight specific key events in a policy timeline that, by its very nature, has been evolving almost organically – starting from a base group of experts that developed a gradual knowledge base and sought to bring it to the policy level. Yet, publications on environmental migration questions were relatively rare until the last decade, and IOM's sustained efforts to develop and share influential work on a topic little understood and little treated at the time were significant. They had impacts on both research and policy communities – prompting in turn a wealth of new work on the topic as interest grew.

One concrete example of the influence of these works is at the terminology level: IOM has put forward a definition of environmental migrants that reads as follows:

> Environmental migrants are persons or groups of persons who, predominantly for reasons of sudden or progressive changes in the environment that adversely affect their lives or living conditions, are obliged to leave their habitual homes, or choose to do so, either temporarily or permanently, and who move either within their country or abroad.
>
> (IOM 2007: 1).

The above definition attempts to capture the complexity of environmental migration without normative implications – as the question of terminology for defining environmental migrants still poses great challenges for the conceptual and legal framework (for a full discussion on the issues around the question of terminology, please refer to IOM 2014a: Brief 3–4). This definition is now widely referred to – and also critically discussed – in other works at the academic level, in policy works, in the media and by other actors (such as McAdam 2011; Piguet *et al.* 2010; Warner *et al.* 2013, 2014). There is no international consensus on the validity of this definition – as on any other terminology attempts – but it provides a fairly neutral conceptual starting point.

Another substantive contribution is the promotion of a message that migration can represent a form of adaptation to environmental and climatic changes. IOM was among the first players to promote, encourage and take concrete action on the basis that environmental migration could be framed in a positive light to achieve positive outcomes (IOM 1992a, 1996). This paradigm is now widely accepted by other actors.

The emergence of the migration, environment and climate change nexus within IOM: a two level process

IOM's strategy on migration, environment and climate change was shaped through two parallel processes at the operational and the policy levels. Through these two entry points, environmental migration has gradually become a specific working theme in itself. If this double approach reflects the richness of IOM's institutional position, it also raises unique challenges.

Analysing IOM's experiences hold value in itself as an example of institutional growth and development of a new policy area within an established organization. But it also allows examining broader challenges associated to the conceptualization, theorization and operationalization of an emerging theme in a consistent and coherent way. Looking into IOM's experience helps further comprehension of the numerous challenges that arise with the development of an emerging policy area at operational, political and research levels – and of possible elements of solutions. In many ways, IOM's experience reflects the hurdles experienced at the global level in achieving a full understanding of environmental migration as a phenomenon and identifying effective courses of action.

Informing internal and external policy processes through the operational strand

IOM's operational activities in the field have allowed the organization to gradually understand, first of all that environmental and climatic factors had an impact on human mobility and vice versa, and secondly, to examine the nature of these connections. Initially, responses related to environmental migration were designed on an ad-hoc basis. In 1998, the humanitarian response to Hurricane Mitch in Central America helped improve awareness of the linkages between large-scale displacement and natural disasters. On this occasion, IOM was able to assist a significant number of displaced persons by developing an extensive humanitarian plan of action. But beyond immediate life-saving responses, the organization started to gauge the full scale of the problem and understand that it was necessary to further comprehend the specificities of displacement in natural disasters – as it presented a set of challenges at the operational level that differed from conflict-induced displacement. IOM was one of the first intergovernmental entities to engage this conceptualization process, and to base this process on already acquired expertise.

That operational realization was developed in parallel to IOM's initial conceptualization efforts on the migration, environment and climate change nexus. As mentioned above, in the 1990s the organization was commissioning and publishing innovative research on the topic. Meanwhile, more and more field projects were developed and implemented – and operational awareness of the need to acknowledge the specific nature of environmentally-induced migration and to propose solutions that would take into account the environment and climatic factors grew. As mentioned earlier, IOM is at the global level, the CCCM lead agency to assist people displaced by natural disasters. This mandate also demands the organization develops new tools that facilitate the provision of humanitarian assistance.

One important example is the development of a data collection methodology – the DTM – that allows not only to estimate the number of displaced people, but to also collect a wealth of other information that can, inter alia, establish displaced populations' socio-economic profiles, their displacement history, to evaluate their primary needs etc. The methodology is sufficiently standardized to ensure that key information is captured whatever the country or type of natural disasters, but flexible enough that only the information that is needed in a specific context is collected.

It has always been customary to collect data to guide responses, but the DTM exercise now goes beyond providing the most basic necessary information to act as it can be read at different levels and the data collected can inform longer-term policy-making for durable solutions. This is especially evident in the context of displacement linked to natural disasters, at a time when the lack of empirical data is frequently cited as a key challenge and the development of empirical research studies as a priority. In that respect, the DTM exercise represents one key source of operational data that is already widely relied upon in key publications within and outside of IOM, notably the annual Global Estimates reports produced by the Internal Displacement Monitoring Centre (IDMC) (IDMC 2013, 2014).

Knowing that 1,500,000 people were displaced during the Haiti earthquake in 2011 allows estimation of the amplitude of the needed response. Knowing that where these 1,500,000 displaced people are located ensures that assistance is directed to the right place quickly and diminishes loss of life. Analysing DTM information to establish households and individual vulnerabilities helps in targeting the most in need first. Extracting the displaced priority needs helps to ensure that assistance provided is coherent and establishes the hierarchy of needs, as articulated by the population. Understanding how displacement interacts with individual and societal characteristics and making links to the wider socio-economic context, provides 'food for thought' to start thinking of longer-term durable solutions that are appropriate to a given context.

IOM is principally a field-based agency – the vast majority of IOM's work is conducted at regional and country level, and while its headquarters are host to about 200 staff, over 8,000 employees are working in over 480 field missions. In concrete terms, this often means that connecting field activities with wider political, policy, research and legal implications can be a difficult and lengthy effort. Attempts to link up operational and policy understanding in the migration, environment and climate change area were no exception. Yet, as has been the case with the migration and development area, the organization decided to build upon its operational base to develop its policy efforts and expand its expertise and credibility in this area, to ultimately contribute at operational but also at policy level to wider global processes.

In that respect, a pivotal step that made the link between theory, policy and operational activities was embodied in the initiative to take stock of IOM migration, environment and climate change activities worldwide, centralize the information and make it available. IOM produced in 2009 a first Compendium of activities related to climate change and environmental degradation (IOM 2009). This compilation work revealed that the organization had secured funding for and implemented over 500 projects that addressed environmental migration in its various forms. Beyond confirming IOM's operational capabilities to develop activities in a relatively new domain of action, these figures also provided a very good indication of donors' appetite for this type of intervention. Most importantly, the sheer number of projects developed and implemented demonstrated that there was a need to be met for this type of project.

The Compendium also provided another key operational indication that would have repercussions at the policy level. The work highlighted that between 2000 and 2009, 54 per cent of projects implemented by IOM in relation to environmental migration were in the context of humanitarian emergency assistance. But it also revealed that the other 46 per cent of the projects targeted the challenges of adaptation and development – such as community stabilization projects in areas of high migration pressure that offered people alternative solutions to migration (IOM 2009: 34). Although today, many promote the concept of migration as an adaptation strategy to climate change, this concept was slow to gather support. Within IOM – and, possibly, beyond – empirical proof of the scope of the challenges of environmental migration in a context of adaptation, accelerated the decision to promote an institutional message centred on the notion that migration could offer adaptation alternatives.

Evidence-based policy-making on migration, environment and climate change

A new edition of the Compendium was produced in 2013 (IOM 2013). This publication represented another milestone in the continuous efforts of the organization to build a coherent and comprehensive approach that integrates operational expertise into theoretical and conceptualization frameworks. This new edition revealed that over the course of four years, between 2009 and 2013, IOM received about $720 million to implement 257 projects in 31 countries, supporting at least 23 million individuals in response to both sudden and slow-onset natural disasters in more than 30 countries worldwide. What also came to light is that IOM's activities in environmental migration continued to expand and took many forms: from emergency response to prevention of forced migration, planned relocation outside of risk areas, establishment of communication systems to reduce risks, development of information and early warning systems and so forth. Examples are numerous and include large-scale operations in a variety of contexts such as Haiti, Papua New Guinea, Sri Lanka, Nepal, Pakistan and in Micronesia.

The 2013 edition of the Compendium did more than simply account for field activities. It represented an important step in the conceptualization and refinement of IOM's institutional approach to environmental migration, as it defined a vulnerability approach to the migration–environment nexus and proposed a set of key policy messages on migration and disasters.

Even acknowledging the inherent limitations of such exercises, this new conceptual effort was successful in contributing to what is generally called 'evidence-based policy' – in concrete terms, policy that seeks to harness already existing knowledge and evidence to offer realistic and efficient solutions to existing problems. It seems obvious that policies developed on the basis of evidence are more likely to have desirable impacts and meet the needs of the beneficiaries – yet, too often, policy-making bodies are divorced from the realities and challenges of the field. In that respect, IOM's extensive field experience allows a concrete assessment of how the migration, environment and climate change nexus can be translated into a wide range of activities in the field and to illustrate both the opportunities and challenges inherent to managing environmental migration. It is clear this knowledge is beneficial not only to the organization but also to outside partners – especially in a thematic area where the lack of empirical information is recognized as a key limitation to overcome.

IOM's institutional approach: bridging the gap between theory, policy and operationalization to prompt action

As mentioned earlier, the organization has pioneered studies on the relationship between migration, environment and climate change since the early 1990s, and ever since, and regularly publishes the results of its research. From an institutional perspective, it is important to note that the first examples of research and policy discussions on the topic were linked to the organization of two specialized conferences in 1992 and 1996 (IOM 1992a, 1996). Afterwards, IOM continued to engage its member states in different policy forums, using field evidence to bring the issues of environmental migration to the attention of its member states at the political level while simultaneously highlighting the fact that more evidence was needed for concrete action. Also of interest is that policy efforts have accelerated since 2007, and that they are driven by member states themselves as they repeatedly elect environmental migration as a topic that needs discussion in political arenas. The section below provides a brief overview of the key institutional landmarks in IOM and its member states' dialogues on migration and environment.

In 2007, IOM presented its first policy approach on environmental migration to its member states and highlighted eight hypothetical scenarios to guide policy decisions (IOM 2007). One key global policy forum that provides states a space to discuss migration policy is the IOM International Dialogue on Migration (IDM). The IDM, an informal and inclusive dialogue organized twice yearly, provides a forum for discussion to encourage the emergence of new themes or to review various migration issues. In 2011, the IDM workshop represented another important step in IOM's efforts to bring migration, environment and climate change to the attention of policy-makers, resulting in the dissemination of policy recommendations (IOM 2012a).

Policy efforts on environmental issues continued in 2012 with the extensive body of work conducted by the organization on migration crises and the adoption by member states of the IOM Migration Crisis Operational Framework (IOM 2012b). In 2014, IOM member states continued to highlight the importance of environmental migration issues as they selected to debate on the progress of the topic within IOM's institutional framework at the IOM Standing Committee on Programmes and Finance (SCPF) in June 2014 (IOM 2014b) and the IOM 105th Council Session in November 2014 (IOM 2015). The decision to create the migration, environment and climate change Division was recognized during the 2014 105th Council Session. In 2015, IOM member states have requested, once again, the organization of a policy dialogue on environmental migration, scheduled for June 2015 within the framework of the 2015 SCPF session.

Migration, environment and climate change: internal and external challenges

The advances and accomplishments described throughout the previous chapters are accompanied by many challenges. The obstacles faced by the organization internally are numerous and the following section will highlight three main hurdles that impact and continue to influence the institutional development of environmental migration as a policy area – institutional perceptions, the scope of the environmental migration topic that is relevant to different policy areas and, directly linked to this, the challenge of finding funding sources to finance actions across distinct policy areas. Taking account of these challenges and thinking of possible solutions will be critical if the organization is to step up its efforts to inform the global governance of environmental migration at large, especially as some of these challenges mirror those felt at the global level.

The challenge of an institutional image and perceptions

For some scholars, IOM is perceived as an institution associated with the development of the so-called Washington Consensus. Historically the organization has developed in the context of the neoliberal reforms prescribed by the Washington Consensus[2] and always had American leadership. Moreover, IOM is an operational agency with no normative mandate anchored in international law, an institution that works first and foremost to support its member states. IOM gets most visibility for operational matters such as its interventions for sea-stranded migrants in Lampedusa than for its agenda-setting achievements. All in all, this means that IOM is easily perceived from the outside as a service provider and implementer which follows guidelines established by others with little room for original conceptualization and policy work.

It is important to note that this perception originates not only from external partners. IOM has for a long time positioned itself as a 'can do' organization rather than a 'can think' entity and for this reason might not be able to benefit from the image that normative agencies, with a mandate enshrined in international law, can commend, as is the case with the UNHCR. Yet this state of affairs is clearly evolving as member states are increasingly asking for policy recommendations of IOM in its different areas of work. In turns, the organization responds to this demand by stepping up its policy efforts in more systematic ways to bridge the divide between perception and the growing reality that IOM is both a 'can do and can think' entity.

In that respect, the institutional development of the environmental migration theme followed IOM's classic pattern of building policy and political credibility from the bottom up – largely basing its policy development efforts on the expertise accumulated through decades of field experience. But the organization went beyond merely reacting to global developments and member states' demands and also attempted to play a leading role in policy efforts, notably by pioneering research to guide the international substantive debate on environmental migration. It is also clear the organization will have to continue its efforts to encourage this shift of perception from a purely operational agency to a key policy player beyond its member states, notably with its non-governmental and academic partners, in order to enhance its credibility as a key player in the international governance of environmental migration. And in turn, external actors, especially academia, should make efforts to take into account the evolution of the organization. Although it is clear that IOM's nature is, and is to remain, field-oriented and non-normative, it is important to acknowledge the policy advances driven by the organization that also have global policy implications.

The challenge of dealing with transversal policy issues

Another issue that relates to the very nature of the migration, environment and climate change nexus is that it spans many policy areas that are for the most part treated within disparate institutions, at national, regional or global levels: climate and environment, forced and voluntary migration, disaster risk and disaster management, emergency and development. Even if IOM has been relatively successful in designing and occupying a politically sensitive space, it remains difficult for the organization – and environmental migration actors at large – to identify and engage with the multitude of interlocutors that have a stake in environmental migration. The difficulty is not inherent to migration, environment and climate change questions – migration questions cannot be studied in, and for, themselves, they always touch upon different domains of competences and legal frameworks. The complexity of the migration phenomenon is even compounded when this notion is coupled with other themes that are policy areas in themselves, such as migration *and* 'development', migration *and* 'health', migration *and* 'labour'.

In the case of migration *and* 'environment and climate', this means developing collaboration with entities that are not IOM's traditional interlocutors, such as ministries of environment or disaster management. In the larger framework of environmental migration governance, it remains difficult for states to coordinate internally between their different institutions that have a stake in the issue. Secondly, even if a consolidated approach is reached, it is not easy to coordinate with other states and intergovernmental and non-governmental entities that experience the same kind of issues with the cross-cutting nature of the theme and also find it difficult to identify and reach out to the most relevant interlocutors. Thus, it can be seen that it is hard for IOM to identify the most appropriate interlocutors – and in turn IOM experiences difficulties with being identified by relevant entities as a frontline policy interlocutor in the environmental and climate change area.

The challenge of funding coherent action on migration, environment and climate change

The financial structure of IOM is extremely specific – the majority of its budget is allocated by donors – mostly member states – for specific and time-bound projects and the organization only relies on a comparatively limited core administrative budget. This funding model represents a strength in many aspects – such as keeping administrative costs low and providing 'value for money' to donors that expect and receive tangible project-specific results. But it also means that resources are limited to finance structures that have no immediate operational mandate – that is also why the organization is so decentralized and functions with a small headquarters. In this light, it is all the more significant that IOM signalled its interest in environmental migration policy – and committed to it – by setting up a new dedicated institutional entity in the form of the migration, environment and climate change Division. Yet, questions on the means of financing such platform on the longer term are inevitably rising. Again, 'projectization' is an IOM-specific challenge, but it links to the wider question of how to finance policy, normative and advocacy work at the global level in parallel to concrete projects and programmes on environmental migration.

As briefly analysed above, challenges are numerous and moving past them will require careful thinking and action. However, it is also important to take stock of what has worked, as a contribution to the global knowledge base on environmental migration.

Conclusion

Relating back to the fact that the organization's mandate makes provision for, and encourages debate on, new migration policy areas, this brief overview of IOM's engagement in the area of environmental migration allows a number of assumptions that are relevant to the global governance of environmental migration more generally to be drawn.

Firstly, it is important to recall that the majority of states worldwide (157 member states) are members of IOM, which highlights the universal nature of the dialogues on migration policy conducted within IOM's governing bodies. IOM member states' repeated engagement and interest in debating this topic, at the policy and institutional levels, highlights the fact that environmental migration matters to most states, whether they are developed, middle income or developing countries. However, it is certain that securing political will on this topic in the complex field of migration policy remains very challenging. Consequently, the availability of a non-binding space for dialogue that an institution such as IOM provides to states, allows them to explore highly political issues in a bid to develop possible solutions.

Secondly, this engagement also validates IOM's unique approach of 'learning by doing', as this original policy-making and agenda-setting approach sparks political interest, and to an extent, political engagement. Furthermore, the fact that these developments have accelerated since 2007, in line with global interest on the topic, shows that IOM has not only been able to *react* to new challenges but to also *lead* on developing policy in a new area – and that the organization can respond to states' appetite for information and guidance.

Finally, the fact that these different efforts culminated in the institutional development of a fully-fledged IOM Division tasked with leading on the policy development and advice to operational activities represents also an achievement when questions around the global governance of environmental migration are debated, as is the case in this volume. At the time of writing, IOM is the only intergovernmental agency that has been conferred a mandate on environmental migration by its members through the creation of a dedicated Division.

Taken altogether, these developments represent a window of opportunity for political action. Once again, it is important to examine IOM's internal experience in a wider context. What is also at stake here is the recognition of environmental migration not as an *emerging* topic any longer, but an *emerged* issue where the need for understanding, knowledge and action is recognized. However, despite important and positive developments, the organization faces many challenges in its efforts to meaningfully inform and influence the global governance of environmental migration.

Notes

1 For more information on IOM activities and approaches on migration, environment and climate change, please visit http://environmentalmigration.iom.int [Accessed 12 March 2015].
2 More information can be found in academic works such as Geiger and Pécoud (2010).

References

Geiger, M. and Pécoud, A. eds. (2010) *The politics of international migration management*. Basingstoke: Palgrave Macmillan.

Internal Displacement Monitoring Centre (IDMC) (2013) *Global estimates 2012: people displaced by disasters*. Geneva: IDMC.

Internal Displacement Monitoring Centre (IDMC) (2014) *Global estimates 2014: people displaced by disasters*. Geneva: IDMC.

International Organization for Migration (IOM) (1953) *Constitution*. Geneva: IOM.

International Organization for Migration (IOM) (1992a) *Migration and the environment*. Report based on a conference jointly sponsored by the Swiss Department of Foreign Affairs, the International Organization for Migration (IOM) and the Refugee Policy Group (RPG). Geneva: IOM.

International Organization for Migration (IOM) (1992b) *Migration: development linkages – some specific issues and practical policy measures*. Geneva: IOM.

International Organization for Migration (IOM) (1992c) *Migration and development: Uganda's experience*. Geneva: IOM.

International Organization for Migration (IOM) (1992d) *Migration and development in the EC southern countries*. Geneva: IOM.

International Organization for Migration (IOM) (1996) *Environmentally-induced population displacements and environmental impacts resulting from mass migrations*. International symposium, Geneva, 21–24 April 1996. Geneva: IOM.

International Organization for Migration (IOM) (1997) *Ecological migrants in Belarus: returning home after Chernobyl*. Geneva: IOM.

International Organization for Migration (IOM) (1998) *Mapping of risk areas of environmentally-induced migration in the Commonwealth of Independent States (CIS)*. Geneva: IOM.

International Organization for Migration (IOM) (2007) *Discussion note: migration and the environment* [online]. Ninety-fourth session of the IOM council, MC/INF/288, 1 November 2007. Available: https://www.iom.int/jahia/webdav/shared/shared/mainsite/about_iom/en/council/94/MC_INF_288.pdf [Accessed 12 March 2015].

International Organization for Migration (IOM) (2009) *Compendium of IOM's activities in migration, climate change and the environment*. Geneva: IOM.

International Organization for Migration (IOM) (2011) *IOM's role in the humanitarian response to displacement induced by natural disasters*. Standing Committee on Programmes and Finances, SCPF/71. Geneva: IOM.

International Organization for Migration (IOM) (2012a) *Climate change, environmental degradation and migration*. International Dialogue on Migration. (18). Geneva: IOM.

International Organization for Migration (IOM) (2012b) *IOM's migration crisis operational framework*. IOM Council, 101st Session, MC/2355. Geneva: IOM.

International Organization for Migration (IOM) (2013) *Compendium on IOM activities in disaster risk reduction and resilience*. Geneva: IOM.

International Organization for Migration (IOM) (2014a) *Outlook on migration, environment and climate change.* Geneva: IOM.

International Organization for Migration (IOM) (2014b) *SCPF report of the 14th session.* Standing Committee on Programmes and Finances, S/14/18. Geneva: IOM.

International Organization for Migration (IOM) (2015) *Draft report of the 105th session of the council.* IOM Council, 105th Session, C/105/49. Geneva: IOM.

Intergovernmental Panel on Climate Change (IPCC) (1990) *First assessment report* [online]. Available: https://www.ipcc.ch/publications_and_data/publications_and_ data_reports.shtml [Accessed 12 March 2015].

Intergovernmental Panel on Climate Change (IPCC) (2007) *Fourth assessment report* [online]. Available: https://www.ipcc.ch/publications_and_data/publications_and_ data_reports.shtml [Accessed 12 March 2015].

Intergovernmental Panel on Climate Change (IPCC) (2014) *Fifth assessment report* [online]. Available: https://www.ipcc.ch/publications_and_data/publications_and_ data_reports.shtml [Accessed 12 March 2015].

McAdam, J. (2011) Environmental migration governance. In *Global migration governance*, ed. Alexander Betts. Oxford: Oxford University Press.

Piguet, E., Pécoud, A. and de Guchteneire, P. (2010) *Migration and climate change: an overview* [online]. Centre on Migration, Policy and Society Working Paper no. 79, University of Oxford. Available: https://www.compas.ox.ac.uk/fileadmin/files/ Publications/working_papers/WP_2010/WP1079%20Piguet-Pecoud-de%20 Guchteneire_01.pdf [Accessed 20 March 2015].

United Nations General Assembly (UNGA) (1991) Strengthening of the coordination of humanitarian emergency assistance of the United Nations. *UN Doc. A/RES/46/182* [online]. Available: www.un.org/documents/ga/res/46/a46r182.htm [Accessed 12 March 2015].

Warner, K., Afifi, T., Kälin, W., Leckie, S., Ferris, B., Martin, F.S., and Wrathall, D. (2013) *Changing climates, moving people: framing migration, displacement and planned relocation* [online]. Policy Brief no. 8. United Nations University, Institute for Environment and Human Security (UNU-EHS). Available: https://www.ehs.unu.edu/ file/get/11213.pdf [Accessed 22 March 2015].

Warner, K., Kälin, W., Martin, F.S., Nassef, Y., Lee, S., Melde, S., Entwisle Chapuisat, H., Frank, M. and Afifi, T. (2014) *Integrating human mobility issues within national adaptation plans* [online]. Policy Brief no. 9. United Nations University, Institute for Environment and Human Security (UNU-EHS). Available: https://www.ehs.unu.edu/file/get/11213. pdf [Accessed 22 March 2015].

8 Environmental migration and the International Red Cross/ Red Crescent Movement

Kerstin Rosenow-Williams

Introduction

Humanitarian organizations work closely with vulnerable populations, and are often among the first groups responding to local needs in their relief operations. Their engagement with the topic of environmental migration, both in their projects on the ground and their advocacy work, forms the core of this chapter. The aim is to analyse the underlying organizational challenges and opportunities in addressing the needs of environmental migrants from a humanitarian perspective.

'I believe that humanitarian actors have much to contribute to these discussions because of their commitment to and experience with working with refugees and displaced people' (Ferris 2011: 1). This observation from Ferris, speaking from her position as the Co-Director of the Brookings-LSE Project on Internal Displacement, underlines the starting point of the following analysis. Thus, Ferris' observation frames the following questions: how have humanitarian organizations used their knowledge gained from their proximity to the most vulnerable populations including refugees and internally displaced persons (IDPs) to contribute to the discussion on environmental migration? How far has the increasing political and legal attention on environmental migration influenced their organizational agenda? And which other factors might shape a humanitarian approach towards environmental migration from an organizational point of view?

To answer these questions, this study focuses on the positions developed towards environmental migration within the International Red Cross/Red Crescent (RC/RC) Movement, particularly within the International Federation of Red Cross and Red Crescent Societies (IFRC), the RC/RC Climate Centre in The Hague, and the German Red Cross (GRC). As a key player in the humanitarian field, the motivations and hurdles faced by the International RC/ RC Movement in addressing environmental migration as a humanitarian challenge and its related response strategies provide a model for deriving conclusions on challenges and opportunities for the organizational field of humanitarian actors in general.

The analysis is embedded in the theoretical framework of organizational sociology. To explain the organizational positioning towards a new topic, the analysis focuses on the influences of external and internal expectations directed at organizations. Combining insights from neo-institutionalism and the theoretical concept of change agents, this study examines not only the historical developments of the organizational positioning towards environmental migration, it also highlights opportunities, challenges and future paths for addressing environmental migration from the perspective of humanitarian organizations as outlined in the conclusion of this chapter.

Theoretical framework

The complexity of environmental migration as a topic and the difficulties in addressing it adequately have been emphasized both by empirical researchers and in the relevant political and legal debates (see 'Introduction' to this volume). The reasons why certain actors are involved in this discourse and which motives they pursue with their engagement, however, remains a relatively recent research question (Hall 2013; Mayer 2014) that is central to the chapters gathered in this volume. In this context, an analysis of the organizational motives and context factors from an organizational sociology perspective is a useful approach that is also undertaken by Blocher and Pilath in their respective chapters in this volume.

   To outline the reasons for the development of a humanitarian perspective on environmental migration, this research highlights the changes taking place in the external institutional environment and at the internal organizational level. The reasons for engaging with the topic of climate change are discussed along the axes of top-down and bottom-up perspectives, which can be linked to external and internal factors explaining organizational development.

   While external factors are situated in the organizational environment that is comprised of other actors in the organizational field,[1] such as NGOs, governments, the general population, and beneficiaries, the internal factors are linked to the members of the organization and the organizational structures at various levels. For the International RC/RC Movement this includes local chapters, national headquarters, and international bodies such as the RC/RC Climate Centre, the IFRC, or the International Committee of the Red Cross (ICRC).

   With regard to the external organizational environment and its impact upon organizations, neo-institutional theories argue that organizational actors, interests, and rationalities are products of the institutional environment of organizations. Neo-institutionalism assumes that regulative and normative pressures as well as cognitive constraints influence organizational behaviour (DiMaggio and Powell 1983). While the regulative frame is legally sanctioned, the cognitive frame is characterized by cultural support, and the normative frame is morally governed (Scott 1995: 35). However, although 'institutions control actors by providing definitions of situations and identities', organizations are not seen as passive rule followers but as active participants who interpret and construct their own worlds (Scott 1995: 22ff., 132).

   With regard to the internal organizational environment, various theoretical approaches exist in organizational sociology. Contingency theories, for example, highlight contextual factors such as organizational size, history and organizational aims, while resource dependency approaches stress the need for organizational resource acquisition. Actors pushing for internal organizational change can also be referred to as change agents, while the social movement literature speaks of norm entrepreneurs (Finnemore and Sikkink 1998; cf. Thomann in this volume), and political sciences of policy entrepreneurs (cf. Pilath in this volume).

According to Buchanan and Badham (1999: 610) 'change agents' are defined as 'any individual seeking to reconfigure an organization's roles, responsibilities, structures, outputs, processes, systems, technology, or other resources'. While their analysis focuses on the individual perspective of change agents, this research aims to identify whether certain individuals have functioned as change agents with regard to the development of an organizational position towards the topic of environmental migration from a humanitarian perspective.

Research methods

Case study selection

The International RC/RC Movement was chosen as an empirical case study because of its recent engagement with the topic of environmental migration, which culminated in the publication *World Disasters Report 2012: Focus on Forced Migration and Displacement* (IFRC 2012), and because of its key position within the global organizational field of humanitarian action. The International RC/RC Movement consists of 189 National RC/RC Societies, the IFRC and the ICRC (IFRC n.d.).

> As the custodian of the Geneva Conventions, the ICRC has a permanent mandate under international law to visit prisons, organize relief operations, reunite separated families and undertake other humanitarian activities during armed conflicts. The ICRC also works to meet the needs of internally displaced persons, raise public awareness of the dangers of mines and explosive remnants of war and trace people who have gone missing during conflicts.
>
> (ICRC and IFRC n.d.: 3–4)

According to the Seville Agreement from 1997, the ICRC acts as lead agency 'in situations of international and non-international armed conflicts, internal strife and their direct results', while the IFRC has this role for 'natural or technological disasters and other emergency and disaster situations in peace time which require resources exceeding those of the operating National Society' (ICRC 1998).

> The International Federation is a global humanitarian organization, which coordinates and directs international assistance following natural and man-made disasters in non-conflict situations. Its mission is to improve the lives of vulnerable people by mobilizing the power of humanity. The International

Federation works with National Societies in responding to catastrophes around the world. Its relief operations are combined with development work, including disaster preparedness programmes, health and care activities, and the promotion of humanitarian values.

(ICRC and IFRC n.d.: 3–4)

The supreme deliberative body is the International Conference of the RC/RC Movement. Every four years, it brings together representatives of the ICRC, the IFRC, the 189 national RC/RC Societies and representatives of the 196 state parties to the Geneva Conventions (IFRC n.d.). The 189 national RC/RC Societies have a special status as auxiliaries to the public authorities in the humanitarian field (ICRC and IFRC 2008: 828–47).

The analysis focuses on the IFRC's programmatic position on environmental migration. This is supplemented by a study on the perspectives of both the RC/RC Climate Centre, selected because of its influential role in guiding the RC/RC Movement's position on climate change adaption (CCA), and the GRC because of its recent advocacy work about persons relocating in response to climatic changes.

Data basis

The research has combined different methods of data gathering to analyse why these three components of the International RC/RC Movement (the IFRC, the RC/RC Climate Centre and the GRC) have developed their current positions on environmental migration. Eleven expert interviews were conducted between 2012 and 2014 with representatives of RC/RC Climate Centre and GRC staff in Germany and abroad. In addition, background interviews with international scientists engaged in environmental migration research, German humanitarian affairs policy-makers and humanitarian practitioners from German NGOs were conducted.

Participatory observations were also carried out in 2013 and 2014 during three events, including two national workshops on the topic of environmental migration led by the German Red Cross youth organization (GRCY) (GRCY 2013) and one international workshop by the GRC in Kampala, Uganda in September 2013. The workshop focused on disaster risk reduction (DRR) and CCA related topics and included 35 participants from ten National RC/RC Societies from sub-Saharan Africa, the GRC, the RC/RC Climate Centre and from two Ugandan government ministries.

Finally, a qualitative analysis was conducted on organizational documents concerning environmental migration by the IFRC, the RC/RC Climate Centre, the GRC and the GRCY, comparing their frames of argumentation to the interviews and participatory observation data. In addition, insights from secondary studies are referred to in order to situate the observations on the International RC/RC Movement in the wider context of the academic, political and legal debates.

The entire dataset was analysed using the computer assisted qualitative data analysis tool MaxQDA to identify the interviewees' perspective on environmental migration while outlining the internal and external factors that impact upon the organization's role and positioning towards the topic within the organizational field of humanitarian action.

Results

The following section traces the historical developments of environmental migration as a theme within the International RC/RC Movement. Firstly, the main developments in the CCA discourse are outlined, followed by a discussion on the arguments characterizing the IFRC's humanitarian position towards environmental migration, and finally the GRC's national advocacy approach is introduced. The subsequent section then discusses both the internal and external factors that can shape an organization's positioning towards the topic of environmental migration.

Situating environmental migration within the CCA discourse of the International RC/RC Movement

In 1999, the participants of the 27th International Conference of the RC/RC Movement agreed for the first time to 'undertake a study to assess the future impact of climatic changes upon the frequency and severity of disasters and the implications for humanitarian response and preparedness' (ICRC 2011: annex 2, final goal 2.1 (3)). This initiative marked the beginning of an organizational reorientation of the International RC/RC Movement towards an active engagement with the topic of climate change as a humanitarian issue.

Consequently, an important structural change, a 'milestone' according to the GRC's DRR and CCA Advisor (Interview, 22 November 2012), took place after the turn of the century: the RC/RC Climate Centre – the influential reference centre of the RC/RC on climate change – was founded in 2002 in The Hague by the Netherlands Red Cross in cooperation with the IFRC. It provides information and education activities about climate change and extreme weather events, supports climate adaptation activities within the existing context of DRR programs, analyses climate change risk reduction issues and is also engaged in advocacy work about the impacts of climate change on vulnerable people, for example within the international policy context of the United Nations Framework Convention on Climate Change (UNFCCC) (RC/RC Climate Centre n.d.).

In 2007, the RC/RC Climate Centre published the seminal *Climate Guide* – a handbook to prepare the RC/RC Movement for the humanitarian implications of climate change. At this stage, the issue of migration was not particularly prominent (mentioned 16 times). It appears mainly as an example of the effects of climate change on economic vulnerability or in case studies from Africa, where extreme droughts impact on migration patterns. At the same time, the report reiterates the concerns raised by academics regarding the complex causes underlying environmental migration (RC/RC Climate Centre 2007: 18). Further, the guide firmly rooted the topic of CCA within the humanitarian mandate:

> As the global climate is changing, the Red Cross/Red Crescent Movement needs to change as well. Climate change directly affects the Red Cross and Red Crescent's core mandate: assistance to the most vulnerable. Inaction is not an option: either we address the rising risks, or we fail to address our own mandate.
>
> (RC/RC Climate Centre 2007: 17)

Defining a humanitarian perspective on environmental migration within the International RC/RC Movement

Two years later, in 2009, a key document, *Climate Change and Human Mobility: A Humanitarian Point of View*, was published in which the RC/RC Movement's mandate to address the topic was established:

> As displaced persons and migrants often encounter situations of need, vulnerability, and distress, the impact that climate change may have on human mobility is also of concern to the Red Cross Red Crescent Movement.
>
> (IFRC 2009: 1)

The three-page statement repeats the argument that mobility patterns are mostly influenced by factors not directly related to climate change, such as economic, social and political factors. It also identifies three main issue areas for RC/RC action: 'Keep a humanitarian focus, and respond flexibly', that means, to take action here and now and to respond to needs and vulnerabilities as they evolve. A second goal is to 'protect populations through DRR'. This includes preventative work at the local and regional level to protect populations while also focusing on migration return options for displaced migrants. The third goal, to 'contribute to people's resilience at community level', should be reached in cooperation with governments through improved services and sustainable development (IFRC 2009: 3). Overall, the aim to prevent migration is clearly established '[b]y strengthening the resilience of people at community level, RC/RC National Societies are contributing most effectively to the reduction of migratory pressures' (IFRC 2009). Finally, humanitarian advocacy about resource conflicts is called for to reduce tensions over resources before conflicts break out.

In 2012, the official IFRC approach to environmental migration was further emphasized in the *World Disasters Report 2012* (IFRC 2012). The report focused on forced migration and displacement, concluding:

> Of all the emerging challenges, perhaps the largest and the most problematic is the impact of climate and environmental change on population mobility.
>
> (IFRC 2012: 231)

The report stressed the following points in regard to the question 'climate change and displacement – what must humanitarians do?' (IFRC 2012: 231–7). Firstly, the IFRC advocates for international coordination, particularly emphasizing the importance of the United Nations High Commissioner for Refugees' (UNHCR) protection role as well as the need for cooperation between the UNHCR and the International Organization for Migration (IOM) (IFRC 2012: 233–4). Cooperation between national governments and local civil society should be enhanced through capacity building projects on CCA, DRR and inclusive resettlement projects that do not compromise people's rights and entitlements. This also requires coordinating local and national DRR strategies and post-disaster relief recovery.

Secondly, the report calls for special attention on the still unknown impacts that slow-onset disasters will have on environmental migration: 'This is where most needs to be done, but where the scope to innovate and confront existing norms and practices is greatest' (IFRC 2012: 237). Slow-onset disasters, such as increasing desertification or environmental degradation, often do not receive the public and media attention focused on sudden-onset climate-related disasters such as hurricanes, floods, or landslides. At the same time for slow-onset disasters there is a much higher potential for adequate preparedness initiatives, which require advance coordination between multiple stakeholders, such as local communities, governments, meteorological departments and local and international NGOs active in the affected area. The expertise of locally connected organizations, such as the International RC/RC Movement or other NGO networks, can become a key factor in advocating successfully for preparatory measures that might prevent displacement due to slow-onset disasters.

The success of such preparatory measures requires a shift from short-term relief to long-term development. Long-term development is needed to address the multiple causes of environmental migration, as well as the large number of people that will be affected. The IFRC report acknowledges that meeting the multiple needs of environmental migrants will require merging a development and human rights perspective into the humanitarian-disaster discourse:

> Over many decades, displacement triggered by violence, conflict and disasters has been framed as a humanitarian crisis underscored by a funding regime whose vocabulary – 'emergency funds', 'consolidated' and 'flash appeals' – echoes this approach. But forced displacement is also a development challenge.
>
> (IFRC 2012: 201)

Consequently, the likely impacts on the livelihoods of forced migrants alongside the related challenges for human security need to be adequately measured before appropriate response mechanisms can be designed. In this context, the IFRC (IFRC 2012: 202ff.) commends the World Bank (2012) *Guidelines for Assessing the Impacts and Costs of Forced Displacement*, as being a comprehensive methodological toolkit that combines mixed methodology of quantitative and qualitative tools. At the same time, the IFRC stresses the need to focus on livelihood support for displaced populations:

> Responding to migration as a 'crisis' often restricts the migrants' movement, employment and access to basic services and rights, ultimately constraining their ability to pursue livelihood options. It is not sufficient to focus solely on saving lives and consider livelihood support only when the situation has stabilized, especially in protracted displacement. Even in emergencies, the displaced continue striving to protect and recover their livelihood activities and adapting to new circumstances.
>
> (World Bank 2012: 190)

Overall, the IFRC believes that migration is a viable, often proactive, adaptation strategy to environmental degradation and climatic changes. At the same time, the needs of people who do not want, or will not be able, to migrate in the face of environmental change must be addressed. With regard to the legal gaps, it is highlighted that the populist term of 'climate refugees' is profoundly misleading and that extending the 1951 Convention Relating to the Status of Refugees (UNHCR 2010) is not the answer. Instead, the IFRC calls for temporary protection mechanisms for those fleeing disaster. It supports the establishment of regional conventions and the innovative 'Nansen process',[2] while encouraging national governments to embed rights-based initiatives for people displaced due to climate change.

National advocacy on environmental migration in Germany

In addition to the developments at the international level within the RC/RC Movement, the GRC's recent advocacy work on environmental migration (GRC 2013a; GRCY 2014b) provides a unique opportunity to analyse a national advocacy campaign on the topic by a RC/RC Society in a Western donor country. The first RC chapter in Germany was established on 12 November 1863, and on 25 January 1901 all regional RC chapters were united under the GRC umbrella with its headquarters in Berlin. Today 400,000 volunteers and 140,000 employees are active in the GRC. In 2012, the organization had a budget of €149 million, including nearly €44.4 million for international activities in 58 countries (GRC 2013b: 38, 61). In addition, the GRCY, which was established on 27 May 1925, has 113,000 members between 6 and 27 years old (GRCY 2014a). The GRCY's youth campaign 'Climate Helpers – Change something before the Climate Does' (2012–2014) provides an excellent example for this study as it placed the issue of environmental migration on the GRC agenda in 2013 (GRCY 2014b).

Since the turn of the twenty-first century, the GRC has paid increasing attention to the topic of CCA, particularly in international projects developed collaboratively between the GRC and its national RC/RC partner societies abroad. In this context of new DRR and CCA programmes, the GRC representatives interviewed also emphasized the necessity of dealing with environmental migration due to its likely future relevance. The topic of environmental migration was discussed, for example, at the regional DRR and CCA Workshop of the GRC in Kampala, Uganda, in September 2013, which was organized in cooperation with the RC/RC Climate Centre to exchange information on climate change trends and their impacts on GRC project countries in sub-Saharan Africa. Although the workshop did not focus specifically on the topic of environmental migration, nor were the associated challenges addressed in the keynote lecture, the topic did arise in the working groups on lessons learnt from local CCA strategies, for example with nomadic communities. The project presentations on Uganda and Togo, where the German Ministry for Economic Cooperation and Development funds two GRC projects from 2013–2018, with the specific objective of strengthening the resilience of selected communities, for example, through the establishment of early warning systems for floods, also mentioned the need to plan for temporary relocation in case of flooding.

In 2013, environmental migration reached the official organizational advocacy agenda of the GRC, when the General Secretariat included the following paragraph in its demands to the new German government. The statement underlines the International RC/RC Movement's belief in the power of international law and calls for the responsibility of nation states to act together in providing adequate protection mechanisms for climate change-induced migrants:

> The GRC expects that the number of people that leave their home in response to climate changes will increase significantly. For this development neither regional nor national mechanisms provide an adequate solution. The solution can only be global. In the same manner that all states have to bear responsibility for climate changes, all states have to accept responsibility for these people. The GRC advocates for a substantial strengthening of the protection under international law.
>
> (GRC 2013a: 56, author's translation)

Interestingly, the new German coalition agreement, following the elections in September 2013, includes a related statement promising to 'be engaged in the development of international instruments concerning the increasingly important topic of climate refugees' (CDU *et al.* 2013: 125, author's translation). Even before 2013, the German government had internationally supported developing a protection framework for those displaced by environmental or climate disasters since the UNHCR Ministerial Conference in 2011, when the majority of member states refused to extend the UNHCR's mandate in this direction (Hall 2013: 102, 104). This eventually led to the establishment of the Nansen Initiative, where Germany is part of the steering group with eight other countries. In June 2014, the German government, for example, funded a consultation on 'Disasters, Climate Change and Displacement: Regional dynamics of human mobility in West Africa' hosted by the German Foreign Office in Bonn (The Nansen Initiative 2014). According to a high-level representative of the German Federal

Foreign Office, the aim was to strengthen regional processes of knowledge exchange especially between the humanitarian community and the climate change specialists at the UNFCCC secretariat in Bonn. At the same time, it remains a goal of the Foreign Office to expand the environmental migration debate from the topic of refugee protection to the needs of IDPs (Interview German Federal Foreign Office representative, 10 April 2014).

Analysis

The analysis section will highlight internal and external factors that can explain the historical development and the current position of the International RC/RC Movement, especially of the IFRC, RC/RC Climate Centre and GRC towards environmental migration from an organizational sociology perspective.

Explaining the developments at the IFRC and RC/RC Climate Centre

The expectations of other key actors involved in international negotiations on the topic of environmental migration, alongside the related scientific and policy discourse, were influential external factors that facilitated the drafting of key Red Cross documents, such as the 2009 document *Climate Change and Human Mobility: A Humanitarian Point of View* (IFRC 2009) or the *World Disasters Report 2012: Focus on Forced Migration and Displacement* (IFRC 2012).

The general move by the International RC/RC Movement, at the end of the 1990s, towards the topic of climate change as humanitarian challenge was shaped by the negotiation of two international treaties, the UNFCCC in 1992 and the Kyoto Protocol in 1997 [2005]. While their original focus was on emission reduction, the need for effective CCA became an increasingly important pillar within these ongoing policy negotiations.

The treaties were preceded by the first two Assessment Reports of the Intergovernmental Panel on Climate Change (IPCC), which was established as a scientific body under the auspices of the United Nations (UN) in 1988. Its Assessment Reports, the Fifth Report was released in 2014, provide the international state of knowledge on climate change and are endorsed by the 195 member states of the IPCC. While the First Assessment Report in 1990 already suggested that migration and displacement might represent the 'greatest single impact of climate change' (quoted in IOM *et al.* 2009: 1), it was only in 2007 that Working Group II of the IPCC more extensively discussed the topic of environmental migration (IPCC 2007: 365ff.). According to a lead environmental migration scholar the increasing attention given by the IPCC towards migration also had an impact on the global perception of the topic in both civil society and academia:

> The topic of climate change or at least environmental migration has been there forever since at least the 1990s and now there is more and more and more attention being paid to this, and I thought it could be because the

IPCC 2007 report actually started talking about adaptation and also mentioned migration (…) [and] all of a sudden it is okay to talk about this.

(Interview at the Center for International Earth Science Information Network, 5 September 2013)

One year later, in 2008, the UN Inter-Agency Standing Committee (IASC), being 'the primary mechanism for inter-agency coordination of humanitarian assistance' (IASC n.d.), established a Climate Change Task Force and a sub-committee on 'Climate Change and Migration', coordinated by an IFRC delegate. An IASC member explained that both the continual information exchange between sub-committee members, and the sub-committee's decision to develop a joint position in order to best influence the UNFCCC negotiations in Poznan (2008), Copenhagen (2009), and Cancún (2010), stimulated a 'huge learning curve' for the humanitarian community as most IASC agencies 'knew very little about climate change policy and the UNFCCC process' (quoted in Hall forthcoming). This exchange among humanitarian organizations, being the first time many of them were active in this policy arena, and the related expectations placed on the IASC members to provide information and expertise on this issue, can be seen as important external factors in the development of the IFRC publications quoted above (cf., e.g., IASC 2009; Kolmannskog 2008; OCHA *et al.* 2009; UNHCR 2008).

Moreover, discourses and expectations of particular national governments shaped certain framings of the issue of environmental migration within the IFRC publications. Thus, for example, on the topic of environmental displacement prevention (IFRC 2009: 3), the IFRC follows a political discourse logic aiming at reducing global migration pressures through investment in countries of origin (e.g., GMG and UNCTAD 2010). At the same time, IFRC's references to a holistic approach that links humanitarian, development and human rights concepts as well as the call for stronger coordination among agencies can be linked to the extensive collaboration of various stakeholders within the IASC task force and its joint advocacy approach towards the global policy level, especially in the UNFCCC negotiation context.

At the level of internal organizational factors, both supportive and restraining factors can be identified that can explain a humanitarian organization's position on the topic of environmental migration. A challenge is presented, for example, by the struggle to position the topic vis-à-vis other humanitarian challenges caused by a warming climate that are also linked to the mandate of humanitarian organizations. This is connected to the issue of scarce resources and the related need to prioritize organizational activities within the National RC/RC Societies, the IFRC and the RC/RC Climate Centre. At the RC/RC Climate Centre it is also acknowledged, for example, that 'there is only so much we can do, and of course as different topics become more prominent we hope to allocate more people to them but migration has not been our strength (Interview RC/RC Climate Centre staff, 26 September 2013). Further challenging issues are the unclear definition of environmental migration and its complex nature. Pablo

Suarez, a lead RC/RC Climate Centre scientist, for example, emphasized the challenges of identifying the complex push-factors of environmental migration:

> We have been very cautious in claims that have directly allocated or attributed migration to a climate change signal. Having said that it is pretty clear that especially small island development states and so on, they have to think about migration very carefully and it is complicated.
>
> (Interview RC/RC Climate Centre staff, 26 September 2013)

A strong supportive factor, on the other hand, is the role CCA played in organizational restructuring and agenda setting within the International RC/RC Movement since the end of the 1990s. The establishment of the RC/RC Climate Centre in 2002 can be seen as a key event in this context. It was initiated by its founding director, Madeleen Helmer, who later, due to her personal expertise and advocacy work, introduced environmental migration as a topic to the senior IFRC levels, and even had it placed on the IASC agenda (cf. Hall forthcoming). This historical development is described below from the perspective of a lead RC/RC Climate Centre scientist who has been attending UNFCCC meetings since 2004 and, through his work, has decisively contributed to the organization's positioning on CCA:

> Over ten years ago when the founding director of the Climate Centre Madeleen Helmer was in the Pacific Islands and she said 'It looks like the climate is changing and people may suffer, what is the Red Cross doing about it?' And people in the humanitarian sector in general did not even know what climate change was in the early (…) 2000s. It was an obscure scientific complicated long term future almost science fiction topic. But we knew from the science that the problem was real, was already having some manifestations, and was likely to grow. (…). I think that by now in part of course because of our work but also because of the work of many others there is absolute recognition that climate change is a humanitarian topic and there are many things that we can do including addressing the consequences of climate change and helping others reach out or even deliver adaptation at the local level, the provincial level, or even hosting or convening meetings of global importance.
>
> (Interview RC/RC Climate Centre staff, 26 September 2013)

Explaining the developments at the GRC

With regard to the developments at the GRC, the analysis reveals similar factors that can explain the new focus of the GRC 'on people that leave their home in response to climate changes' and its advocacy work in 2013 towards the newly elected German government for 'a substantial strengthening of the protection under international law' (GRC 2013a).

With regard to external organizational factors that can explain this development, the GRCY campaign 'Climate Helpers – Change something before the Climate Does' (2012–2014), which covers the five aspects of civil protection, health, education, climate protection, and climate migration was the key factor influencing the GRC's advocacy work on environmental migration (Informal talk with GRC staff 16 December 2014). The campaign was therefore more influential than the IFRC *World Disasters Report 2012* or the local examples of environmental displacement found across GRC project partner countries.

The GRCY campaign on 'climate migration' asks 'the federal government and international policymakers to enforce laws to protect and accept climate refugees' (GRCY 2013: 55). Throughout the campaign it has become evident that the link between migration and climate change is the most complex topic of the five campaign areas. GRCY members have been confronted with a skeptical public both inside and outside their organization (Interview GRCY representative, 20 January 2014). In a written survey conducted with 25 active GRCY volunteers and employees that have a multiplier role within the organization and who participated in a February 2014 campaign workshop, the following answers were given to the question 'why do you think the topic of climate migration is important', revealing the following reasons that can be linked to external discussions taking place both nationally and internationally.

Table 8.1 Motivation of GRCY workshop participants in advocating the topic of climate migration in their 'Climate Helper' campaign

Reasons why environmental migration is an important topic according to GRCY members	
Timeliness	Future challenge that will become more important
	Very up-to-date and extremely explosive topic that will be a significant problem
Preparedness	Being prepared when the first refugees arrive
	Plan in advance, know how to act, and address the topic in time
Protection	Being aware that climate migrants need help and protection
	The development of international law is universally relevant
National responsibility	Germany as an industrial nation must help where possible, especially in developing countries
Awareness raising	Reduce the fears and prejudices within the general public, increase the openness towards non-Germans
	Topic is relevant for everyone, both nationally and internationally, not only in developing countries
Engagement	Become engaged, active and informed about the topic
	Climate change already takes place in Germany. Due to the disasters in Germany we can put ourselves in the position of climate migrants and decide to help

Source: based on GRCY 2014e: 18, author's translation.

This list of motives shows some linkages to arguments raised in the IFRC publications, although interviewed GRCY volunteers and employees might not have read these publications themselves but been informed via the media, the workshop presentations and their discussions with the general public, which took place throughout their campaign work. The answers refer to empirical observations concerning a future increase of environmental migrants and the need for political action and legal responses. In addition, the survey exposes the issue of societal challenges. Fears in the general public, the lack of information and possible solution strategies in the countries of origin and in Germany or Europe are defined as important motives for becoming engaged in advocacy work.

Overall, advocating for and communicating the needs of the most vulnerable people, who are often among the most strongly affected by climatic changes, is perceived by the GRCY as a task extending beyond humanitarian organizations. For the online petition for the German Parliament that demands better protection mechanisms for climate induced migrants this has also led to the cooperation with the NGOs *Naturschutzjugend* and *BUNDjugend*, two environmental protection youth organizations (GRCY 2014c). The campaign also resulted in a youth conference on climate migration with representatives from the major political youth parties on 22 July 2014 in Berlin (GRCY 2014d), the handing over of 3,451 signatures in a petition to two Parliamentarians of the Green Party who will pursue the issue further, and a unanimous resolution of the German Federal Youth Council entitled 'Recognize the consequences of climate change as a reason for flight!' (DBJR 2014). Overall, the position of the German government and its Federal Office towards the issue of environmental migration, which became visible in its support for an extended UNHCR mandate and the subsequent support of the Nansen Initiative, have provided an enabling environment for bottom-up initiatives like the GRCY campaign to develop and gain influence.

At the level of internal organizational development, change agents who influence the organizational agenda can also be identified. The establishment of the position of Head of Division on DRR and CCA at the GRC headquarters in Berlin in 2009 was a decisive factor in the internal organizational development of a CCA agenda. With regards to the practical implications of environmental migration, the GRC consequentially decided to strengthen its already existing expertise in combining relief and preparedness initiatives, as described by Thorsten Klose, DRR and CCA Advisor at GRC since 2009, and from 2015, Head of Resilience Unit and Integrated Programming:

> I think it will lead to the fact that what we already do in this area will become more important. If it is clear that people will migrate because of more extreme weather events then it is important in my opinion to strengthen emergency relief capacities to provide adequate provisions for the fleeing population (...). At the same time, this is again very reactive. That means, that the measures that we are already implementing in the areas of food security,

establishment of early warning systems, water infrastructure, have to be focused more on the future climate risks. This will be important I believe.
(Interview GRC staff, 22 November 2012, author's translation)

Another change agent in the context of the GRCY is the coordinator of the 'Climate Helper' campaign, Jessica Fritz, who does not only coordinate the internal campaign development but also builds networks with other NGOs active on the issue of environmental migration, such as *Brot für die Welt*, Oxfam and the *Klima-Allianz* (participatory observation at a joint workshop in Berlin, 23 September 2013), and the above-mentioned environmental youth organizations. Her motive 'to bring this debate to the public' (Interview, 4 February 2013) was developed in various campaign workshops by the GRCY volunteers in cooperation with external experts on the topic from civil society, politics and academia, thus, meeting the demand for inter-organizational cooperation raised by the IFRC.

Conclusion

The International RC/RC Movement, most notably the IFRC, has increasingly focused on environmental migration in its rhetoric and advocacy work over the last decade. This coincides with the academic, political, and legal debates that have also received heightened attention in the last five years. The IFRC *World Disasters Report 2012* is particularly noteworthy as it clearly linked the topic of environmental migration with the humanitarian obligation to help the most vulnerable. While IFRC's focus lies mainly on prevention of displacement through DRR and CCA mechanisms, which are increasingly supported by National RC/RC Societies in cooperation with national governments, the IFRC has also strongly advocated the issue of protection for displaced persons (IFRC 2012).

The IFRC and the National RC/RC Societies, in their roles as auxiliaries to national authorities, have continuously demanded changes at the political level for environmental migrants either through cooperation and capacity building mechanisms in affected countries or through direct public advocacy work both internationally and nationally. Most advocacy campaigns on environmental migration focus on promoting solutions through international law. To what extent decisions to migrate because of natural disasters will receive legal protection, especially in cases of international border-crossing, remains a political and legal challenge. However, this challenge is being currently addressed by the intergovernmental Nansen Initiative, which is also consulting civil society organizations throughout its regional meetings (cf. The Nansen Initiative n.d.).

With regard to future opportunities and challenges, one can conclude that the issue of environmental migration requires a holistic approach that links the humanitarian perspective to other perspectives, such as the development agenda or the human rights point of view (IFRC 2012: 237). Humanitarian organizations have various advantages in this regard: they are often already engaged in advocacy work for displaced populations and embedded in multi-level organizational coordination networks that allow them to focus attention on those being displaced by man-made or natural environmental changes. This includes resettlement issues as well as immediate and flexible responses to the occurrence of new environmental displacements and related needs that might exceed national coping capacities. In addition, humanitarian organizations have increasingly developed their expertise in the areas of DRR and CCA, stressing the need for a preventive agenda that could be linked to the issue of environmental migration. Their contacts to vulnerable populations and related organizational knowledge concerning their needs, often acquired during or after disasters such as natural extreme events or wars, also enables humanitarian organizations to advocate for programmes that could prevent environmental migration in the future through the improvement of local living conditions and basic needs.

The above analysis of the internal and external factors that can explain the organizational engagement with the topic of environmental migration showed that while migration is an important topic for the International RC/RC Movement, the decision to broaden its agenda to address environmental migration also raised practical questions concerning the feasibility of such an engagement in light of limited financial and structural resources and increasing numbers of refugees and IDPs. Consequentially, it is argued that, particularly in the context of slow-onset disasters, the reduction of pressures leading to migration requires more humanitarian and development attention to prevent forced environmental migration. The analysis showed that the question, how humanitarian organizations address the topic of environmental migration, depends on the one hand, on individual actors within the organization and their perception of local needs and organizational capacities and on the other hand, on the overall discourse development at the national and international level which can have a decisive influence on both organizational projects and advocacy work.

Notes

1 According to DiMaggio and Powell (1983: 148) an organizational field consists of 'the totality of relevant actors' that 'in the aggregate, constitute a recognized area of institutional life'.
2 The Nansen Initiative was established under the leadership of Switzerland and Norway pledging to address disaster-induced cross-border displacement (The Nansen Initiative 2014). The first Nansen Conference on Climate Change and Displacement was held in Oslo in June 2011 and the Nansen Initiative was officially launched in October 2012. With a projected duration of three years, five sub-regional consultative groups from the most affected regions (i.e. Pacific, Central America, Horn of Africa, South Asia and South-East Asia) are planned to take place leading up to a global consultative meeting in 2015.

References

Buchanan, D. and Badham, R. (1999) Politics and organizational change: the lived experience. *Human Relations.* 52(5): 609–29.

Christlich Demokratische Union Deutschlands (CDU), Christlich-Soziale Union Deutschlands (CSU) and Sozialdemokratische Partei Deutschlands (SPD) (2013) *Deutschlands Zukunft gestalten: Koalitionsvertrag zwischen CDU, CSU und SPD* [online]. Available: www.bundesregierung.de/Content/DE/_Anlagen/2013/2013-12-17-koaliti onsvertrag.pdf [Accessed 9 March 2015].

DiMaggio, P.J. and Powell, W.W. (1983) The iron cage revisited: institutional isomorphism and collective rationality in organizational fields. *American Sociological Review.* 48(2): 147–60.

Ferris, E. (2011) *Humanitarian silos climate change-induced displacement: Brookings-LSE Project on Internal Displacement* [online]. Available: www.brookings.edu/research/papers/2011/11/01-climate-change-displacement-ferris [Accessed 19 December 2014].

Finnemore, M. and Sikkink, K. (1998) International norm dynamics and political change. *International Organization.* 52(4): 887–917.

German Federal Youth Council (DBJR) (2014) *Folgen des Klimawandels als Fluchtgrund anerkennen!* [online]. Available: http://mein-jrk.de/fileadmin/user_upload/11-Klimahelfer/2014-VV-Beschluss-Klimaflucht.pdf [Accessed 19 December 2014].

German Red Cross (GRC) (2013a) *Erwartungen an den 18. Deutschen Bundestag* [online]. Available: www.drk.de/fileadmin/Presse/Erwartungen_des_DRK_an_den_18._Deuts chen_Bundestag.pdf [Accessed 19 December 2014].

German Red Cross (GRC) (2013b) *Das Jahrbuch 2012: 365 Tage Menschlichkeit* [online]. Available: www.drk.de/fileadmin/Ueber_uns/Zahlen_Fakten/Jahresberichte/Jahrbuch _2012/DRK_Jahrbuch_2012.pdf [Accessed 10 March 2015].

German Red Cross Youth (GRCY) (2013) *The climate journal: the campaign magazine of the Red Cross Youth* [online]. Available: http://mein-jrk.de/fileadmin/user_up load/11-klimahelfer/KlimaJournal_engl_RZ07_webversion_ansicht.pdf [Accessed 19 December 2014].

German Red Cross Youth (GRCY) (2014a) *Deutsches Jugendrotkreuz: Im Zeichen der Menschlichkeit* [online]. Available: http://jugendrotkreuz.de/jugendrotkreuz/ [Accessed 19 December 2014].

German Red Cross Youth (GRCY) (2014b) *Klimahelfer* [online]. Available: http://mein-jrk.de/klimahelfer [Accessed 19 December 2014].

German Red Cross Youth (GRCY) (2014c) *Online Petition* [online]. Available: http://mein-jrk.de/fileadmin/user_upload/11-Klimahelfer/Petition_zum_Schutz_von_ Klimamigranten.pdf [Accessed 19 December 2014].

German Red Cross Youth (GRCY) (2014d) *Not hat viele Ursachen* [online]. Available: http://mein-jrk.de/themen/klimahelfer/aktuelles-events/news/vom-klima-wandel-vertrieben/ [Accessed 19 December 2014].

German Red Cross Youth (GRCY) (2014e) *Fluchthelfer Seminar: Multiplikatoren Schulung zur Klimahelfer Kampagne. 07.–09. Februar 2014 in Göttingen.* Berlin: Deutsches Rotes Kreuz.

Global Migration Group (GMG) and United Nations Conference on Trade and Development (UNCTAD) (2010) *Fact-sheet on contribution of migrants to development: trade, investment and development linkages* [online]. Available: www.globalmigrationgroup. org/sites/default/files/uploads/documents/UNCTAD_GMG_factsheet_trade_ investment_development_May2010.pdf [Accessed 9 March 2015].

Hall, N. (2013) Moving beyond its mandate? UNHCR and climate change displacement. *Journal of International Organizations Studies.* 4(1): 91–108.

Hall, N. (forthcoming) A catalyst for cooperation? The Inter-Agency Standing Committee and the humanitarian response to climate change. *Global Governance.*

Inter-Agency Standing Committee (IASC) (n.d.) *Welcome to the IASC* [online]. Available: www.humanitarianinfo.org/iasc/ [Accessed 2 December 2014].

Inter-Agency Standing Committee (IASC) (2009) *Final report: addressing the humanitarian challenges of climate change. Regional and national perspectives findings from the IASC regional and national consultations, May–June, 2009* [online]. Available: www.humanitarianinfo.org/iasc/downloaddoc.aspx?docID=5127&type=pdf [Accessed 19 December 2014].

Intergovernmental Panel on Climate Change (IPCC) (2007) *Climate change 2007: impacts, adaptation and vulnerability. Contribution of working group II to the Fourth Assessment Report of the Intergovernmental Panel on Climate Change.* Cambridge: Cambridge University Press.

International Committee of the Red Cross (ICRC) (1998) *Agreement on the organization of the international activities of the components of the International Red Cross and Red Crescent Movement. The Seville Agreement* [online]. Available: www.icrc.org/eng/resources/documents/misc/57jp4y.htm [Accessed 26 March 2014].

International Committee of the Red Cross (ICRC) (2011) *27th International Conference 1999. Resolution 1* [online]. Available: www.icrc.org/eng/resources/documents/resolution/27-international-conference-resolution-1-1999.htm [Accessed 19 February 2014].

International Committee of the Red Cross (ICRC) and International Federation of Red Cross and Red Crescent Societies (IFRC) (n.d.) *The International Red Cross and Red Crescent Movement at a glance* [online]. Available: www.ifrc.org/Global/Publications/general/at_a_glance-en.pdf [Accessed 9 March 2015].

International Committee of the Red Cross (ICRC) and International Federation of Red Cross and Red Crescent Societies (IFRC) (2008) *Handbook of the International Red Cross and Red Crescent Movement.* 14th edn. Geneva: International Committee of the Red Cross, International Federation of Red Cross and Red Crescent Societies.

International Federation of Red Cross and Red Crescent Societies (IFRC) (n.d.) *The International Red Cross and Red Crescent Movement* [online]. Available: www.ifrc.org/en/who-we-are/the-movement/ [Accessed 19 February 2014].

International Federation of Red Cross and Red Crescent Societies (IFRC) (2009) *Climate change and human mobility: a humanitarian point of view* [online]. Available: https://www.ifrc.org/Global/Publications/disasters/climate%20change/climate_change_and_human_mobility-en.pdf [Accessed 19 December 2014].

International Federation of Red Cross and Red Crescent Societies (IFRC) (2012) *World disasters report 2012: focus on forced migration and displacement* [online]. Available: www.ifrcmedia.org/assets/pages/wdr2012/resources/1216800-WDR-2012-EN-FULL.pdf [Accessed 19 December 2014].

International Organization for Migration (IOM), United Nations High Commissioner for Refugees (UNHCR), United Nations University (UNU), Norwegian Refugee Council (NRC) and Representative of the Secretary-General on the Human Rights of Internally Displaced Persons (RSG on the HR of IDPs) (2009) *Climate change, migration, and displacement: impacts, vulnerability, and adaptation options* [online]. Available: www.unhcr.org/4a1e51eb0.html [Accessed 9 March 2015].

Kolmannskog, V. (2008) *Future floods of refugees: a comment on climate change, conflict and forced migration* [online]. Available: www.nrc.no/arch/_img/9268480.pdf [Accessed 19 December 2014].

Mayer, B. (2014) 'Environmental migration' as advocacy: is it going to work? *Refuge: Canada's Journal on Refugees.* 29(2): 27–41.

Office for the Coordination of Humanitarian Affairs (OCHA), Internal Displacement Monitoring Centre (IDMC) and Norwegian Refugee Council (NRC) (2009) *Monitoring disaster displacement in the context of climate change* [online]. Available: www.refworld.org/pdfid/4ab9cd4e2.pdf [Accessed 19 December 2014].

Red Cross/Red Crescent Climate Centre (RC/RC Climate Centre) (n.d.) *About us* [online]. Available: www.climatecentre.org/site/about-us [Accessed 19 December 2014].

Red Cross/Red Crescent Climate Centre (RC/RC Climate Centre) (2007) *Climate guide.* The Hague: International Federation of Red Cross and Red Crescent Societies, The Netherlands Red Cross.

Scott, W.R. (1995) *Institutions and organizations: foundations of organizational science.* Thousand Oaks: Sage Publications.

The Nansen Initiative (n.d.) *About us* [online]. Available: www.nanseninitiative.org/ [Accessed 19 December 2014].

The Nansen Initiative (2014) *Disasters, climate change and displacement: regional dynamics of human mobility in West Africa* [online]. Available: www.nanseninitiative.org/disasters-climate-change-and-displacement-regional-dynamics-human-mobility-west-africa [Accessed 9 March 2015].

United Nations High Commissioner for Refugees (UNHCR) (2008) *Climate change, natural disasters and human displacement: a UNHCR perspective* [online]. Available: www.unhcr.org/4901e81a4.html [Accessed 19 December 2014].

United Nations High Commissioner for Refugees (UNHCR) (2010) *Convention and protocol relating to the status of refugees.* Geneva: United Nations High Commissioner for Refugees.

World Bank (2012) *Guidelines for assessing the impacts and costs of forced displacement* [online]. Available: www.worldbank.org/forced-displacement [Accessed 19 December 2014].

Part 4

The point of view of practitioners

9 Displacement in the context of disasters, climate change and environmental degradation

The Norwegian Refugee Council

Lena Brenn

Introduction

The Norwegian Refugee Council (NRC), Norway's largest humanitarian organization and the fifth largest in the world, operates in approximately 25 countries delivering humanitarian assistance and protection to people displaced by conflict, violence, disasters, or a combination thereof. Disasters and effects of climate change are, and will continue to be, a major driver of displacement – which is why the topic has become increasingly important for NRC in the recent years. This chapter will give an overview of the issue's development over the past few years and provide a snapshot of NRC's current activities in this regard. It will also reflect on good practices and achievements so far and show how NRC as an organization delivering programme activities in the field, advocacy and expert deployment will continue to position itself in the discourse on displacement in the context of disasters, climate change and environmental degradation in the future.

Climate change is our generations' biggest challenge

Every year, millions of people are displaced by disasters and the effects of climate change. NRC's Internal Displacement Monitoring Centre (IDMC) indicated in its 2014 'Global Estimates report – People displaced by disasters' that 166 million people were newly displaced by disasters between 2008 and 2013 (NRC and IDMC 2014). This is the figure from sudden-onset disasters only, the number of displaced persons from slow-onset disasters, such as droughts and environmental degradation, is not included but is additional to the mentioned figure. According to the Intergovernmental Panel on Climate Change (IPCC), climate change is expected to increase the frequency and intensity of natural hazard events, and will consequently lead to more displacement in the future.

The risk of displacement is estimated to have more than doubled since the 1970s (NRC and IDMC 2014: 8ff.). One of the reasons for the rising trend is that more people are exposed to natural hazards and affected by disasters than 40 years ago, particularly in urban areas of more vulnerable countries. Furthermore, disaster preparedness and response measures, including early warning systems and emergency evacuations, have improved, which means that more people survive disasters – but many of the survivors become displaced. Most of the displaced people remain within their countries, but cross-border displacement also occurs in the context of climate change, disasters and environmental degradation. The cross-border displacement creates a protection gap since such persons are not normally considered refugees under international refugee law, and human rights law does not address critical issues such as their admission, stay and basic rights.

NRC's perspective on disasters, climate change and environmental degradation

As a displacement organization, NRC protects the rights of displaced and vulnerable people during crisis, irrespective of whether the displacement is driven by conflict, human rights violations, war and/or disasters and the effects of climate change. Up to now, NRC's work focused more on displacement in the context of conflict and violence rather than disasters and climate change. However, as the displacement figures show, currently more people are displaced by disasters than conflict and it is projected that the effects of climate change will continue to be a major driver of displacement. For this reason, NRC has scaled up its engagement in recent years to work more systematically on these issues.

NRC recognizes that it is often difficult to draw the line between conflict and disaster-induced displacement as the drivers are multi-causal and interlinked. For instance, a person who fled a conflict may subsequently be displaced by a disaster, or individuals may have fled from an area affected by both conflict and disaster. Natural hazards and environmental degradation can also create tensions over scarce resources.

In disaster contexts, NRC is looking at both sudden-onset and slow-onset disasters, including the impacts of climate change and environmental degradation. The relevant entry point for NRC's engagement is not the character of the disaster, but rather that it triggers displacement or may lead to displacement in the future.

Following the logic of the organizational set up of NRC, which includes delivering programme activities in the field, advocacy and expert deployment, NRC is working on the various levels: first on preparedness and prevention measures to reduce the risk of displacement, second to provide assistance and protection during the displacement phase after a disaster has occurred, and finally to finding long-term solutions.

The section below will provide an overview about NRC's current activities related to disasters, climate change and environmental degradation.

Advocacy

For several years NRC has advocated for increased recognition and understanding among policy and decision makers to make them aware of the displacement and protection concerns related to disasters and the impacts of climate change. One key pieces of evidence for advocacy includes producing reliable statistics and analysis on displacement situations and trends worldwide caused by disasters and effects of climate change through the annual IDMC Global Estimates report and displacement database. This data helps to inform and influence international, regional and national decision-makers. Together with Climate Interactive,[1] IDMC also developed probabilistic models that estimate the likelihood of future displacement associated with floods, droughts or other slow-onset disasters such as environmental degradation (for more information about the system dynamics model see NRC and IDMC 2014: 42–3).

Furthermore, NRC is conducting specific research on displacement in the context of disasters and climate change, for example on urbanization, community-based resilience and the displacement of pastoralists. NRC is also advocating for the inclusion of disaster-induced displacement into policy and practice at the national and regional level and is working to integrate these issues into strategic global processes, such as the UNFCCC, the post-2015 framework for disaster risk reduction (DRR) and the World Humanitarian Summit.

Programme activities in the field

NRC has a wide range of programmes addressing disasters, climate change and environmental degradation in the field, especially in countries where displacement is likely to occur in the future, such as in the Horn of Africa. In Somalia, for example, the resilience project *Building Resilient Communities in Somalia* has been established. Since resilient communities, households and individuals are better able to withstand shocks and stresses such as natural hazard events, NRC has, together with other agencies, developed this pilot project that aims to strengthen the capacity of vulnerable groups in areas such as DRR, climate change adaptation and poverty reduction.

Expert deployment

For several years, NRC has recruited, trained and deployed a steadily increasing group of DRR/disaster risk management (DRM) experts, who have contributed to develop DRR/DRM capacity of UN agencies, such as the United Nations Development Programme (UNDP) or the United Nations International Strategy for Disaster Reduction (UNISDR), regional organizations such as the African Union, the Intergovernmental Authority on Development, or the Secretariat of the Pacific Regional Environment Programme, and some national governments and institutions in disaster-prone countries. NRC is also deploying relevant technical experts such as meteorologists, hydrologists, DRR specialists and so forth to strengthen the national and regional capacity within early warning and climate services.[2]

Good practices

Nansen Initiative on disaster-induced cross-border displacement

There are no legal protections for people who are displaced across borders in the context of climate change and environmental degradation. These people are in most cases not refugees under international refugee law, and human rights law does not address critical issues such as their admission, stay and basic rights. With the adoption of paragraph 14 (f) of the Cancún Outcome Agreement in December 2010, states recognized climate change-induced migration, displacement and relocation as an adaptation challenge, and agreed to enhance their understanding and cooperation in this respect. This served as the basis for the Nansen Initiative on cross-border displacement in the context of disasters and climate change. This initiative is a state-led, bottom-up consultative process headed by the Norwegians and Swiss and intends to build consensus on the development of a protection agenda addressing the needs of people displaced across borders in the context of disasters. To inform the Nansen Initiative process with practical experiences, intergovernmental Regional Consultations and Civil Society Meetings are taking place in the Pacific, Central America, the Horn of Africa, South-East Asia, and South Asia between 2013 and 2015. The results of the Nansen Initiative Regional Consultations and Civil Society Meetings will be consolidated and discussed at a global intergovernmental consultation in October 2015. The Nansen Initiative does not seek to develop new legal standards, but rather to discuss and build consensus among states on the potential elements of a protection agenda, which may include standards of treatment.[3]

NRC is engaged in this process through its membership of the Consultative Committee, providing empirical evidence and thematic research on disaster-induced displacement, deployment of experts to the regions where the Nansen Initiative consultations took place, and managing various grants to support the Nansen Initiative activities as the Nansen Initiative is not a legal entity. NRC is therefore working very closely with the Nansen Initiative Secretariat, United Nations High Commissioner for Refugees (UNHCR), the European Union, Switzerland and Norway to support the process. This state-led initiative is an excellent example of how states, organizations and institutions with different backgrounds and expertise can work together to develop a better understanding of the human mobility and displacement dynamics in the various regions in a bottom-up way, identify good practices and tools for the protection of people displaced across borders, and finally find solutions to deal with the challenge.

Arab network for environment and development

Together with the Arab Network for Environment and Development, NRC is working to influence the policy and decision makers in the Arab region to ensure that displacement is integrated into the DRR activities and policies. To achieve this, disaster-induced displacement studies and vulnerability assessments in selected climatic hotspot regions are conducted and discussed at workshops with local and national government representatives, civil society organizations, land owners, the local community and experts. This participatory approach has been successful not only in improving the capacity of the stakeholders to better apply DRR measures, but also to create ownership about the process in order to develop adequate policy solutions at the national and local levels.[4]

Advisory Group on Climate Change and Human Mobility

The Advisory Group on Climate Change and Human Mobility is composed of like-minded organizations, such as UNHCR, International Organization for Migration (IOM), United Nations University Institute for Environment and Human Security (UNU-EHS), UNDP, International Labour Organization (ILO), NRC including IDMC, Sciences Po – Center for International Studies and Research (CERI) and Refugees International, that advocate for including human mobility aspects in the UNFCCC process, the post-2015 framework for DRR and the post-2015 development agenda. Through joint submissions, side events, press conferences and monthly coordination meetings, the Advisory Group is a good example of how various organizations with different mandates are working together instead of competing with each other. The main objective is to bring the issue of human mobility into the key global policy processes and through joining forces and using the various networks of the group members, the Advisory Group tries to fully maximize its outreach to achieve this objective.

Looking to the future

The year 2015 will be an important phase in guiding the future discussion on climate change because many global processes will be concluded or have major milestones: the new Sendai framework for DRR 2015–2030,[5] the new climate change agreement coming out of the UNFCCC process,[6] and the Nansen Initiative's global meeting with the discussion about the protection agenda on cross-border displacement in the context of disasters.[7] At the same time, it is important to look not only at the international but also at the regional, national and local levels. The dynamics vary from region to region and call for tailored responses. NRC is therefore engaging on all levels through its advocacy work, the programme activities in the field, the expert deployment, and the provision of reliable data on disaster-induced displacement by NRC/IDMC. To ensure coordination and a holistic approach between these different foci, NRC has recently created an internal working group consisting of seven staff members from these various departments. With regard to external coordination, NRC will continue to build on its partnerships with various stakeholders, share experiences, good practices and lessons learned with other actors in order to not 're-invent the wheel'. Through joining forces, it is much easier and more effective to push for the same goal: to prevent and minimize displacement in the context of disasters, climate change and environmental degradation, to provide assistance and protection to the displaced people when a disaster occurs and finally to find durable solutions.

Notes

1 www.climateinteractive.org/ [Accessed 16 March 2015].
2 http://norcapweb.no/ [Accessed 16 March 2015].
3 http://nanseninitiative.org/ [Accessed 25 February 2015].
4 www.raednetwork.org/ [Accessed 16 March 2015].
5 www.wcdrr.org/ [Accessed 27 March 2015].
6 www.cop21.gouv.fr/en [Accessed 16 March 2015].
7 www2.nanseninitiative.org/global-consultations/ [Accessed 16 March 2015].

References

Norwegian Refugee Council (NRC) and Internal Displacement Monitoring Centre (IDMC) (2014) *Global estimates 2014: people displaced by disasters* [online]. Available: www.internal-displacement.org/assets/publications/2014/201409-global-estimates2.pdf [Accessed 25 February 2015].

10 The United Nations Convention to Combat Desertification and the International Organization for Migration Partnership

Addressing land, sustainable development and human mobility

Barbara Bendandi, Clara Crimella and Sven Walter

Introduction

Land management has a deep impact on the ability of individuals and communities to thrive and prosper. Both in rural or urban areas, land and access to land are closely intertwined with security as well as social, economic and political stability. This is especially true for developing countries as a large share of their economies depend on climate-sensitive sectors, namely agriculture, forestry and water management. Desertification, land degradation and drought can threaten these sectors and lead to internal and international migration and, when not appropriately and timely managed, to displacement. Decisions to migrate are influenced by the presence or lack of tenure rights and productive land both in places of destination and origin. While land abandonment and out-migration of people of working age are major issues for places of origin, a number of serious issues in destinations are raised regarding food and water availability and land property. While natural resources decline and land disputes increase, food crises, ethnic clashes and conflicts are also on the rise, especially in those areas confronted with the impacts of climate change.

Land management has significantly increased over the past decades. Today, some 1.9 billion hectares and 1.5 billion people are affected by desertification and land degradation globally, with approximately 50 per cent of agricultural land either moderately or severely degraded (Barsk-Rundquist 2014). The reasons are multiple and complex, including climatic variations, such as violent winds and heavy downpours, and human activities, such as over-cultivation, deforestation, overgrazing, agricultural expansion, or poorly drained irrigation systems. All this is leading to soil salinization and environmental degradation, including downstream flooding and silting, poor water quality as well as sand and dust storms. This shrinking resource base is undermining the livelihoods of millions of people wordwide, forcing many to leave their homes.

Yet the inter-linkages between land degradation and migration, including the security and human right implications, have so far not been appropriately addressed in the international development and environmental arena. To fill this gap, the United Nations Convention to Combat Desertification (UNCCD) and the International Organization for Migration (IOM) are building a strong, inter-agency partnership to gather evidence of the different aspects of the challenge and working together to turn challenges into opportunities, in order to improve lives, advance development patterns and facilitate adaptation actions.

What is IOM bringing to the land discussion?

As the leading intergovernmental migration agency, IOM is particularly concerned with human mobility matters in the context of climate change and environment, an area which IOM recognizes as a key emerging issue to be addressed. IOM is committed to stepping up efforts, together with its partners, to place migration and the environment at the heart of international, regional and national concerns.

In the last two decades, IOM has developed a comprehensive operational, research, policy and advocacy programme on human mobility, environment and climate change with the overall objective of improving the evidence base on the topic and supporting governments in enhancing their capacities to deal with complex migration management issues and disaster risk reduction in the context of environmental change.

In this context, IOM deals with the inter-linkages between desertification, land degradation and drought and migration from different angles, since these environmental factors can have impacts on human mobility, and migration can in turn be expected to either aggravate or mitigate land degradation. On the one hand, migration can increase competition over natural scarce resources and lead to further land degradation. On the other hand, migration could provide a positive solution to land degradation when it occurs as a viable and efficient adaptation strategy that helps individuals and communities to better manage risks and to cope with environmental and climatic changes. It is known that many households engage in migration not only to improve their economic situations, but also as part of an income diversification and 'insurance strategy'. Therefore, temporary migration and remittances can also be seen as a strategy to increase resilience, as remittances, skills and investments can serve for adaptation purposes at the household and community level. In terms of adaptation, families that receive remittances have proven to be more resistant to external stressors, including environmental stressors, as remittances not only improve consumption but families can also make investments or savings with a long-term perspective (IOM 2014).

What is UNCCD bringing to the migration discussion?

The UNCCD is the sole legally binding international agreement linking environment and development to sustainable land management. As one of the three Rio Conventions, it aims to reverse and prevent desertification and land degradation and to mitigate the effects of drought in affected areas in order to support poverty reduction and environmental sustainability. It provides a unique framework for country Parties and other stakeholders to:

- achieve land degradation neutrality at all levels;
- promote land-based adaptation to climate change; and
- address the linkages between land and security in order to promote national security, food security as well as land and water security.

Migration can be considered both as a cause and effect of desertification, land degradation and drought, which is why country Parties, which adopted the UNCCD in 1994, were 'mindful that desertification and drought affect sustainable development through their interrelationships with important social problems such as poverty, poor health and nutrition, lack of food security, and those arising from migration, displacement of persons and demographic dynamics' (United Nations Convention to Combat Desertification 1994).

Desertification, land degradation and drought are major drivers of forced and environmentally-induced migration. Therefore, the UNCCD is using its areas of competence to promote sustainable land management practices, which are environmentally sound, socially acceptable and economically viable, to reduce forced migration towards urban centres or to other countries and to provide viable livelihood options.

Competition for land is growing significantly, leading to conflicts and migration in many countries. In order to reduce possible conflicts and forced migration:

- Sound land use planning must be put in place, not only at national, but also at transboundary levels. This requires functioning coordination mechanisms at national, sub-national and sub-regional levels.
- Land and user rights must be granted in order to secure returns to any investments made, both for the encouragement of stewardship and private investments.
- Efforts must be increased to rehabilitate and restore degraded and abandoned land. With a growing global population expected to reach 9 billion by 2050, more than 4 million hectares may be needed per year for increased food production.

While action is required to reduce forced migration induced by desertification, land degradation and drought, 'voluntary migration can be part of the solution [since] migrants' remittances and skills are becoming vital for their survival (…) [and] bridge acute financial and human resource skill shortfalls in rural areas' (Barbut 2014; IOM 2014). Therefore, diaspora communities are crucial partners supporting the establishment and upscaling of sound and viable agricultural management systems in their places of origin and thus contribute to sustainable development of their countries of origin as called-upon by the Rabat Process, the Euro-African Dialogue on Migration and Development, which aims to:

- Improve the mobilization of migrant remittances to the benefit of their country of origin; [and]
- Realize the potential for migrant engagement with countries of origin. (Euro-African Dialogue on Migration and Development n.d.)

The IOM–UNCCD partnership to jointly address the vicious cycle of land degradation and forced migration

With the vision of building social and environmental resilience, decreasing tension over land resources and helping countries to improve understanding of the inter-linkages between human mobility and land degradation, the IOM and UNCCD signed a Memorandum of Understanding at the 105th session of the IOM Council that took place in Geneva from 25 to 27 November 2014.

Both organizations will benefit from the strengthened cooperation through reciprocal sharing of expertise in non-traditional fields of intervention. IOM will enhance its capacity to consider and deal with environmental threats such as desertification, land degradation and drought. UNCCD will improve understanding of human mobility and its impacts and feedbacks on ecosystems in view of contributing to a larger number of political and developmental fora conventionally more focused on people's rights and vulnerabilities.

A joint project in West Africa

IOM and the Global Mechanism of the UNCCD are already implementing a joint initiative through the project 'West Africa: Promoting sustainable land management in migration-prone areas through innovative financing mechanisms' funded by the Italian Development Cooperation (Barsk-Rundquist 2014).

Taking into account the fact that many countries in the region of the Economic Community of West African States (ECOWAS) are seriously affected by the effects of desertification, land degradation and drought, and with West Africa counting the highest number of international migrants in the entire African continent, the project explores both the potential benefits and challenges posed by environmental migration and aims to contribute to the prevention of land degradation as well as to the restoration and rehabilitation of degraded land by increasing investments in sustainable land management in migration-prone areas of the ECOWAS region in general, and the countries of Burkina Faso, Niger and Senegal in particular, predominantly through the use and up-scaling of innovative financing mechanisms.

In the three project countries, the so-called 'countries of origin', the project targets four key areas of intervention:

1   *Analysis of the interrelations between migration and the environment and their effects on development and security in West Africa.*

This assessment helps all concerned stakeholders to better understand the multiple interrelations, causes and effects of the migration–environment nexus and to identify responses required at the policy level.

2   *Identification of policy options to effectively address the migration–desertification, land degradation and drought nexus.*
    Based on the lessons learned through the project, we will be able to propose policy options to decision-makers for their consideration. These options will include the issues of sustainable land management, enabling environment, sound land-use planning, restoration, coordination and effective use of remittances to manage desertification, land degradation and drought.

3   *Analysis of the opportunities to increase investments in sustainable land management and land rehabilitation in West Africa.*
    Promising investment opportunities in land-based production systems, such as agriculture, livestock management and forestry, in the three countries of origin will be assessed and options for up-scaling will be promoted.

4   *Facilitation of the application and testing of innovative financing mechanisms, including channelling remittances and promoting diaspora investments, in migration-prone areas in Burkina Faso, Niger and Senegal.*
    These innovative mechanisms and regulations to promote migrant investments in land rehabilitation will be tested in coordination with ongoing initiatives such as TerrAfrica (www.terrafrica.org/) and the Great Green Wall Initiative for the Sahara and Sahel (FAO n.d.) in order to facilitate and to promote economic opportunities as well as the public–private investment climate for sustainable land management and for local communities and local authorities.

In the country of destination, namely Italy, the project engages with the diaspora from Senegal as well as Burkina Faso and Niger in order to:

5   *Offer support to migrant entrepreneurs willing to invest in sustainable land management and land rehabilitation in their countries of origin.*

The studies will provide an overview of the current opportunities for channelling diaspora investments and remittances towards sustainable land management and land-based adaptation initiatives in the three countries and propose solutions to overcome the main challenges in Burkina Faso, Niger and Senegal.

Preliminary project results indicate that, in order to effectively facilitate investments in sustainable land management, four conditions have to be in place, not only for diaspora, but for any private investment:

1   An enabling environment must be in place in the countries of origin.
2   Viable investment opportunities and instruments must exist in these countries for adapting to the effects of climate change and increase the resilience of local populations.
3   The diaspora must be aware of these investment opportunities.

4   The diaspora must have a vested interest in investing in sound land-based systems.

In order to promote sustainable development in a holistic way and to properly address the interrelations between migration and environment and their effects on food security, new and innovative partnerships, such as the one between IOM and UNCCD, are required between institutions that have not traditionally cooperated to better mitigate the negative effects of migration, such as insecurity, while promoting the positive contribution of migration for development as a whole. The project is aiming to do both, facilitating new and innovative partnerships, improving livelihoods in migration-prone areas threatened by desertification, land degradation and drought and facilitating the positive contribution of the diaspora for the sustainable development of their countries of origin.

References

Barbut, M. (2014) Migration for the good. *Huffington Post*. 23 December 2014.

Barsk-Rundquist, E. (2014) Land, migration and development: a new dimension for UNCCD implementation. *IOM Conference 'Integrating Migration into Development'* [online]. Available: www.italy.iom.int/conf/panel3/Session2/GMspeech.pdf [Accessed 25 February 2015].

Euro-African Dialogue on Migration and Development (n.d.) *Rabat Process* [online]. Available: www.processusderabat.net/web/uploads/cms/Rabat-Process.pdf [Accessed 25 February 2015].

Food and Agriculture Organization of the United Nations (FAO) (n.d.) *Great Green Wall for the Sahara and Sahel Initiative: an African partnership to tackle desertification and land degradation* [online]. Available: www.fao.org/partnerships/great-green-wall/en/ [Accessed 18 March 2015].

International Organization for Migration (IOM) (2014) *IOM outlook on migration, environment and climate change* [online]. Available: http://publications.iom.int/ bookstore/index.php?main_page=product_info&cPath=34&products_id=1429 [Accessed 18 March 2015].

United Nations Convention to Combat Desertification (1994) [online]. Available: www. unccd.int/en/about-the-convention/Pages/Text-overview.aspx [Accessed 25 February 2015].

11 Mobilizing action on climate change and migration

The UK Migration and Climate Change Coalition

Alex Randall

Introduction

The UK Migration and Climate Change Coalition is a project that works with refugee and migration rights groups on migration and displacement linked to climate change. I have worked with the project for three years. This chapter explores some of the dilemmas advocacy groups face when working on this topic, and some issues we encounter when working with environmental organizations. I want to draw out how different parts of the green movement talk about migration linked to climate change and how they use the idea of people displaced by climate change in their campaigning and activism. I also want to unpack how green organizations and the progressive media borrow and repeat messages about migration and climate change that are often seemingly opposed to their values.

The 'Old guard' and the 'New radicals'

Several intellectual traditions within the green movement have shaped its thinking on migration and climate change. My purpose here is not to critique any part of the green movement, but rather to draw out the different ways they conceptualize migration linked to climate change. Many environmental thinkers have a neo-Malthusian concern that growing populations will destroy the ecosystems we depend on for life. The Club of Rome's famous *Limits to Growth* (Meadows 1972) challenged the idea that infinite growth was possible on a finite planet. It became a powerful early text shaping much environmental thinking in the English-speaking world. Parts of the green movement also have an approach to environmentalism informed by the early conservation movement that saw humans as the destroyers of pristine ecosystems, protected only by saviour conservationists creating reserves. I will label this group the 'Old Guard'.

However, there are also strands of thinking within the environmental movement based on entirely dissimilar intellectual and activist traditions. These have produced very different ways of thinking about migration linked to climate change. A new generation of activists finds their inspiration not in Malthus, the Club of Rome and conservation; but in Paulo Freire (1996), Naomi Klein (2015), the Suffragettes and the anti-slavery movement. Climate change is seen as a justice issue. High emitting countries are often seen as the perpetrators of disasters in poorer low emitting countries. The solution is seen as a movement for justice spanning North and South, and through international agreements reflecting this movement's demand for justice. For simplicity, I will call this crowd the 'New Radicals'.

The 'Old Guard' and the 'New Radicals' can exist within the same organizations. This is more likely to occur in the established big, green NGOs, such as Friends of the Earth UK, World Wide Fund for Nature and Greenpeace. There are some new organizations that have little time for the 'Old Guard', or barely know they exist, such as 350.org, and the International youth climate movements. Both groups talk about climate change and migration in similar ways, but there are also some important differences.

Both the 'Old Guard' and the 'New Radicals' tend to characterize migration linked to climate change in the following ways. First, as massive: Norman Myer's assertion that climate change will create 250 million migrants (Myers 2002) is frequently repeated. Second, rather than seeing migration as a complex phenomenon with many causes, they often see it as simple, inevitable and driven by climate change. Third, as creating an emergency in the UK; either an emergency requiring compassion and help – the position of the New Radicals, or an emergency requiring the defence of the UK's borders – the position of the 'Old Guard'. Additionally, the 'Old Guard' often characterize migration linked to climate change as a threat to the UK's ecosystems as more people create more demand for services and more carbon emissions. Further, the 'Old Guard' also utilizes public fear of migration as an opportunity to convince people of the need for action on climate change.

The green movement: a complicated relationship

As part of our work on migration and climate change I have spoken to a number of people within green organizations who believe that climate change will create an inevitable and massive flow of refugees into the UK, and for some of them this view seems to be held despite them knowing there is strong evidence indicating otherwise. During one conversation, a senior figure in a green organization told me that he simply did not believe the evidence on migration and climate change. He was convinced that climate change would force millions of people into the UK. I pointed him towards the 5th Assessment of the IPCC (Adger *et al.* 2014), which having assessed the evidence argues that this kind of movement is unlikely. He was totally dismissive of the IPCC's assessment on human movement and climate change, in spite of wholeheartedly trusting its assessment of almost every other aspect of climate change.

The green movement's other key narrative linking climate and migration is one in which climate change drives people into new areas and this has a detrimental impact on ecosystems. An extension of this concern is that as people move from poorer to richer countries, their emissions will increase making climate change even harder to deal with. Jonathon Porritt captures perfectly this sentiment. Porritt is a senior and respected figure in the UK green movement. He was director of the Blair Government's Sustainable Development Commission, founder of the green think tank, Forum for the Future, and is a former director of Friends of the Earth. He publicly called for the UK to have a 'net zero' immigration policy (Clover 2008). As part of broader concerns about 'population pressure', he believes that Britain should have zero net migration to keep carbon emissions low and destruction of ecosystems to a minimum.

The vast anti-migrant sentiment in the UK has also led some greens to see opposing immigration as a strategy to encourage right-leaning voters to support climate change policies. A clean tech investment trader and commentator wrote in the *Independent*, '[i]f you're worried about immigration, then you should be terrified by climate change' (Razzouk 2015).

These sentiments were echoed by a Green Party parliamentary candidate in a blog post (Read 2014) asking 'Why are those so opposed to migration so blind to something that will cause it to increase so dramatically?' The Green Party of England and Wales is divided on the issue. Senior party figures have been some of the few politicians to make positive statements about migration. Natalie Bennett (2014), the party leader, very publicly welcomed new Romanian and Hungarian migrants when the countries joined the EU, against a backdrop of scaremongering by every other party. Bennett's statements represent a typical 'New Radical' position. However, another group of senior Green Party figures published a letter in the *Guardian* (Padley 2013) arguing that migration was adding to UK carbon emissions and making protecting the UK environment even harder – a typical 'Old Guard' stance.

Direct action: protesting in solidarity or tapping anti-refugee sentiment?

The group that I have characterized as the 'Old Guard' are not the only section of the green movement that see migration linked to climate change as both massive and problematic. The 'New Radicals' equally see migration linked to climate change as being huge, inevitable and creating an emergency. Through our advocacy work I have had the chance to speak to many people in this camp. My sense, having spent a lot of time in these activist groups, is that their motivations are very different from the 'Old Guard'.

In the run-up to the Copenhagen climate negotiations in 2009, UK climate activism enjoyed a resurgence, and scored a couple of key wins on coal and aviation. Previously disparate activist groups came together around the Climate Camps. These protests produced a number of 'climate refugee' direct actions, which were deeply problematic. They portrayed 'climate refugees' as hapless victims and perpetuated a number of myths about migration linked to climate change. In 2009, a group of activists chained themselves to the entrance of Southampton Airport. Several of them used tents to obstruct the entrance. The tents were used as banners and were painted with phrases like 'Climate Refugee Camp' and '250 million climate refugees by 2050' (Plane Stupid 2009). A similar protest saw activists create another 'climate refugee camp' on the banks of the river Thames in central London. Banners stated 'Big business burns carbon, the poor become climate refugees'. Rather than seeing refugees as a threat or a source of environmental degradation, the protesters intended to create an act of solidarity. Other messages on their websites (Campaign Against Climate Change 2011) stated they saw their protests as acting on behalf of the 'climate refugees', campaigning for justice and even for reparations for historical carbon emissions. However, looking at the photos of the protests it is also possible to see refugees portrayed as objects of pity. These campaigners clearly see refugees and migrants very differently to the 'Old Guard'.

However, we can still ask what impression the passing public might have of the 'climate refugees' portrayed in these protests. Within activist circles, the idea that these protests were acts of solidarity and demands for justice would have been well understood. However, outside of this world, the public may simply have taken away the idea that climate change is going to create a refugee crisis in the UK. If the passing public were already hostile towards migrants and refugees, the protest may simply have reinforced this feeling. The calls for justice, solidarity and reparations would have been lost. In other words, what the public takes away from the protests of the 'New Radicals' may not be very different from what the public takes away from the statements of the 'Old Guard'.

Openness to change: how the 'Old Guard' and the 'New Radicals' react to challenge

The difference in intention is important for working with parts of the green movement in the future. The way that we have tried to work and engage with these different parts of the green movement is based on the messages they intended, rather than messages they actually created. When speaking to people who have been involved in protests similar to the 'climate refugee camps', I feel there is potential for cooperation. Demands for justice and acts of solidarity are needed. If these groups are prepared to communicate about migration linked to climate change in a nuanced and intelligent way then this is positive. There is nothing wrong with framing migration linked to climate change as a justice issue, and similarly nothing wrong with bringing the issue to public attention using protest. The fact that such protests and messages have been created with this motivation has usually meant that the campaigners and protesters are open to dialogue regarding how affected communities feel about the issue. They have also been open to thinking more deeply about accuracy and about the risks to existing refugees and migrants.

Through our advocacy work on migration and climate change we have also been in dialogue with many environmentalists that fit the 'Old Guard' ideology. These people have seemed much less receptive to our arguments. I have challenged several people who hold the 'Old Guard' outlook on migration and climate change. In these conversations they have always been hostile to the idea that the relationship between migration and climate change is incredibly complex, and also to the idea that migration is not a bad thing. They almost always resorted quickly to familiar tropes about migrants 'pushing down wages' or 'putting pressure on the school system'. Finally, they are usually hostile to the idea that migration linked to climate change is anything other than a crisis requiring the tightening of the UK's borders. My sense from these conversations is that this imagined crisis is simply too good for the environmentalist 'Old Guard' to let go of. They believe that an immigration crisis caused by climate change is going to be their ticket to influence. They hope that presenting climate change as creating a refugee crisis on Britain's shores will finally wake up the government to lowering emissions. However, it is not just tactics that keep them clinging to their messages. Their way of thinking about migration and climate change is also informed by the influential texts of their movement: *Limits to Growth, Small is Beautiful* (Schumacher 1973) and *The Whole Earth Catalogue* (Brand 1968). These texts imagine a slower, more rural existence. More people would work the land, live in small communities and become self-sufficient in food and energy. The idea of a more mobile, more urban, more multicultural world seems antithetical to their hopes for the future.

For these reasons, I have given up on trying to win arguments with the 'Old Guard'. I still challenge them, but I do not hope to convince them. I see great hope in building connections between parts of the green movement inhabited by the 'New Radicals'. Since 2012 we have organized a number of events to try to bring climate change and refugee activists together. The purpose has been to build a group of people who can speak out intelligently on the issue from a standpoint of social justice.

Military messages: green speakers

Throughout 2014 and 2015 I watched several green organizations and progressive media outlets repeat some very unhelpful messages about the link between climate, migration and armed conflict. The origins of these messages have been various military institutions and figures. During 2014 a number of military institutions (CNA 2014; Hagel 2014) produced assessments of the risk posed by climate change. These assessments have looked at the security implications of climate change. They have also presented migration and displacement linked to climate change as a security problem, but have been rather vague about why migration might create new armed violence. However, the suggestion is that people will move because of climate change, compete over resources and this will end in armed conflict. The militaries of Western nations will then be forced to intervene in these conflicts. At other points in these reports the authors simply claim their military will have to take a greater role in dealing with natural disasters.

My intention here is not to focus on whether this analysis is correct (although I believe that it is not), but rather to focus on how these messages have been adopted, used, challenged or modified by actors within civil society. As part of our advocacy work we frequently engage with other campaigners on this issue. This assessment is largely based on my experience of challenging people and organizations when they borrow these messages, and then listening to how they react. What, for example, should campaigners and activists make of former Royal Navy Rear Admiral Neil Morisetti? He has been a vocal supporter of action on climate change, supporting strong international agreements to reduce emissions. His key argument is that unchecked climate change will create situations in which the UK is forced to commit troops to overseas conflicts (Carrington 2014). He believes climate change will create new conflicts, and the UK will have no choice but to use its armed forces to stabilize these situations. One of the key drivers of these conflicts will be the movement of people. Displacement, migration and then conflict over resources will be a key factor in creating these violent situations, which will require armed intervention by the UK.

There are plenty of critiques of Morisetti's position (Randall 2015) but what I want to examine here is how campaigners and activists have responded to and used his comments, rather than whether his arguments are valid or not. Morisetti made these remarks most recently at a climate change event organized by a new organization (ECIU 2014) hoping to counter climate change skepticism. By inviting Morisetti, and providing a platform for his views, they made a strategic campaign decision that they hoped would shift climate policy at the highest levels in the UK. Who, after all, might a government minister listen to more than a retired Navy Admiral? What better way to bring about swifter government action than to present climate change as an expensive and deadly security problem? What surprised me was the excitement with which a number of radical and progressive organizations unquestioningly repeated his assertion that human mobility linked to climate change would result in conflict. The usually 'progressive' *Huffington Post* ran a story, written by a Friends of the Earth staffer, repeating the claims (Shrubsole 2014). Similarly, the Environment section of the *Guardian* – usually deeply critical of UK military intervention – gave an entirely uncritical airing of Morisetti's opinions (Carrington 2014). It seemed that campaigners and media outlets who are often deeply cynical of the military's motives for *anything*, were now repeating the claims of senior military figures. The concern usually expressed for those most vulnerable to climate impacts was suddenly replaced by a narrative that saw migrants as the cause of violence, a vector for armed conflict and security problem that would tie up UK forces.

The dilemma faced by progressive activists here is between their own values and the prospect of influence at the highest levels. There is a feeling that repeating the assertions of military figures, by adopting their language and framing, might open doors for them – or if not for them personally, for the idea of speedier reductions in carbon emissions.

What kind of crisis might lead to action on climate change?

When I speak to campaigners and activists about these issues, what I often see are people caught in an imagined dilemma. They imagine that presenting apocalyptic messages about migration and climate change will bring them influence; important people will listen and the public will wake up if they can turn climate change into a security or immigration crisis. They also seem to imagine that without this narrative (or a similarly dramatic one) they are destined to obscurity, along with their wholly legitimate and pressing fears about climate change. When I can, I try to speak to people for long enough to convince them that their dilemma is an imagined one. The supposed threat of a climate-induced immigration crisis will not actually help engage the public on climate change. Almost every other dire warning about climate change has failed to galvanize public and political action on climate change. So why would this one?

References

Adger, W.N., Pulhin, J.M., Barnett, J., Dabelko, G.D., Hovelsrud, G.K., Levy, M., Oswald Spring, Ú. and Vogel, C.H. (2014) *Human security*. In *Climate change 2014: impacts, adaptation, and vulnerability. Part A: global and sectoral aspects*, ed. Intergovernmental Panel on Climate Change (IPCC). Working Group II contribution to the fifth Assessment Report of the Intergovernmental Panel on Climate Change. New York: IPCC.

Bennett, N. (2014) *Natalie Bennett speech: immigration policy – time for facts, time for humanity* [online]. Available: https://www.greenparty.org.uk/news/2014/02/10/natalie-bennett-speech-immigration-policy-time-for-the-facts,-time-for-humanity/ [Accessed 12 March 2015].

Brand, S. (1968) *The whole earth catalog*. Menlo Park: Portola Institute.

Campaign Against Climate Change (2011) *Stand up for climate justice* [online]. Available: www.campaigncc.org/standupforclimatejustice [Accessed 13 March 2015].

Carrington, D. (2014) Climate change will see more UK forces deployed in conflicts around world. *The Guardian*, 10 November 2014.

Centre for Naval Analyses (CNA) (2014) *National security and the accelerating risks of climate change*. Alexandria: CNA Corporation.

Clover, C. (2008) Jonathon Porritt: Britain should have 'zero net immigration' policy. *Daily Telegraph*, 6 June 2008.

Energy and Climate Intelligence Unit (ECIU) (2014) *Climate change: risks and opportunities for the UK* [online]. Available: http://eciu.net/press-releases/2014/climate-change-risks-and-opportunities-for-the-uk [Accessed 13 March 2015].

Freire, P. (1996) *Pedagogy of the oppressed*. London: Penguin.

Hagel, C. (2014) *Quadrennial defense review*. Washington, D.C.: The White House, Department of Defense.

Klein, N. (2015) *This changes everything: capitalism vs. the climate*. London: Penguin.

Meadows, D. (1972) *Limits to growth*. New York: Signet.

Myers, N. (2002) Environmental refugees: a growing phenomenon of the 21st century. *Philosophical Transactions of Biological Sciences*. 357(1420): 609–13.

Padley, C. (2013) Many greens worried by high immigration. *The Guardian* [online], 25 July 2013. Available: www.theguardian.com/politics/2013/jul/25/greens-worried-high-immigration [Accessed 18 March 2015].

Plane Stupid (2009) *Plane stupid turns Southampton Airport into climate refugee camp* [online]. Available: www.planestupid.com/content/plane-stupid-turns-southampton-airport-climate-refugee-camp [Accessed 13 March 2015].

Randall, A. (2015) *Infographic: exploring evidence for the climate change and conflict connection* [online]. Available: http://climatemigration.org.uk/infographic-exploring-evidence-for-the-climate-change-and-conflict-connection/ [Accessed 13 March 2015].

Razzouk, A. (2015) If you're worried about immigration, then you should be terrified about climate change. *The Independent* [online], 3 November 2015. Available: www.independent.co.uk/voices/comment/if-youre-worried-about-immigration-then-you-should-be-terrified-about-climate-change-9835475.html [Accessed 18 March 2015].

Read, R. (2014) *Climate: how UKIP and the Tory right will defeat themselves* [online]. Available: https://www.opendemocracy.net/ourkingdom/rupert-read/climate-how-ukip-and-tory-right-will-defeat-themselves [Accessed 12 March 2015].

Schumacher, E.F. (1973) *Small is beautiful: economics as if people mattered*. New York: HarperCollins.

Shrubsole, G. (2014) *'Adapt and survive': the British establishment's answer to the security threat of climate change* [online]. Available: www.huffingtonpost.co.uk/guy-shrubsole/climate-change_b_6138654.html [Accessed 13 March 2015].

12 Climate-induced migrants need dignified recognition under a new protocol

Perspective from Bangladesh

Aminul Hoque

Bangladesh: a critical landscape on population and climate vulnerability

Bangladesh is the eighth most populated country in the world, at 160 million people, with an average of 950 people per square kilometre. Of this population, more than 50 million live below the poverty line (BBS 2010) and many of these occupy remote and ecologically fragile parts of the country, such as floodplains and river islands, or the coastal zones where cyclones are a major threat. The increasing trend in population growth has also created problems across the country for disaster preparedness for the future negative climatic changes and coping strategies.

Climate change, alongside environmental degradation, in Bangladesh is expected to exacerbate many existing vulnerabilities, potentially resulting in mass migration shrinking present opportunities and being beyond possible future adaptation. Internal migration has already commenced due to climate-induced problems across the country, but in many cases, the policies and institutional frameworks, especially measures taken by the Bangladesh Climate Change Strategy and Action Plan (BCCSAP), are not sufficient to protect the displaced people.

Therefore, there is a need to review the relevant policies and institutional frameworks, especially the BCCSAP and its current measures, to identify the protection gaps and adopting new policies to protect the climate-induced migrants.

The scenario on climate-induced migration: empirical evidences

Bangladesh is already regarded as a highly vulnerable country because of sea-level rise, overpopulation and high population in low-lying coastal zones (Pender 2008). Currently, almost 40 million people live in the coastal areas. It is predicted that coastal land erosion will displace 3 per cent of the population by the 2030s, rising to 6 per cent in the 2050s (Tanner *et al.* 2007).

A recent study (Rabbani 2009) in Bangladesh anticipated over 35 million people being displaced from 19 coastal districts in Bangladesh if 1 metre of sea-level rise occurs this century. IOM (2010) has reported that many people have already migrated to the urban slums from the coastal zones of Bangladesh due to frequent cyclone and river erosions.

More than 50 million people live below the poverty line in Bangladesh (BBS 2010), mostly living in coastal areas and in the northern part of the country. These areas are treated as ecologically fragile due to flood and river erosion and desertification. Apart from this, increasing population growth puts growing pressure on basic needs and environmental issues, presenting a threat to our future coping strategies.

The rising environmental changes and extreme weather events have been influencing population migration in Bangladesh in many ways. The observation and analysis of Space Research and Remote Sensing Organization, Bangladesh (SAPRSO) reveals that the trend of extreme weather events, i.e., sudden-onset events like flood and cyclone, has been increasing over the last 30 years, which causes mass displacement with permanent migration across the country. Apart from this the impact of environmental degradation, the slow-onset processes such as salinity in coastal areas, coastal and river erosion, and drought and desertification, contribute significantly to population movements. This report briefly provides the empirical correlation of these events to migration:

Floods are a fact of life for many people in Bangladesh, with around a quarter of the country normally inundated by flood every year. Most people living in flood areas have adapted, raising their houses on high stilts and adjusting their farming systems. However, once every few years there is a severe flood that covers a considerably greater area, with much more significant damage to lives and livelihoods. In the last 25 years, Bangladesh has experienced six severe floods, with the 1988 and 1998 floods alone causing around 6,500 and 1,100 deaths respectively and displacing as many as 45 and 30 million people (BARCIK n.d.). The experience has also spread over the last few years with 850,000 people in 2009, 250,000 in 2010 and nearly 450,000 people in 2011 being displaced, and forcibly migrating both permanently and temporarily due to flood.

a   Tropical cyclones hit Bangladesh, on average, every three years. They are accompanied by high winds and storm surges of up to seven metres, leading to extensive damage to houses and loss of lives and livelihoods. Tropical cyclones in 1970 and 1991 (Cyclone Marian) killed 500,000 and 140,000 people respectively. Cyclone Marian led to the forcible displacement of at least 15 per cent of people in coastal areas and 4 per cent across the nation. Similar to floods, tropical cyclones cause widespread mass displacement of people both during and after the storm itself. The most recent cyclone, Aila, affected 3.9 million people with 200,000 people migrating.

Although Bangladesh has made significant progress over the years, in terms of early warning systems, cyclone shelters and other disaster preparedness, the country still lacks the assets to return to pre-disaster livelihood standards. The empirical evidence shows that there was a reduced death toll following the cyclone SIDR in 2007 (approximately 3,500) but it still resulted in very widespread damage to houses, crops, livestock and other assets costing US$3 billion, constituting 5 per cent of the GDP (Joint UN Multi-Sector Assessment and Response Framework 2010) at that time. Un-estimated asset loss also puts pressure on poor people, and forces at least 650,000 to move temporarily from their domiciles, with a recorded 20 per cent not returning after the disaster.

b   River and coastal erosion is a constant threat and forces people to leave their homes. While no established data conclusively links river erosion to climate change, it is assumed that increasing temperatures contributes to glacier melting in the Himalayan range, creating unpredictable water flows and severe flash floods in the Ganges–Brahmaputra–Meghna system. Heavier and more erratic rainfall has also been observed from the negative climate change impacts. Bangladesh, as a lower riparian country, has to bear the burden of huge melted water and erratic rainfall that increases the downward river flow with high tidal waves and causing severe river bank erosion in coastal and non-coastal rivers. A study by the Centre for Environment and Geographic Information Services (CEGIS) has shown that 100,000 people become homeless every year, lose 10,000 hectares of agricultural and homestead land due to river bank erosion and are forced to permanently migrate.

c   The IPCC assessment narrates that droughts will affect 8 million people by 2050 in Bangladesh. The droughts in Bangladesh are products of two related factors: rising temperature which is intensified by climate change and causes reduction of both surface and ground water. The droughts pose threats to livelihoods of the affected areas, agricultural production, and economy of both the rural and urban areas.

Drought occurs mostly in the northwestern part of the country. An enormous impact has been observed on crop production as the production of all winter crops goes down with the arrival of droughts. Droughts also result in land degradation, low livestock population, unemployment, and malnutrition and people migrating to other areas where opportunities are available as a final adaption strategy. Since 1973, Bangladesh has experienced repeated droughts, which have affected 47 per cent of area and 53 per cent of people. Evidence suggests that each drought affects at least 3 per cent of the total population (Akter 2009). Similar to other disasters, drought is a recurrent event in Bangladesh.

Government practice to deal with the climate migrant issue in Bangladesh

In addressing the problems associated with climate change, the government prepared the BCCSAP, a 10-year programme in 2008 which was revised again in 2009 (MoEF 2009). The BCCSAP is a knowledge-based document with a 10-year action plan to build capacity and resilience in the country to meet climate change challenges over the next 20–25 years under six thematic areas for action. These thematic areas are: (i) food security, social protection, and health; (ii) comprehensive disaster management; (iii) infrastructural development; (iv) research and knowledge management; (v) mitigation and low-carbon development; and (vi) capacity building and institutional strengthening. The BCCSAP is an approved government programme, which has been incorporated within the Sixth Five Year Plan as well as the Perspective Plan 2021 for the country.

To operationalize the BCCSAP planned activities, the government also established the Bangladesh Climate Change Trust Fund and has allocated more than US$300 million to date. Furthermore, a Bangladesh Climate Change Resilience Fund/Multi-Donor Trust Fund was established to pool funds from the donors and development partners to implement a long-term strategy to adapt to the adverse effects of climate change in Bangladesh.

Despite all this, there are concerns regarding how the BCCSAP will address the management of climate migration issues. The BCCSAP clearly mentions the state's responsibility to resettle climate displaced people and advocates for the free movement of these people worldwide. Their movement should be monitored by the state and adequate institutional support should be provided to turn the displaced population into trained and useful citizens for any country in the world (MoEF 2009: 2, 16). But this responsibility did not translate into any particular point of action and implementation under any of these six thematic development pillars last year.

EquityBD's campaign on migrant issues

EquityBD has been engaging in campaigns and advocacy activities through following the BCCSAP as a base document on climate change issues in Bangladesh, as BCCSAP, in encompassing the six thematic development areas, provides an almost holistic development approach. But there is a major concern that the BCSSAP has ignored mass participation, especially participation of climate victims, and been prepared by experts with very little knowledge of the reality on the ground. Hence, the questions have been raised whether the BCCSAP will be able to fulfil the demand of climate victims and vulnerable people. Addressing this concern, we aim to develop a proactive civil society organization (CSO) role for different climate change issues, and campaign for the prioritization of migration at local and national planning levels.

Hardly any advocacy is taking place in Bangladesh on issues of climate justice, a gap identified by EquityBD. The concept of 'Climate Justice' includes the issues of: i) payment of climate change compensation by rich countries as they are responsible for the warming of Earth; ii) new international protocol for climate-induced migrants as they have very little alternatives to cope with climate adverse impact within a country like Bangladesh; and iii) a climate integrated national development plan that will support sustainable management of the environment along with economic activities in future.

Taking this in view, EquityBD has been campaigning for climate justice and undertaking the following objectives. Firstly, to develop a critical civil society alliance in Bangladesh to influence government policies in light of the 'equity and justice principle' of climate change, Secondly, provide the facts and figures to different national and international civil society alliances, so that claims for climate justice and compensation, reparation from the developed countries will be strengthened, and finally, conduct advocacy through disseminating on the country's ground-level climate change impacts at the international level to establish the appropriate development support strategies from donors.

Challenges in future dealing with climate migrants

Bangladesh is not able to manage the future climate-displaced people

According to future projection, Bangladesh will become the sixth most populated (250 million) country in 2050, with a population density of around 1,300 people per kilometre. This high population will create burdens on the land, food, water and the natural systems. Apart from this scenario, environmental degradation as a result of climate change would intensify the situation leading people to migrate in the near future. There will be further opportunities for internal migration of new 'climate migrants'[1] within Bangladesh as the landmass will have shrunk due to rising sea levels.

The government's failure to reconstruct sea embankments will further intensify the displacement (Ahmed and Neelormi 2008), demonstrated by Cyclone SIDR in 2007, Cyclone Mohasen in 2008 and even more violently, Cyclone Aila in 2009, which caused both displacement and subsequent migration. An estimated 100,000 people migrated to a nearby district because of acute shortage of essential food, drinking water, sanitation and outbreak of skin diseases.

International policy is not adequately dealing with the issue

Due to the lack of appropriate international policy framework, the issue of climate-induced migrants has not received proper global recognition over recent years. The present United Nations and international policies for protecting internally displaced persons are insufficient. As per the normative frameworks under the 1998 United Nations (UN) Guiding Principles on Internal Displacement, the respective states have the primary responsibility to help internally displaced persons. However, there are challenges on the ground to ensure the protection of internally displaced persons. This is because the affected countries are sometimes unable to protect the displaced people, with Bangladesh as an example. In some cases many countries, especially developed countries, deny the entry of migrated people and their international protection referring to the so-called principle of national sovereignty and non-interference.

Global response has failed in dealing with the climate migrant issue

There has been little output in the observed global climate negotiation process, especially in the Conference of the Parties (COP) to address the issues of climate migrants and protection of their livelihoods. After a long debate, all country parties adopted the 'Cancún Adaptation Framework' in the COP 16 and agreed to undertake action to reduce vulnerability and build resilience of developing country parties, taking into account their urgent and immediate needs. This adaptation framework includes one agenda related to climate migrant management, implemented under the working definition of internally displaced person (IDP), which means respective country parties will have to manage the IDPs through their own efforts within their territory.

But in principal, the Cancún Adaptation Framework has emphasized taking into the account the Common But Different Responsibilities (CBDR) principle by all country parties, especially developed country parties, for enhancing their action through enhancing understanding, coordination and cooperation with regard to climate-induced displacement, migration and planned relocation where appropriate at national, regional and international levels (UNFCCC 2011: art. 14.f). The exercise of the CBDR principle is absent in the latest global negotiations. The Cancún Adaptation Framework instead focuses on a wide range of adaptation activities that country parties may undertake. These activities include: adaptation planning, prioritizing and implementation activities; impact and vulnerability assessments; institutional capacity strengthening; building of socio-economic and ecological systems; disaster risk reduction strategies and public awareness. Thus, climate migrant issues, both internal and across borders, are perceived as being ignored in the global negotiation process.

Thus, the Cancún Adaptation Framework has failed to address the climate migrant issue. The developed countries hold major responsibilities due to their excessive emission of greenhouse gases. Accepting this liability, the Cancún agreement proposed to establish an international adaptation committee, that was a fundamental requirement for enhancing global adaptation policies, process and supporting mechanism. This committee, however, has not yet been established.

The latest global negotiation (COP 19) has ignored the climate migrant issue and included it under the framework of 'Loss and Damage'. There has been no measurable achievement towards the Loss and Damage issue in COP 19, except forming a committee, which in fact has been deferred for the next three years to 2016.

Our way forward on the climate migrant issue

A legislative document (internal displacement policy) imperative for Bangladesh

Bangladesh has yet to develop policies for mass displacement in the context of internal migration or resettlement. However, climate-induced displacement has been officially recognized by its government through the BCCSAP 2009. The state has responsibility and primary duty to protect forcibly migrating persons and ensure their basic needs. Before demanding international responsibility, the state must formulate its own policy on internal displacement. The Ministry of Environment and Forests (MoEF) of Bangladesh has declared it will review the BCCSAP 2009 along with formulating a legislative document on 'Internal Displacement Policy' but has not yet started the process.

Mainstreaming the climate-induced migrant in BCCSAP Action and Implementation Plan

The present BCCSAP is not cost allocated and has no priority-based delivery framework to address climate-induced migrants and their management. Given this absence, BCCSAP needs to be reviewed and further developed as an effective instrument that would be capable of providing guidance on how migrant issues should be treated and implemented on a priority basis, while serving the climate migrants' interests. The latest information indicates that no particular action or resources have been mobilized to address the migrant issue despite the plan of action to 'Monitor of internal and external migration of adversely impacted population and providing support to them through capacity building for their rehabilitation in new environment' under BCCSAP.

Developed countries have to recognize their historical responsibilities to GHG emission and pay compensation to deal with the climate migrants issue

The annex-1 countries (rich countries according to the Kyoto Protocol list) are historically responsible for emitting greenhouse gases (GHG), which are the main cause of warming the planet. The annex-1 countries have been extracting and transferring the natural resources from developing countries, often without concern for local needs, and contributing to the GHG emission for the last two centuries in the name of industrial development. As a result, developing countries have suffered the negative impacts of the climatic change despite having limited responsibility for GHG emissions. Changing climatic patterns have caused extreme weather events (super cyclones, river erosion, salinity and so forth) in developing countries resulting in life loss, severe damage to resources and forced displacement. We think that there are no structural and economic capacities of poor developing countries to further recover from these damages. In this context, it would be just if annex-1 countries recognize their historical responsibilities for global warming and must give a proactive commitment to compensate accordingly.

Expanding the UN definition of refugee, focusing on climate-induced factors

The 1951 Refugee Convention (which reflects its post-World War II context) and 1967 Protocol provides the current definition of refugee, which does not recognize climate migrants as refugees. It defines refugees as people who are outside their country of origin, with a well-founded fear of persecution on account of their race, religion, nationality, political opinion or membership of a particular social group. The Convention mandates protection for those whose civil and political rights are violated. However, it does not protect persons whose socio-economic rights are at risk, thus the United Nations High Commissioner for Refugees (UNHCR) currently denies it has a mandate for assisting persons displaced by climate change.

Given this, a new protocol to the Geneva Convention was already requested during a meeting with representatives of governments, environmental and humanitarian organizations, and United Nations agencies organized by the government of the Maldives in 2006 (Biermann and Boas 2008).

Jessie Cooper, an American lawyer, proposed the extension of the definition of a refugee and an amendment of Article 1A of the Geneva Convention by adding degraded environmental conditions that endanger life, health, livelihoods and the use of resources (Cooper 1998). She justified her analysis by reference to Article 25(1) of the Universal Declaration of Human Rights ('Everyone has the right to a standard of living adequate for the health and well-being of himself and of his family, including food, clothing, housing and medical care and necessary social services, and the right to security in the event of unemployment, sickness, disability, widowhood, old age or other lack of livelihood in circumstances beyond his control') (UN 1948).

Climate migrant issue must be integrated with post-2015 development goal

The agenda on climate-induced forced displacement has not been included in many important global development discourses, such as Post-2015 Sustainable Development Goals (SDGs), Rio+20 and so forth. EquityBD is concerned about the dual policy where UN and other international discourses have been talking about future sustainable development, without addressing the underlying problem and the responsibility of those creating crises such as the climate-induced displacement issue. Thus, we demand the UN include the issue in all future global development discourses and framing of appropriate responsibility, based on the respective country scenario.

This provides an opportune moment for our global policymakers to ensure the climate-induced displacement issues are better addressed in post-2015 goals and other frameworks for international action on disaster risk reduction and sustainable development. The post-2015 goals are currently under preparation and must assure that developing and developed countries and donors will give due attention to climate change adaptation plans and to the increasing risk of displacement, including by facilitating migration and planned relocation locally and globally that respect the rights and dignity of vulnerable populations.

Note

1 In Article 27 of the BCCSAP, it is anticipated that, 'the imminent threat of displacement of more than 20 million people in the event of sea-level change and

resulting increase in salinity coupled with impact of increase in cyclones and storm surges, in the near future' (MoEF 2009: 16).

References

Ahmed, A.U. and Neelormi, S. (2008) *Climate change, loss of livelihoods and forced displacements in Bangladesh* [online]. Available: www.csrlbd.org/resources/climate change/doc_download/47-climate-change-loss-of-livelihoods-and-forced-displacements-in-bangladesh- [Accessed 11 May 2015].

Akter, T. (2009) *Climate change and flow of environmental displacement in Bangladesh: Unnayan Anneshan – the innovators.* Dhaka: Center for Research and Action on Development.

Bangladesh Bureau of Statistics (BBS) (2010) *Report on the house hold income & expenditure (HHIE) survey 2010 in Bangladesh* [online]. Available: www.bbs.gov.bd/PageReportLists. aspx?PARENTKEY=66 [Accessed 11 May 2015].

Bangladesh Resource Centre for Indigenous Knowledge (BARCIK) (n.d.) *National adaptation programme of action (NAPA) and people's adaptation plan* [online]. Available: www.klima-und-gerechtigkeit.de/fileadmin/upload/Dialogforen/summary_NAPA_study.pdf [Accessed 9 April 2015].

Biermann, F. and Boas, I. (2008) Protecting climate refugees: the case for a global protocol. *Environment: Science and Policy for Sustainable Development.* 50(6): 8–17.

Cooper, J.B. (1998) Environmental refugees: meeting the requirements of the refugee definition. *New York University Environmental Law Journal.* 6: 480–529.

International Organization for Migration (IOM) (2010) *Assessing the evidence: environment, climate change and migration in Bangladesh* [online]. Available: http://publications.iom. int/bookstore/free/environment_climate_change_bangladesh.pdf [Accessed 9 April 2015].

Joint UN Multi-Sector Assessment & Response Framework (2010) *Cyclone Aila* [online]. Available: www.lcgbangladesh.org/derweb/Needs%20Assessment/Reports/Aila_UN_AssessmentFramework_FINAL.pdf [Accessed 11 May 2015].

Ministry of Environment and Forests, Government of the People's Republic of Bangladesh (MoEF) (2009) *Bangladesh Climate Change Strategy and Action Plan 2009* [online]. Available: http://cmsdata.iucn.org/downloads/bangladesh_climate_change_strategy_and_action_plan_2009.pdf [Accessed 11 May 2015].

Pender, J. (2008) Community-led adaptation in Bangladesh. *Forced Migration Review.* (31): 54–5.

Rabbani, M.G. (2009) Climate forced migration: a massive threat to coastal people in Bangladesh. *Clime Asia: Climate Action Network-South Asia Newsletter.* Dhaka: BCAS.

Tanner, T.M., Hassan, A., Islam, K.M.N., Conway, D., Mechler, R., Ahmed, A.U. and Alam, M. (2007) *ORCHID: piloting climate risk screening in DFID Bangladesh – summary research report* [online]. Available: https://www.ids.ac.uk/files/dmfile/ORCHID BangladeshResearchReport2007.pdf [Accessed 11 May 2015].

United Nations (UN) (1948) *Universal declaration of human rights* [online]. Available: www.un.org/en/documents/udhr/ [Accessed 11 May 2015].

United Nations Framework Convention on Climate Change (UNFCCC) (2011) *The Cancún Agreements: outcome of the work of the Ad Hoc Working Group on Long-term Cooperative Action under the Convention* [online]. Available: http://unfccc.int/resource/docs/2010/cop16/eng/07a01.pdf [Accessed 6 May 2015].

Part 5

The role of advocacy work

13 Civil society advocacy and environmental migration in Zimbabwe

A case study in public policy

Innocent Chirisa and Elmond Bandauko

Introduction

Imbued in most environmental migration matters are issues of public policy and spatial planning. Practice shows that detachment, resistance, compensation and climate change mitigation are at the centre of environmental migration. In seeking to redress these pivotal concerns, civil society organizations (CSOs) enter the debate, thereby providing an oppositional function, bringing conflict and friction with the state. The affected populations (the migrants) are often caught in between and, sometimes, tend to be the 'big losers' as the state and CSOs fight each other over the issues that arise. The present study seeks to unravel the terrain of CSO advocacy in matters of environmental migration in Zimbabwe, highlighting the major thrusts, issues and constraints in the execution of effective resettlement of the affected communities. The study applies the case study design, for in-depth analysis of issues (Baxter and Jack 2008).

In urban settings, the case of urban gentrification is discussed in situations where the state has engaged in, or promoted, forced displacement of urban migrants, often resulting in the ultimate demolition of their dwellings, on the grounds of environmental health improvement. The post-independence cases of the Porta Farm in 1990 and Operation Murambatsvina in 2005 are presented. From the rural side, the major triggers of environmental migration have been mineral exploitation (for example, Murowa and Marange diamonds), large dam constructions (for example, Tokwe-Mukosi Dam) and, more recently, plantation farming (for example, the case of Chisumbanje Ethanol Plant). While the state's argument has focused on equity, investment and employment creation towards furthering the national interests, the argument by the civil society has been narrow in its approach, just looking into the issues of adequate security and protection of households and affected communities. In certain instances, the CSOs have played a 'midwifery' role in trying to ensure that the sentiments, physiological needs and esteem of the affected people are met. This has happened, sometimes, in direct conflict with the interests of the state.

The chapter is organized according to the following sections: the introduction sets the tone for the discussion, by highlighting the facets of the concept of environmental migration. The theory section discusses the concepts of civil society advocacy, environmental migration, public policy and spatial planning, and provides an outline of the theoretical framework that informs the discussion of this chapter. The results section then details the urban and rural-based cases of environmental migration in Zimbabwe. It focuses on the Porta Farm case, Operation Murambatsvina, Marange and Tokwe-Mukosi cases. A discussion, including practical implications, then relates the results and the theory and tries to distil the key observations from the study. Finally, the conclusion and 'Way forward' section rounds off the debate by retelling the key messages in the chapter and providing recommendations regarding the issue of environmental migration in Zimbabwe.

Theory

The concepts of civil society advocacy, environmental migration, public policy and spatial planning inform the discussion of this chapter. The relationship of these concepts to this study is explained in the forthcoming paragraphs. Civil society advocacy entails the campaigns for justice by organizations championing human rights promotion. Environmental migration, the basis of the argument in this chapter, explains the movement of people from defined local areas due to forces of environmental change or the private or public sector seeking to exploit environmental resources, such as minerals and forest reserves. Lastly, spatial planning is a public policy activity that determines where activities should be located and why. Overall, the concept of environmental migration is multi-dimensional in nature involving an environmental challenge in an area (for example flooding), or a project which takes up new land. Once the site is 'invaded' by the project, communities are displaced. In the process of displacement human rights may be violated, creating a gap where civil society groups advocate for fair treatment of the victims and pressure the government or private business at work to consider adequate compensation for the victims. In certain instances, public policy about this involves relocation programmes of which planning for the resettlement of the victims is a critical subject.

Civil society advocacy

First, it is important to give a conceptual reflection on the meaning of civil society. Civil society refers to associations and/or groups of individual citizens who represent different sectors of society in exclusion of, and independent from, the government's control. Civil society includes, among others, non-governmental organizations (NGOs), community-based organizations, professional associations, philanthropic and religious organizations, academic institutions, the media, workers' unions and both ordinary and elite individuals (Tumushabe and Mugyenyi 2002). Taken as a whole, civil society represents a diversity of identities, issues and perspectives (Tumushabe and Mugyenyi 2002). CSOs are organizations who work closely with the local communities: hence the need for CSOs to advocate for the needs of the poor with whom they work (Tumushabe and Mugyenyi 2002). Civil society can draw strength from its diversity, even though it cannot speak for the interests of all people all of the time, or even some of the time (Pact Tanzania 2005). Civil society creates and uses public free spaces to gather, think, exchange and refine views, organize and take action.

CSOs have a key role in the development of policies and laws that affect all citizens (Pact Tanzania 2005). They usually do this through their advocacy work. CSOs have a critical role in influencing policy makers on behalf of the poor. They must engage policy makers to take action on the needs of the poor regarding specific issues through mutual agreement and/or negotiation to reach a compromise position which best serves the perceived needs. There will therefore be positions of agreement, disagreement or compromise (Tumushabe and Mugyenyi 2002).

There are also various theoretical and philosophical foundations of the concept of civil society. John Locke (1632–1704) was the first theorist in modern times to stress that civil society is a body in its own right, separate from the state. People form a community, in which their social life develops and in which the state has no say. This sphere is pre- or unpolitical. The first task of this civil society is to protect the individual – his/her rights and property – against the state and its arbitrary interventions (Merkel and Lauth 1998: 4; Schade 2002: 10). Charles Montesquieu (1689–1755) elaborated his model of separation of powers (*De l'esprit des lois* 1748) where he distinguished, as Locke did, between political society (regulating the relations between citizens and government) and civil society (regulating the relations between citizens), but presents a far less sharp contrast between the two spheres. Instead, he stresses a balance between central authority and societal networks (corps intermediaries), where the central authority (monarchy) must be controlled by the rule of law and limited by the countervailing power of independent organizations (networks) that operate inside and outside the political structure (Merkel and Lauth 1998: 5). Tocqueville (1835/1840) stressed even more the role of these independent associations as civil society. He saw these associations as schools of democracy in which democratic thinking, attitudes and behaviour are learnt, with the further aim of protecting and defending individual rights against potentially authoritarian regimes and tyrannical majorities in society (Pietrzyk 2003). According to Tocqueville these associations should be built voluntarily and at all levels (local, regional, national). Thus, civic virtues, such as tolerance, acceptance, honesty and trust are deeply integrated into the character of civic individuals.

As Putnam later describes it, social capital contributes to trust and confidence (Putnam 2000: 19–26). Antonio Gramsci (1891–1937) focused on civil society from a Marxist theoretical angle. He stressed the potentially oppositional role of civil society as a 'public room', separate from state and market, in which ideological hegemony is contested. According to him, civil society contains a wide range of organizations and ideologies, which both challenge and uphold the existing order. The political and cultural hegemony of the ruling classes and societal consensus is formed within civil society. Gramsci's ideas influenced the resistance to totalitarian regimes in Eastern Europe and Latin America (Lewis 2002). Moreover, Jürgen Habermas (*1929) focused his concept of civil society on its role within the public sphere. The political system needs the articulation of interests in the public space to put different concerns on the political agenda, but this function cannot be left entirely to established institutions, such as political parties. Marginalized groups tend to organize and find a way to articulate their interests. This is necessary because political parties and parliaments need to 'get informed public opinion beyond the established power structures' (Habermas 1992: 374).

Advocacy has several meanings and explanations. Some definitions of advocacy refer to actual policy change; some refer to the activity, while other definitions refer to who does the advocacy and who is meant to receive the advocacy (Pact Tanzania 2005). Advocacy is a strategy, act or process aimed at bringing about change of attitude, policies, traditions, laws and ideologies for a desired positive result (Pact Tanzania 2005). It can also be defined as an effort made towards decision makers on changing a specific policy or law at different levels.

CSOs do policy advocacy for a number of reasons. Tumushabe and Mugyenyi (2002) point out that sometimes, it is better to justify the need for policy advocacy by citing examples of some of the best development plans for grassroots development being undermined by existing policies or lack of appropriate policies. The role of policy advocacy is to set up a counter dialogue or promote policy dialogue to demonstrate to policy makers where policy change is required (Tumushabe and Mugyenyi 2002). Holloway (1998: 15) argues that 'advocacy' means 'organised efforts to effect systematic or incremental change'. This definition could therefore cover the activities of any pressure group within business, government or civil society, which is pushing for change. This might mean pushing for reform within a particular organization or it might mean pushing for the interests of a particular group vis-à-vis others, and it might mean the practice of politics. A number of CSOs are involved in advocacy work and these include representative organizations, public service organizations, employment-related organizations and cause-related organizations.

Civil society advocacy is implemented through a number of strategies (Fox and Helweg 1997), which include transformational, developmental and instrumental strategies. Instrumental advocacy – or the process by which concrete policy outcomes or reforms are achieved – is what is normally associated with advocacy, as are the well-defined steps and set of skills and techniques that make the achievement of these outcomes possible (Fox and Helweg 1997). If 'doing advocacy' or being an effective advocacy organization was as simple, inter alia, as knowing how to mount a campaign, using the media, or 'mapping' power actors and their relationships, there would probably be no policies or reforms left to influence, and we would all be living in some conception of our own ideal world.

Holloway (1998) points out that there are basic strategies that can be used by civil society organizations in executing their advocacy work. These strategies include mass movement and powerful lobby. Mass movement involves a situation where an NGO will try to identify other organizations that are sympathetic to what it is doing, and form coalitions with them (Crisis Group 2005). The members of all these organizations become, in turn, members of a coalition, and will form a mass movement that can be shown to express the concerns of the citizens for or against the cause for which the NGO stands – environment, corruption, human rights, and women to mention but these few. An example might be a coalition of churches, trade unions, chambers of commerce and youth clubs – with the advocacy NGO as a catalyst helping to bring them together and give them direction. The power of the advocacy NGO is thus expressed through the way it has been able to raise people's awareness about an issue. Powerful lobby involves a situation whereby an advocacy NGO will try to identify people who are very well placed in key positions and convince them of the power and right of their arguments. Such few, but key individuals, once convinced of the power of the cause espoused by the advocacy NGO will be able to effect change because of their reputation and their positions. They do not necessarily need a large membership behind them (Holloway 1998).

Civil society advocacy often faces a number of obstacles such as limited technical capacity, poor democratic space among others. Obstacles to effective policy advocacy vary from campaign to campaign. There are key limitations to NGOs and practitioners engaged in policy advocacy. Policy advocacy NGOs such as community-based organizations often complain of lack of democratic space, questions about the legitimacy of NGOs to advocate for the poor, lack of 'relevant' policy advocacy information, limited access to policy makers, lack of appropriate advocacy skills and having a good understanding of the politics of the policy making process (Tumushabe and Mugyenyi 2002).

Environmental migration

The issue of what links exist between environmental change and migration has been attracting increasing attention both in the media and in the scientific community in recent years. There is still a lot of uncertainty about how exactly environmentally-induced migration and its effects should be defined (Dun and Gemenne 2008; German Development Institute 2012; Maystadt and Mueller 2006). There is often confusion in literature on terms such as environmental migration, climate change-induced migration, ecological refugees and environmentally induced migration (Stojanov and Kavanová 2009). The major cause for this confusion is because there is a challenge in separating environmental factors from other drivers of migration (Dun and Gemenne 2008). A number of international research projects, such as those conducted by the International Organization for Migration (IOM) and Centre for Environmental Security, have concluded that the link between environmental change and migration can be summarized as follows:

- Migration is rarely caused by ecological factors alone. In the vast majority of cases, it is the result of a complex interplay between political, social, economic and ecological factors.
- In areas facing creeping or rapidly occurring environmental changes, migration is an adaptation rather than a survival strategy.

- Migration that takes place in the context of environmental change largely occurs within national borders or sub-regions but not between continents (German Development Institute 2012).

To this date, however, there is no universal consensus on what environmental migration is. What remains critical is that a large number of people are affected (Osterwalder 2008). Laczko (2010: 6) defines 'environmental migrants' as 'those persons or groups of persons who, for compelling reasons of sudden or progressive changes in the environment that adversely affect their lives or living conditions, are obliged to leave their habitual homes, or choose to do so, either temporarily or permanently, and who move either within their country or abroad'. Laczko observes that climate change does not necessarily displace people but it creates conditions that make it challenging for people to live where they are.

There are many linkages between conflicts, disasters and human mobility. A study conducted by Kolmannskog (2009) suggests that in countries such as Somalia, floods and droughts create very unfavourable conditions that cause pastoralists to move to regions that receive rains. This is an example of typical environmental migration. Another example is China, where the major causes of environmental disruption or displacement include reservoir development, transport infrastructure investments and urban resettlement (Stojanov and Kavanová 2009).

Public policy and spatial planning

Public policy and spatial planning are closely related. The concept of public policy has two distinct components, which are 'public' and 'policy'. The term policy designates the behaviour of some actor or set of actors, such as an official, a governmental agency, or a legislature, in an area of activity such as public transportation or consumer protection. Public policy also may be viewed as whatever governments choose to do or not to do (Anderson 2003). Such definitions may be adequate for ordinary discourse, but because we set out in this chapter to undertake a systematic analysis of public policy, a more precise definition or concept is needed. Public policies, as the name suggests, are those categories of policies that are formulated by national governments or local public officials (Anderson 2003). Public policies do not just come into being, but are formulated to achieve pre-determined goals and objectives and often are not fulfilled. Phulisani (2009) highlighted that the word 'policy' can be used to cover matters ranging from high order strategy to administrative detail. This indicates that policy is a very complex word to comprehend, as it has no single simplified explanation in literature (Phulisani 2009).

Public policy and spatial planning are closely connected. As explained earlier public policy is formulated by public agencies or bodies. Spatial planning is also a public sector activity, mainly implemented by local governments. Spatial planning is concerned with the problem of coordination or integration of the spatial dimension of sectoral policies through a territorially-based strategy

(Cullingworth and Vincent 2006: 91; UNECE 2008). Spatial planning is more complex than simple land use regulation since it addresses the tensions and contradictions among sectoral policies, for example for conflicts between economic development, environmental and social cohesion policies. The key role of spatial planning is to promote a more rational arrangement of activities and to reconcile competing policy objectives. Though the scope of spatial planning differs from one context to another, there are common characteristics of this activity (Chirisa and Dumba 2012). It can therefore be argued that spatial planning is concerned with the formulation of policies, strategies and instruments to manage land use and physical development of a defined territory.

The practice of spatial planning for urban areas is almost always seen only as a means for creating and justifying policies for the control of land development because decentralization policies and practice are drawing more and more attention to the provision of public services at local government level (Mattingly 2001). It is appropriate at this point to acknowledge that the spatial planning referred to is physical in its nature. Its subjects are land, buildings and physical space. These are subjects it shares with town planning, city planning, town and country planning, and other commonly recognized forms of urban planning.

Results

Baker *et al.* (2014) have discussed at length the role of civil society organization assisting in responding to natural disasters in Zimbabwe, for example during flooding events and famine. The same has also applied to development, and thus, human-made induced environmental displacements (cf. Tibaijuka 2005). This paper adopted document analysis and discourse analysis of cases in environmental migration in interrogating the case of civil society advocacy in urban cases and rural-based cases in Zimbabwe. This chapter will explore different case studies to highlight their common features. The following are the details of cases of environmental migration that are of concern to CSOs in Zimbabwe. The first section deals with urban cases, with a focus on Porta Farm residents, Chirambahuyo of Chitungwiza, and Operation Murambatsvina. Porta Farm is a place where people who were evicted from Harare in 1991 to pave way for the visit by Queen Elizabeth II of England and members of the CHOGM were moved to. The farm is near Norton, which is a satellite town of Harare, the capital city of Zimbabwe. Chirambahuyo was a settlement that emerged in the 1970s close to Chitungwiza, a dormitory town of Harare, some 40 kilometres away from the city centre. Here, the colonial government destroyed the settlement although attempts were made to regularize it through town planning (Patel and Adams 1981). Lastly, Operation Murambatsvina was the Government of Zimbabwe's massive clean-up campaign that saw the razing down of all urban informal settlements in a bid to clean up the urban centres which the government blamed for bringing many 'dirty activities' (Tibaijuka 2005).

After the urban cases, rural-based cases are described, with particular attention given to the Chiadzwa Diamond fields, Tokwe-Mukosi Dam displacements and the Chisumbanje Ethanol Plant.

Urban cases: tracking the voice and concerns of CSOs

The cases of Porta Farm migrants and Operation Murambatsvina are clear cases of people being forced out of a place and the civil society groups advocating for their fair treatment albeit against a 'strong state'. In the case of Operation Murambastvina, a good number of the civil society groups, such as Crisis Coalition and Humana raised their voice against the government's activities (Crisis Group 2005; Westgate 2007). The UN special envoy, Mrs Anna Kajumulo Tibaijuk arrived several days after the Operation had started on a fact-finding mission and to persuade the government to change its approach to urban informality. Her mission was to try and persuade the Government of Zimbabwe to tolerate informal settlements rather than be brutal to its people (Tibaijuka 2005).

Porta Farm migrants in the 1990s

Porta Farm was an informal settlement, which in June 2005 was home to between 6,000 and 10,000 people. It was established by the Zimbabwean government in 1991 following a series of forced evictions in Harare, originally started as part of an exercise to 'clean up' Harare ahead of a Commonwealth Heads of Government Meeting. Those relocated to Porta Farm were informed by Harare City officials that their stay there would be temporary and Harare City Council, with the assistance of central government, would permanently resettle them elsewhere. While some people were resettled, the population of Porta Farm grew over the years as new people – many made homeless because of other forced evictions around Harare – moved to the area.

Although the experiences of the people of Porta Farm are similar in many respects to other communities affected by Operation Murambatsvina, the residents of Porta Farm had faced several previous attempts by local and national authorities to evict them forcibly and have fought to secure their right to housing, including through looking to the courts for protection. In separate rulings on planned evictions at Porta Farm in 1995 and again in 2004, the High Court of Zimbabwe clearly stated that the people of Porta Farm should not be evicted unless and until the authorities ensured the provision of suitable alternative accommodation.

The case of Porta Farm therefore highlights the Government of Zimbabwe's increasing willingness to subvert the authority of the courts. This erosion of the rule of law has seriously undermined the role of the legal system in protecting human rights in Zimbabwe. Victims of violations have been left with little choice but to seek justice at the international level.

Having given the residents of Porta Farm less than 24 hours' notice of the impending forced eviction, heavily armed police in riot gear started to bulldoze the houses early on the morning of 28 June 2005 and continued on 29 June. In intervening days, thousands of people were forced to sleep outside in the rubble in mid-winter. On the 29th, the police also began to remove people forcibly on the back of trucks. During the chaos several deaths occurred, including those of two children. The Porta Farm evictions took place while the UN Special Envoy, Mrs Anna Tibaijuka, was in Zimbabwe. Members of the Special Envoy's team visited Porta Farm. They witnessed demolitions and forced removal of the people in police and government trucks. The subsequent report of the UN Special Envoy describes how the team was 'shocked by the brutality' of what they witnessed (Tibaijuka 2005: 2).

Operation Murambatsvina in 2005

Operation Murambatsvina was launched in May 2005 by the Government of Zimbabwe as a clean-up operation of its cities, known as 'Murambatsvina', a programme to enforce bylaws to stop all forms of 'illegal activities in areas such as vending, illegal structures, and illegal cultivation' (Tibaijuka 2005: 4) among others (cf. Human Rights Watch 2005). Murambatsvina is a Shona name that can be dismantled into two main parts, *Muramba* ('the one who refuses') and *tsvina* ('dirt' or 'filth') (Vambe 2008). One of the justifications for implementing the nationwide operation was to reverse the chaotic urbanization and improper agricultural practices and associated health implications (Tibaijuka 2005). Urbanization results in overcrowding in urban centres which makes it easy for the transmission of communicable diseases, such as cholera, dysentery and other diarrhoeal infections. The government's actions were probably driven by a rationale of dealing with this problem by forcing people out of the cities and towns, thus in keeping with the precautionary principle in spatial planning. This indicates that Operation Murambatsvina was a real environmental issue to some extent. Executed with the combined force of the police, the army and youth militias, it started in Harare and quickly spread to practically all urban centres, including Bulawayo, Mutare, Gweru, Marondera, Kwekwe, Kadoma and Chinhoyi. While originally targeting vendors in Harare's central districts, it soon included demolition of illegal structures of informal traders, shanty homes of the poor and unauthorized residential extensions of more well-to-do residents of low density suburbs (Crisis Group 2005). According to United Nations estimates, about 700,000 people were affected by Operation Murambatsvina (Crisis Group 2005).

Operation Murambatsvina did not occur in a policy vacuum and was seen, in many ways, as a genuine attempt to cope with rapid urbanization and urban governance (Tibaijuka 2005). The campaign was because of a chain of events. The events can be traced back to 1994 when Statutory Instrument 216 was published. Statutory Instrument 216 of the *Regional Town and Country Planning Act* effectively allowed for the development of non-residential activities in residential areas and sent a clear signal to local authorities of the government's desire to promote the informal economy in residential areas (Tibaijuka 2005). There was an increase in flea markets, vending stalls and home-based service industries. The cities and towns throughout Zimbabwe witnessed an unprecedented growth in the volume of street hawkers and makeshift stands, many of which were supplying the same range of goods sold by stores in front of which they plied their business, clearly violating the rights of the formal sector, which continued to pay taxes (Tibaijuka 2005).

Between 2 June and 20 July 2006, five civil society organizations in Botswana formed the Botswana Civil Society Solidarity Coalition for Zimbabwe and organized a schedule of events as a first anniversary commemorative campaign to increase understanding in Botswana about Operation Murambatsvina. Arbitrary evictions are being documented and monitored worldwide by UNHABITAT and its partners. Nevertheless, such evictions are under way in several African countries. In Zimbabwe, Operation Murambatsvina rendered people homeless and economically destitute on an unprecedented scale. Tibaijuka (2005: 27) argues:

> Most of the victims were already among the most economically disadvantaged groups in society, and they have now been pushed deeper into poverty and have become even more vulnerable. The scale of suffering is immense, particularly among widows, single mothers, children and orphans, the elderly and disabled persons. In addition to the already significant pre-existing humanitarian needs, additional needs have been generated on a large scale, particularly in the shelter, water, sanitation and health sectors.

The operation attracted the attention of CSOs, such as the Zimbabwe Lawyers for Human Rights (ZLHR) and the Centre on Housing Rights and Evictions (COHRE).

A report prepared by Westgate in 2007, on behalf of the COHRE and ZLHR, indicates that the evictions in Zimbabwe may constitute a crime against humanity since the Statute of the International Criminal Court clearly prohibits the deportation and forcible transfer of population under certain conditions that appear to be present in the Zimbabwean operation. According to the Rome Statute, deportation or forcible transfer of population is the forced displacement of person from the area in which they are lawfully present, without any grounds permitted under international law, and in the context of a widespread and systematic attack against civilians. The ZLHR notes that forcefully evicted people were 'left in the open' after the eviction. This is because the Operation provided no alternative accommodation for the people. The unplanned and over-zealous manner in which the Operation was carried out has unleashed chaos and human suffering. It has created a state of emergency as tens of thousands of families and vulnerable women and children are left in the open without protection from the elements, without access to adequate water and sanitation or healthcare, and without food security. Such conditions are clearly life-threatening. In human settlements terms, the Operation has rendered over half a million people, previously housed in so-called substandard dwellings, either homeless or living with friends and relatives in overcrowded and health-threatening conditions. In economic terms, the Operation has destroyed and seriously disrupted the livelihoods of millions of people (Westgate 2007).

Rural-based cases: tracking the voice and concerns of CSOs

Relocation of rural communities due to development-induced displacements owing to, but not limited to the extraction of natural resources, is not a novel development in Zimbabwean history. However, it should be noted that in most cases, the relocation of communities has taken place because of what has come to be termed as 'development-induced displacements'. Development-induced displacement is linked to environmental migration because people in a given location are forced to move out of the place and location which they are now used to in order to pave the way for the proposed development (Terminski 2013). Examples of such developmental projects that have displaced and resettled many communities in Zimbabwe include, but are not limited to, the construction of the Kariba Dam and the Osborne Dam in Mutare. Of the recorded cases of displacements that had occurred in Zimbabwe, the highest case is that of the 86,000 Tonga people who were displaced from the Zambezi Valley to pave the way for the construction of the Kariba Dam. In itself development-induced relocation in Zimbabwe clearly reflects the interaction between law, policy and politics (Mwonzora 2011).

Murowa and Marange diamonds

Terminski (2013) has highlighted mining-induced displacement and resettlement as a highly diverse global socioeconomic issue occurring in all regions of the world, as a human rights issue, and as a source of challenges to public international law and institutions providing humanitarian assistance. It has become well known that the largest portion of the displacement is caused by open-pit mining with diamonds being one of the minerals. This has been evident in Zimbabwe with the large-scale diamond mining project, Murowa and Marange (Chiadzwa). The Marange diamond area dates back to the early 1990s when De Beers secured an Exclusive Prospecting Order for parts of Marange but did not certify the area suitable for mining activities (CNRG 2012). Mining in the Marange area then started to be considered seriously from March 2006 when African Consolidated Resources filed claims, going through periods of illegal mining prior to the intervention of the state.

The Government of Zimbabwe then entered into mining partnerships with private investors following the formalizations of mining operations at Marange diamond fields in 2009. The government announced in early 2009 that plans were in motion to relocate about 4,321 Marange families who were to be affected by the diamond mining to a farm owned by the Agricultural and Rural Development Authority at Transau in Odzi, 24 kilometres west of the city of Mutare (CNRG 2012). The poor villagers have been exposed to perennial poverty, coupled with disrupted income generation from their farming and forestry projects (cf. CNRG 2012).

On another angle, the discovery of diamonds in Chiadzwa led to the internal and international scramble to either mine, buy or sell the Marange diamonds by both state and non-state actors. People from Chiadzwa, and other surrounding areas, rushed to the mining fields in 2006 to pan for diamonds after having heard 'rumours that diamonds had been discovered in their area' (Human Rights Watch 2009: 14). In the same vein, Kabemba (2010: 4) argues 'the Chiadzwa diamond rush should be understood in the broader context of the governance problems afflicting Zimbabwe'.

The mining of diamonds in the Chiadzwa area and the displacement of local communities has attracted the concerns of CSOs, especially those working on issues of human rights, such as the Human Rights Watch (Mwonzora 2011). Some of the human rights organizations working on the Marange diamond issues have used a combination of legal literacy training, legal representation, research, documentation, grassroots mobilizations and lobby and advocacy campaigns in intervening for the Chiadzwa community (Mwonzora 2011). This case is a reflection of civil society advocacy in environmental migration. CSOs take a leading role in representing communities experiencing environmentally-induced migration. A proposal for development in an area where a community is already settled will eventually lead to the displacement of the community of which relocation and compensation plans must be in place if the communities are not going to suffer (Human Rights Watch 2009). While all development obviously occurs within an environment, it is pre-historic environmental factors that influenced the formation of valuable assets, such as good farming soils or mineral streams. When the discovery of a mineral occurs, the development becomes the 'cog' that drives people off their lands, being the 'environmental' aspect of the migration. In the case at hand, the CSOs in the Chiadzwa community were trying to defend the human rights of the environmental migrants. The forced movement of the community violates human rights, such as their entitlement to land and livelihoods in their environment, which the various CSOs aimed to defend and protect. The civil society groups in Manicaland, such as Mutare Monday by Centre for Research and Development, Zimbabwe Natural Resources Dialogue Forum and Marange Development Trust have expressed serious concerns about the mining operations in Chiadzwa. The civil society groups are much more worried with environmental degradation and rampant human rights violations that have seen the displacements of local communities and disruption of livelihoods with alternatives.

Tokwe-Mukosi Dam

The rivers Tokwe and Mukosi have also enhanced environmental migration through the construction of Tokwe-Mukosi Dam. The colonial government originally conceived the idea of building a dam in the good catchment area offered by the intersection of these two rivers. Plans for construction started in 1998 but they stopped temporarily due to financial constraints, but commenced again early in 2014 (Mutangi and Mutari 2014). The motive behind this project is to generate electricity for Masvingo province as well as water for irrigation to south-eastern lowveld estates, including Triangle, Hippo valley, Mweneze and Mkwasine (Mutangi and Mutari 2014). The dam is located 80 kilometres south of Masvingo town.

However, there have been calls by developmental practitioners, including civil society organizations to undertake an Environmental Impact Assessment (EIA) before the project is implemented. The government is regulating the assessment through its Environmental Management Agency created under the Environmental Management Act (Chapter 20: 27) of 2002 (Government of Zimbabwe 2002). EIAs are critical in informing the likely impacts development projects like dam construction will have on the environment and the communities. A study by Mutangi and Mutari (2014) clearly shows some of the effects induced by development projects in a given place or site. The purpose of the study was to examine the socio-cultural implications of forced migration and the changes in livelihood strategies because of the relocation of the surrounding community. Evidence from the research indicates that forced migration would cause a profound unravelling of existing patterns of social disintegration. When people are forcibly moved, production systems are dismantled, long-established residential communities and settlements are disorganized, while kinship groups and family systems are often scattered. The moved individuals said that forced relocation breaks down their family relations and disadvantages other vulnerable members of their families such as orphans and elders. Kinship ties held by people living around Tokwe-Mukosi Dam were often disturbed through forced relocation (Mutangi and Mutari 2014). They noted that because of the relocation some social connections were lost because they were relocated to different areas from some of their relatives and friends. It is also evidenced that life-sustaining social networks that provide mutual support are rendered non-functional because of forced migration. Formal and informal associations and self-organized services are wiped out by the sudden scattering of their membership. The respondents noted that they used to have their community gardens (mishandirapamwe) as well as some credit clubs (mikando) which they had established because of mutual trust that had developed because of living together for a long time in the community. This entails that forced displacement destroys local people's social networks, which usually act as social safety nets in providing social security to local people in times of uncertainties such as drought, hunger and death. These social networks range from extended family members, church members, friends and village neighbours and their significance was undermined due to the displacement of some members. It has also been observed that the relocation programme at Tokwe-Mukosi was done randomly, that is people were not moved as collectives, which acted as safety nets to various members and resulted in extended family breakdowns (Mutangi and Mutari 2014). Therefore, forced migration can tear apart the existing social fabric, leading to socio-cultural disarticulation.

In the case of Tokwe-Mukosi displacements, CSOs intervened in a number of ways. The Zimbabwe Red Cross Society has been closely monitoring the unfolding humanitarian situation since the first alert by the provincial office (29 January

2014) and the team for community disaster response in the affected areas (IFRC 2014). Local and international organizations, community-based organizations, NGOs and the UN have indicated the need to carry out assessments and start appealing for support. The civil protection department is playing a key role in coordinating the response actions. The Ministry of Local Government has been making daily press briefings of the situation to keep the local and international community updated. This initiative by the Ministry is attuned to ensuring that the communities are safe and well catered for.

Chisumbanje Ethanol Plant

The Chisumbanje Ethanol Plant project consists of sugarcane plantations in Chisumbanje and Middle Sabi, with the ethanol plant being located in Chisumbanje. The relevant area stands on 50,000 hectares of land (10,000 hectares in Middle Sabi and 40,000 in Chisumbanje and Chinyamukwakwa). Migration in the Chisumbanje ethanol project affected people from both Chisumbanje and Chinyamukwakwa communities. A company called Green Fuel started the ethanol project. It has become a contested issue, creating a 'saga' as the incompatible goals at play between the local communities affected the company, the government and local politicians. The case of Green Fuels has raged on since 2008. The villagers involved have a number of grievances against the company, which, among others, include unpaid compensation, the manner in which they were disposed of their ancestral lands, toxicity of waste discharged into the environment and the risk of food insecurity in the area (Crisis in Zimbabwe Coalition 2014). By the end of 2012, four years into the project, out of the total 1,754 households displaced from their communal lands in Chisumbanje (1,060) and Chinyamukwakwa (694) communal lands, only 516 had been resettled with 1,238 households yet to be relocated (Mutambara 2012).

A study conducted by Konyani (2014) unearthed that the civil society in Chisumbanje is not against the development of the ethanol plant. The concern of the community and traditional leadership is on the massive displacements that were perpetrated through the implementation of this ethanol project. Their agricultural fields were taken over by the investment. Such a project resulted in human rights violations involving forced evictions, displacement and even loss of life when social unrest and conflict over natural resources control and expropriation erupt. In Chisumbanje, there are often conflicts between corporations, indigenous peoples and the state over development projects, which are initiated without proper consultation or the consent of the very people who are dispossessed of their habitats. The dispossession also implies loss of livelihoods.

Discussion and practical implications

Critical to note, however, is that the urban environmental migration narratives in Zimbabwe have had an element of promoting the health and amenity of the people and environment, respectively; they are indeed stories embedded in syntax between prevention of possible health risks and disasters and the fears of political turmoil among the restive populations. Besides, Zimbabwe has always tried to avoid accommodating 'urban messes' as observable in a number of other African states after gaining independence (beginning from the late 1950s). Urban areas in most sub-Saharan countries, such as Zimbabwe are characterized by high levels of informality. From the perspective of government, and in particular, the Government of Zimbabwe, this makes the settlements 'messy' and less aesthetic. Despite Zimbabwe launching Operation Murambatsvina to try and deal with this problem, the issue continues. This implies that dealing with informality in a ruthless manner, as the Government of Zimbabwe did, does not always work. This shortcoming is partly explained by the lack of capacity to tackle employment and urban poverty, including housing and poverty, which often sees the poor urban households producing slums.

The debates on environmental migration in Zimbabwe have not been adequately handled, at least from a scholarly perspective. There is very limited research on these issues in Zimbabwe. However, given the multi-dimensional nature of the concept of environmental migration, there is evidence in Zimbabwe that some populations are exposed to environmentally-induced migration. The urban cases of environmental migration in Zimbabwe exemplify typical forced migration, where civil society organizations sometimes intervene to protect and defend human rights. From the rural side, the major triggers of environmental migration have been mineral exploitation (for example, Murowa and Marange diamonds), large dam constructions (for example, Tokwe-Mukosi Dam) and, of late, plantation farming (for example, the case of Chisumbanje Ethanol Plant). While the state's argument has focused on equity, investment and employment creation towards furthering the national interests, the argument by the civil society has been atomistic, looking for the adequate security and protection of households and communities affected. In certain instances, the CSOs have played a 'midwifery' role in trying to ensure that the sentiments, physiological needs and esteem of the affected people are met. This has happened, sometimes in direct conflict and interest of the state, which has subsequently often felt exposed or betrayed.

Public policy and spatial planning have a role to play in the debate on environmental migration. This is the role of the state in safeguarding environmental health through regulations, policies and spatial planning. It is this planning and policy that CSOs sometimes stand against, highlighting human rights abuses and failure by the state to take note of the plight of the environmentally-displaced population. CSO advocacy is critical in championing policy change, though sometimes it is a challenging task. From the cases reviewed, several common features emerge. CSOs' voices in all the cases were usually raised to protect the rights of the environmental migrants, whether they were displaced by natural disasters, such as flooding (for example in Muzarabani Area), or disease outbreaks, such as cholera, typhoid and dysentery cases in peri-urban Harare, evictions or mining activities among other scenarios. Diseases mentioned tend to be a perennial tropical problem. The tropics are characterized by hotter climates, and rising temperatures often lead to an increase in diseases. The CSOs have called on the government and other stakeholders to take action for the protection of human rights in line with international protocols, such as the International Convention on the Elimination of All Forms of Racial Discrimination, the International Covenant on Civil and Political Rights, the International Covenant on Economic, Social and Cultural Rights and the Convention on the Elimination of All Forms of Discrimination against Women.

Conclusion

The chapter concludes that environmental migrations in Zimbabwe have taken different shapes, forms and consequences. It has demonstrated that the concept of environmental migration is multi-dimensional. The idea is that environmental change creates unfavourable conditions that make it difficult for people to remain living in their traditional localities. The study recommends the state and CSOs should take a systematic and holistic approach to issues in which negotiation and trust building are the cornerstone of the debate. Public policy and spatial planning can be used to an advantage instead of being misused, as seems to be the case in Zimbabwe. Spatial planning should ensure that before people are displaced, compensation and relocation plans are in place. Physical planning is an aspect of spatial planning and it involves the designs of shelters that suit the needs and requirements of the local communities. Local displacement can cause abuse and human rights violation when local communities disadvantaged because of the private and commercial interests not best representing 'public interest'. Overall, and normally, development should benefit local communities. The central government, through the relevant ministries, should also provide financial and technical support to enable indigenous people to consult with corporations bringing development projects into their area. When indigenous peoples consent to such projects, they should have a right to a fair share of benefits from activities on their lands. Where projects proceed without consent, mechanisms for restoration of lost advantages should be provided and these should be fair and meaningful in order to sustain the lives of the affected persons. National and international institutions financing development projects must ensure that their operational policies and guidelines are consistent with indigenous and international human rights standards and principles.

References

Anderson, J.E. (2003) *Public policymaking: an introduction.* Boston: Houghton Mifflin.

Baker, J., Guevara, M., Peratsakis, C. and Pournik, M. (2014) Diversity of national response: Zimbabwe and Zambia. In *Institutional capacity for natural disasters: case studies in Africa, climate change and African political stability* (CCAPS), ed. J. Bussell. Austin: University of Texas.

Baxter, P. and Jack, S. (2008) Qualitative case study methodology: study design and implementation for novice researchers. *The Qualitative Report.* 13: 544–59.

Centre for Natural Resource Governance (CNRG) (2012) *Marange relocations lead to new poverty* [online]. Available: www.swradioafrica.com/Documents/Marange%20relocations%20lead%20to%20new%20poverty.pdf [12 March 2015].

Chirisa, I. and Dumba, S. (2012) Spatial planning, legislation and the historical and contemporary challenges in Zimbabwe: a conjectural approach. *Journal of African Studies and Development.* 4(1): 1–13.

Crisis Group (2005) Zimbabwe's Operation Murambatsvina: the tipping point? *Africa Report* [online]. (97). Available: www.crisisgroup.org/~/media/Files/africa/southern-africa/zimbabwe/Zimbabwes%20Operation%20Murambatsvina%20The%20Tipping%20Point.pdf [Accessed 16 October 2014].

Crisis in Zimbabwe Coalition (2014) *No green light for green fuels as villagers protest* [online]. Available: www.crisiszimbabwe.org/advocacy/local-advocacy/item/1141-no-green-light-for-green-fuels-as-villagers-protest.html [3 April 2015].

Cullingworth, J.B. and Vincent, B. (2006) *Town and country planning in the UK.* London: Routledge.

Dun, O. and Gemenne, F. (2008) *Defining environmental migration.* Bonn: United Nations University Center for Human Security.

Fox, L.M. and Helweg, P. (1997) *Advocacy strategies for civil society: a conceptual framework and practitioners guide* [online]. Available: http://pdf.usaid.gov/pdf_docs/pnacn907.pdf [Accessed 25 February 2015].

German Development Institute (2012) *Environmental change and migration: perspectives for future action* [online]. Briefing Paper 15. Available: www.die-gdi.de/uploads/media/BP_15.2012.pdf [Accessed 25 February 2015].

Government of Zimbabwe (2002) *Environmental Management Act.* Harare: Government Printers.

Habermas, J. (1992) Zur Rolle von Zivilgesellschaft und politischer Öffentlichkeit. In *Faktizität und Geltung*, ed. J. Habermas. Frankfurt am Main: Suhrkamp.

Holloway, R. (1998) *Supporting citizens' initiatives: Bangladesh's NGO and society.* Dhaka: University Press Ltd.

Human Rights Watch (2005) Zimbabwe: evicted and forsaken – internally displaced persons in the aftermath of Operation Murambatsvina. *Human Rights Watch.* 17(16).

Human Rights Watch (2009) *Diamonds in the rough: human rights abuses in the Marange diamond fields of Zimbabwe* [online]. Available: www.observatori.org/paises/pais_82/documentos/zimbabwe0609web.pdf [Accessed 29 September 2014].

International Federation of Red Cross and Red Crescent Societies (IFRC) (2014) *World disasters report 2014: focus on culture and risk* [online]. Available: www.ifrc.org/world-disasters-report-2014 [Accessed 3 April 2015].

Kabemba, C. (2010) The Kimberley process and the Chiadzwa diamonds in Zimbabwe: challenges and effectiveness. *Perspectives.* 3(10): 4–11.

Kolmannskog, V. (2009) New issues in refugee research: climate change, disaster, displacement and migration. Initial evidence from Africa. *Research Africa.* (180). Geneva: United Nations High Commissioner for Refugees.

Konyani, E.G. (2014) Why development-induced displacement is morally objectionable: an ethical appraisal of the Chisumbanje ethanol project in Chipinge, South eastern Zimbabwe. *Afro Asian Journal of Social Sciences.* 5(1): 1–11.

Laczko, F. (2010) *Migration, environment and climate change: assessing the evidence.* Geneva: International Organisation for Migration.

Lewis, D. (2002) Civil society in African contexts: reflections on the usefulness of a concept. *Development and Change.* 33(4): 569–86.

Mattingly, M. (2001) *Spatial planning for urban infrastructure investment: a guide to training and practice.* London: University College London.

Maystadt, J.F. and Mueller, V. (2006) *Environmental migrants: a myth?* Washington, D.C.: International Food Policy Research Centre.

Merkel, W. and Lauth, H. (1998) Systemwechsel und Zivilgesellschaft: Welche Zivilgesellschaft braucht die Demokratie? *Aus Politik und Zeitgeschichte.* 6(7): 3–12.

Mutambara, A. (2012) *Chisumbanje ethanol project back on track* [online]. Available: www.herald.co.zw/chisumbanje-ethanol-project-back-on-track/ [Accessed 12 March 2015].

Mutangi, G.T. and Mutari, W. (2014) Socio-cultural implications and livelihoods displacement of the moved communities as a result of the construction of the Tokwe-Mukosi Dam, Masvingo. *Greener Journal of Social Sciences.* 4(2): 17–77.

Mwonzora, G. (2011) *Diamond rush and the relocation of the Chiadzwa community: a human rights perspective.* A research paper submitted for masters of arts in development studies. The Hague: International Institute of Social Studies.

Osterwalder, K. (2008) *Migration and desertification* [online]. Available: www.unccd.int/Lists/SiteDocumentLibrary/Publications/Desertificationandmigration.pdf   [Accessed 26 February 2015].

Pact Tanzania (2005) *Civil society and advocacy* [online]. Advocacy Expert Series. Available: www.impactalliance.org/file_download.php?location=S_U&filename=119 28203201Civil_Society_and_Advocacy_(Tz_2005).pdf [Accessed 26 February 2015].

Patel, D.H. and Adams, R.J. (1981) *Chirambahuyo: a case study in low-income housing.* Gweru: Mambo Press.

Phulisani, R.S. (2009) *Approaches to policy development: a rapid scan of the literature* [online]. Available: http//www.phulisani.com [Accessed 4 October 2014].

Pietrzyk, D.I. (2003) Democracy or civil society? *Politics.* 23(1): 38–45.

Putnam, R.D. (2000) *Democracies in flux: the evolution of social capital in contemporary society.* Oxford: Oxford University Press.

Schade, J. (2002) Zivilgesellschaft: Eine vielschichtige Debatte. *INEF Report.* (59). Duisburg: Institut für Entwicklung und Frieden.

Stojanov, R. and Kavanová, K. (2009) El concepto de migrantes medio ambientales (comentariosintroductorios). *Estudios Migratorios Latino americanos.* 23(68): 39–54.

Terminski, B. (2013) *Development-induced displacement and resettlement: theoretical frameworks and current challenges* [online]. Available: https://dlc.dlib.indiana.edu/dlc/bitstream/handle/10535/8833/Bogumil%20Terminski,%20development-Induced%20 Displacement%20and%20Resettlement.%20Theoretical%20frameworks%20and%20 current%20challenges.pdf?sequence=1 [Accessed 4 October 2014].

Tibaijuka, A.K. (2005) *Report of the Fact-Finding Mission to Zimbabwe to Assess the Scope and Impact of Operation Murambatsvina by the UN Special Envoy on Human Settlements Issues in Zimbabwe* [online]. Available: http://ww2.unhabitat.org/documents/ZimbabweReport.pdf [Accessed 12 March 2015].

Tocqueville, A. (1835/1840) *De la Democratie en Amérique.* Chicago: University of Chicago Press.

Tumushabe, G. and Mugyenyi, O. (2002) *Amplifying the role of civil society in the implementation of the plan for modernization of agriculture.* Building Civil Society Policy Advocacy Capacity. PMA Project Briefing Paper. (1).

United Nations Economic Commission for Europe (UNECE) (2008) *Spatial planning: key instrument for development and effective governance.* Geneva: United Nations Economic Commission for Europe.

Vambe, B. (2008) *The hidden dimensions of operation Murambatsvina in Zimbabwe*. Harare: Weaver Press.

Westgate, M. (2007) *Operation Murambatsvina: a crime against humanity. An independent legal opinion whether the 2005 Operation Murambatsvina forced evictions constituted a crime against humanity under the Rome Statute*. Geneva: Centre on Housing Rights and Evictions (COHRE) and Harare: Zimbabwe Lawyers on Human Rights (ZLHR).

14 Towards an 'environmental migration management' discourse

A discursive turn in environmental migration advocacy?

Sarah Nash

Introduction

Dominant discourses concerning environmental migration have in the past been characterized by securitization and apocalyptic tones, portraying migrants as international security concerns. Migration has been treated as inherently problematic and migrants have been afforded little agency. A great deal of attention has been paid to whether environmental drivers of migration can be separated from other factors leading to migration, and to estimating numbers of potential 'environmental migrants' (Myers 1993, 1997, 2002; Suhrke 1994).

The securitized discourse surrounding climate change and migration, within which those migrating were mostly labelled 'environmental refugees' or 'climate refugees', rose to prominence in the context of a general scepticism surrounding migration but also in the context of popular environmentalism (Morrisey 2012). This securitized discourse has been produced by a variety of actors, from academics (Homer-Dixon 1999), to defence departments (US Department of Defense 2010), to think tanks with close links to policymakers (Center for American Progress 2007, 2009), to the UN Security Council (UNSC 2007) and non-governmental organizations (NGOs) (Christian Aid 2007). This particular problematization of climate change and migration was designed, at least in part, to shock the international community into taking action to counteract climate change.

However, it can be argued that this discourse has done exactly the opposite. In addition to opening up the possibility of militarization of the policy area, the legitimization of forced movements of people has also been identified as a risk (Martin 2010). Further to these concerns, the securitized discourse has been perceived as playing into 'other long-standing anti-immigrant narratives that connect migrants with crime, violence and disease' (Morrissey 2012: 42). Finally, the securitized discourse potentially may have had negative effects, rather than the positive effects envisaged by campaigners, on spurring action on climate change. Such a discourse may actually 'forestall solving problems' (Jakobeit and Methmann 2012: 301) and 'post a threat to the kind of peaceful international cooperation and development initiatives needed to respond equitably and effectively to climate change' (Hartmann 2010: 234).

In part as a reaction to these issues, a marked softening of tones has taken place, with migration no longer being conceptualized as inherently problematic. In fact, migration is increasingly being seen as a potential adaptation strategy to the negative effects of climate change, which can and should be optimized by being properly managed. This chapter will analyse this discourse, which is here labelled the 'environmental migration management discourse', in depth. Two central questions emerge:

1   Does the rise of the environmental migration management discourse represent a discursive turn in discussions related to climate change and migration?
2   What options for political action are included or excluded by this discourse?

In order to begin to answer these questions, an analysis of documents has been carried out. The main document corpus consists of ten briefing papers and reports from international organizations (IOs), specifically the International Organization for Migration (IOM) and the United Nations High Commissioner for Refugees (UNHCR), which is then supplemented by a further six documents from the Nansen Initiative, the World Bank, the UK Climate Change and Migration Coalition and the UK Government Office for Science. The documents were all published between 2011 and 2014. This by no means provides a comprehensive account of the discursive landscape related to environmental migration, but the selection was made in order to provide a snapshot into the environmental migration management discourse in particular. The documents are all designed to contribute to advocacy in the area of climate change and migration, mainly stemming from IOs and NGOs, with high levels of interaction with academia.

This chapter will firstly provide an outline of the central components of the environmental migration management discourse, before secondly turning to the involvement of different actors in this discourse. In the third section, this chapter will broach the question of whether the rise of the environmental migration management discourse represents a discursive turn in discussions related to climate change and migration. Finally, the options for political actions that are included or excluded by the environmental migration management discourse are discussed.

The environmental migration management discourse

In contrast to the securitized discourse surrounding climate change and migration, which has until recently prevailed, the environmental migration management discourse recognizes migration as a normal and potentially positive phenomenon. Indeed, some of the early building blocks of the environmental migration management discourse have been critiques of the academic literature, such as the unreliability of the projections of numbers of people who will be displaced by climate change (Black 2001; Gemenne 2011; Kniveton *et al.* 2008; McLeman 2012) and that these projections are based on the numbers of people living in places of risk, without factoring in the degree of resilience and adaptive measures which may be taken (Black *et al.* 2011; Gemenne 2011; Laczko and Aghazarm 2009). This has signalled a move within academia away from the use of projections for numbers of displaced persons, towards a more nuanced discussion and more empirical studies aiming to gain a better understanding of migration dynamics (Warner 2014).

This is a move that has also been visible within organizations undertaking advocacy work, many of which share close links with academic institutions, and projections of numbers of displaced persons are relied on less frequently, with the complexity of the area, the interlinkages between different drivers of movement and the difficulty of making projections being highlighted instead (IOM 2014a; Laczko and Aghazarm 2009; Newland 2011). In addition to this shared background with the academic literature, the emerging environmental management discourse shares many aspects of the more general migration management discourse, which has been well documented in the migration literature (Geiger and Pécoud 2010; Ghosh 2012), often being analysed rather critically (Boucher 2009; Scheel and Ratfisch 2014). However, these aspects are specified and added to with relation to environmental migration, creating a new discourse in the area of environment/ climate change and migration.

Central to the environmental migration management discourse is the 'triple-win argument', which is imported from the migration management discourse. According to this argument, 'migration should be turned into a process benefiting all parties (including receiving states, sending countries and migrants themselves)' (Geiger and Pécoud 2010: 9). Debates within this discourse are therefore no longer centred around whether migration should be authorized or prevented, but rather around how migration can be effectively 'managed' in order to optimize impacts.

This argument can clearly be seen emerging from a range of organizations, such as from the IOM, which describes 'managed population movements' as 'a win–win situation for migrants and also for countries of destination and origin' (IOM 2011a: 5). This argument is made in the most contemporary documents from IOM, where it has been stated that 'migration does not have to be a last resort measure but can also be a positive driver for change' (IOM 2014c: 1). This argument also echoes that of the Foresight Report and, according to that report's recommendations, 'international policy should aim to ensure that migration occurs in a way that maximizes benefits to the individual, and both source and destination communities' (Foresight 2011: 8). This exemplifies the triple-win argument that is at the core of the migration management discourse.

The second central storyline to the environmental migration management discourse provides differentiation from the more general migration management discourse. The storyline is that migration can be regarded as an adaptation strategy in itself:

> While migration can be a manifestation of acute vulnerability, it can also represent an adaptation strategy since it can:
> • help reduce risk to lives, livelihoods and ecosystems;

- contribute to income diversification;
- enhance overall capacity of households and communities to cope with the adverse effects of environmental and climate change. (IOM 2011a: 4)

Therefore, migration is not simply vaguely beneficial to a range of actors, but can alleviate specific negative impacts of environmental phenomena such as climate change. Within this understanding, migration is therefore more than simply a coping strategy but rather, in line with the IPCC definition of adaptation, part of 'the process of adjustment to actual or expected climate change and its effects. In human systems, adaptation seeks to moderate or avoid harm or exploit beneficial opportunities (…)' (IPCC 2014: 5).

Smit *et al.* (2001) have differentiated between autonomous and planned adaptation, where autonomous adaptations are 'considered to be those that take place – invariably in reactive response (after initial impacts are manifest) to climatic stimuli – as a matter of course, without the directed intervention of a public agency' (Smit *et al.* 2001: 18.2.3). Planned adaptations, then, involve this public agency and 'can be either reactive or anticipatory' (Smit *et al.* 2001: 18.2.3).

This distinction is interesting in the context of the environmental migration management discourse. Whereas environmental migration that may already be taking place would be classed as autonomous adaptation due to the absence of directed intervention of public agency, the development of the environmental migration management discourse signals a shift towards planned adaptation, particularly if the storylines within this discourse are coupled with complementary actions on the part of public agencies. Indeed, this has been suggested in the literature: 'autonomous adaptation as illustrated through migration cannot be a singular solution. Policymakers should be more proactive and perhaps have a hand in helping movement, particularly for "trapped" populations (…), to avoid maladaptive measures' (Ober 2014).

The way in which migration is said to be able to help achieve adaptation is due to the fact that 'migration helps people manage risks, diversify livelihoods and cope with environmental changes affecting their way of life' (IOM 2011b: 2). These risk management and livelihood diversification strategies are said to decrease vulnerability and increase people's resilience to climate change and environmental shocks. For example, the 2014 IPCC report states with high agreement that 'expanding opportunities for mobility can reduce vulnerability' (IPCC 2014: 20). Recent empirical studies using the proxy of rainfall variability and its impact on livelihoods have also suggested this role for migration in reducing vulnerability in some contexts (Warner 2014).

There are several ways through which this is said to take place, mainly connected to migrants' role in the international labour market. Typically one member or several members of a household will become labour migrants in order to diversify income sources, acting as an insurance strategy against environmental shocks, with remittances being sent back to the household (Foresight 2011: 18).

This is outlined in a policy research working paper that was written for The World Bank, which states that 'many of the benefits of migration for the adaptive capacity of communities of origin arise through remittances' (Barnett and Webber 2010: 22). The volume of remittances today make this a particularly attractive argument, since 'globally, the volume of remittances may be double the volume of Official Development Assistance (ODA)' (Barnett and Webber 2010: 22). In addition to fulfilling basic needs such as food, remittances have been argued as being able to 'sustain access to basic needs in times of livelihood shocks such as drought, finance the acquisition of human, social, physical and natural capital; and increase demand and so stimulate local production' (Barnett and Webber 2010: 22). The most positive perceptions of remittances look to communal efforts: 'Networks of migrants have been known to pool resources and invest in public good facilities such as schools and health clinics' (Barnett and Webber 2010: 22).

Remittances are therefore viewed as giving communities the ability to survive negative environmental effects even when livelihoods are declining. It has also been argued that allowing this kind of managed labour migration will prevent 'a larger migration of whole households or communities in an unplanned and unpredictable way' (Foresight 2011: 16).

The kind of migration that is preferred within the environmental migration management discourse is migration of a temporary and/or circular nature, rather than the traditional paradigm of permanent migration. This fits particularly well within the triple-win argument of the environmental migration management discourse. Temporary migration is seen as being positive for sending communities, as it allows for the transfer of remittances but without having the negative side effect of a permanent 'brain drain'. This type of migration is also perceived as being positive, or at least not negative, for receiving communities as it provides a source of labour without permanent immigrant communities settling in a community. This aspect is particularly important for winning favour in an atmosphere in which immigration is viewed as increasingly unfavourable. Thirdly, migrants themselves are seen as benefiting from this kind of migration as they have the ability to improve the livelihoods of their households without needing to leave permanently.

Despite an outwardly positive view of migration, the environmental migration discourse is seemingly conversely compatible with a sedentary bias, which generally assumes that migration is negative. This is due to the focus on temporary and/or circular migration as positive, with permanent migration still viewed rather negatively.

The analysis above has suggested that within the environmental migration management discourse, there is a significant difference in how migrants are portrayed in comparison to the threat or victim terminology of the securitized discourse: they are 'less of a victim than the climate change refugee, and more of an industrious individual' (Bettini 2013: 3). Migrants are entrepreneurs who access the international labour market in order to provide for their own resilience or, typically, their households, and sometimes also their communities. This is a parallel to the development literature, where we have seen remittance-sending migrants portrayed as 'heroes' of development.

Actors and the environmental migration management discourse

No discourse develops in isolation. This means that it is also relevant to turn to the actors that are creating and sustaining the environmental migration management discourse. Similarly to the constellation of actors utilizing the securitized discourse which has preceded it, these actors do not make up a homogenous group. However, in contrast to the securitized discourse, the environmental migration management discourse is being spearheaded by one particular actor: IOM (cf. Ionesco and Traore in this volume). IOM has explicitly stated the aim of positioning itself 'as a key player on the management of climate induced migration, in particular on policy, capacity building, research and operationalization of migration and climate activities' (IOM 2014d: 1). As part of this aim, IOM is carrying out training to 'build the capacity of policymakers and practitioners, in order to factor migration into environmental and development policies, as well as climate change adaptation strategies, and to take environmental change into account in comprehensive migration management policies at the national level' (IOM 2014b: 1), which widens the audience for their discourse.

As the previous section has shown, all of the main storylines outlined for the environmental migration discourse have been utilized by IOM in various briefing documents and policy papers. The approach fits very closely with the general philosophy of IOM in maximizing the positives of migration and of offering its services in managing this migration (Georgi 2010; IOM 2012b). IOM is also interestingly positioned, due to its quasi-insider status at the UN, despite not actually being a UN agency. In addition, the role of states in the direction taken by IOM should not be underestimated. IOM is constituted of member states, to which IOM is therefore structurally responsible and dependent for funding. Due to this structure, IOM acts in the interests of states. Furthermore, the majority of IOM funding is provided by rich industrialized states, thus entrenching a bias towards the interests of these particular states (Georgi 2010). Therefore, although IOM itself is promoting the environmental migration management discourse and is in turn positioning itself as an actor in its own right as a provider of environmental migration management services, other (state) actors also come into play due to the organization's structure.

Aside from the organization's own statements of intention regarding their deepening involvement in environmental migration management, there are further suggestions that IOM is indeed actively pursuing a role in the management of environmental migration in some official capacity. For example, the Inter-Agency Standing Committee (IASC) for Internally Displaced Persons (IDPs), which is the main mechanism for coordinating humanitarian assistance for IDPs, places IOM in the role of responsibility for camp management in the case of disaster-generated IDPs (IASC 2006). While responsibility for disaster-generated IDPs is not analogous to responsibility for environmental migrants or even environmentally displaced persons, this is a relevant appointment. In addition to reinforcing IOM's role in migration governance (in this case, specifically related to internal displacement), IOM's membership of the IASC ensures that the organization is involved in a highly-officialized forum for collaboration with UN agencies.

While IOM appears to epitomize the environmental migration management discourse, other organizations can be less straightforwardly categorized. It has been argued that despite maintaining its protection focus, UNHCR has begun to align itself within the broader migration management discourse, particularly in noting the complementarity of migration management with the protection focus (Scheel and Ratfisch 2014; cf. Hantscher in this volume). However, in relation to the environment this is less clear. The mandate of the UNHCR is limited by its official statute which states that the organization:

> shall assume the function of providing international protection, under the auspices of the United Nations, to refugees who fall within the scope of the present Statute and of seeking permanent solutions for the problem of refugees by assisting Governments and, subject to the approval of the Governments concerned, private organizations to facilitate the voluntary repatriation of such refugees, or their assimilation within new national communities.
>
> (UNGA 1950: 1.1)

The fact that UNHCR has not fully internalized the environmental migration management discourse may be down to this clear protection mandate. Therefore, it is questionable whether UNHCR will ever be able to fully adopt the environmental migration management discourse without making its own participation in it obsolete.

Rather than carving out environmental migration as a separate area of work, as IOM appears to be doing, UNHCR integrates environmental concerns to the extent that they affect its existing work: 'As a rights-based and protection agency, UNHCR's concern relates to the enjoyment of human rights by people relocated or displaced by the effects of disasters and climate change, either within their own borders or across borders' (UNHCR 2014: 13). Despite exercising caution in relation to the restrictions of their mandate, UNHCR is active in advocacy related to environmental migration. 'More recently, UNHCR has advocated for a more predictable and consistent approach to address the protection needs of people who may be displaced across borders owing to natural disasters, including those associated with the impacts of climate change' (UNHCR 2014: 4).

Although retaining a problematization of migration (primarily due to the focus on forced migration), there are important differences to the securitized discourse outlined in the introduction to this chapter. Firstly, UNHCR rejects the use of the 'climate refugee' terminology which is characteristic of the securitized discourse (UNHCR 2011: 8–9). Secondly, UNHCR emphasizes that 'it is generally difficult to single out climatic and environmental factors as the sole, unilateral driver of population movements' (UNHCR 2014: 13), instead pointing to the multi-causality of movement and therefore the difficulty of establishing a causal relationship between environmental factors and migration. This echoes the scholarly concerns voiced in response to the simplified understanding of migration privileged by the securitized discourse.

Instead, UNHCR emphasizes human security, highlighting that states may experience both climate change and conflict simultaneously, meaning that 'countries already experiencing conflict may be triply hit, rendering both the humanitarian needs and responses in such situations even more complex' (UNHCR 2014: 13). The important link between climate change and conflict for UNHCR appears to be the protection needs of populations, as 'individuals and communities displaced by disasters and climate change and those displaced by conflicts often experience similar trauma and deprivation. They may have protection needs and vulnerabilities comparable to those whose flight is provoked by armed violence or human rights abuses' (UNHCR 2014: 13).

Although the UNHCR discourse is very much protection oriented when it is operating as a sole actor, UNHCR also operates as a part of coalitions of groups working on climate change and migration, where the discourse varies from this pattern. Along with IOM, the United Nations University Institute for Environment and Human Security (UNU-EHS), the United Nations Development Programme (UNDP), the International Labour Organization (ILO), the Norwegian Refugee Council/Internal Displacement Monitoring Centre (NRC/IDMC), Sciences Po – Center for International Studies and Research (CERI) and Refugees International, UNHCR is a member of the Advisory Group on Climate Change and Human Mobility which is composed of members that 'consider that close cooperation in framing and communicating issues surrounding human mobility in response to climate change is the most effective way to inform policy-making' (Advisory Group on Climate Change and Human Mobility 2014: 14). This group is more closely aligned to the environmental migration management discourse, with a focus on 'human mobility both as an adaptation strategy and as a dimension of loss and damage' (Advisory Group on Climate Change and Human Mobility 2014: 14). The Advisory Group has identified the potential for migration to be 'a positive coping and survival strategy', with elements such as 'remittances used to take resilience measures at household level' and 'the global labour market' being identified as elements of such strategies. According to the Advisory Group, 'this would support migration as an informed choice, rather than as a forced decision in the absence of alternative adaptation options that would enhance their resilience' (Advisory Group on Climate Change and Human Mobility 2014: 5).

This position is not necessarily contradictory, with UNHCR itself having previously pointed to the distinct yet complementary nature of protection and migration management approaches more generally (UNHCR 2006). However, the clear line that IOM takes on environment and migration by its promotion of the environmental migration management discourse is missing in UNHCR's approach, which appears more ad hoc.

The Nansen Initiative has also emerged as particularly active in advocacy concerning the environment and migration nexus, with the aim of the Initiative being 'the development of a protection agenda addressing the needs of people displaced across international borders by natural disasters, including the effects of climate change' (Nansen Initiative 2013: 1; cf. Brenn in this volume). The focus is that 'national and international responses to this challenge are presently insufficient for meeting the protection and assistance needs of these affected people' (Nansen Initiative 2013: 1). The focus on protection has strong parallels with that of UNHCR and there are indeed strong links between the two organizations, with UNHCR occupying the position of a Standing Invitee to the steering group of the Nansen Initiative. While also perhaps a question of mandate restriction, the convergence between these two organizations could also suggest the emergence of another alternative discourse specifically related to disasters and cross-border displacement. However, IOM is also a Standing Invitee to the steering group, therefore not ruling out the compatibility of these discourses.

Outside of IOs, the environmental migration management discourse has also become more prevalent among think tanks such as the Migration Policy Institute (Newland 2011) and in some NGO related publications (Ober 2014). With more flexible mandates than organizations such as IOM and in particular UNHCR, think tanks and NGOs have more scope to adopt new discourses, however their impact is also more limited. NGOs working on environment and migration are also far from a homogenous group. While some NGOs have a protection focus and similar discourse to organizations such as UNHCR (see, for example Refugees International), others promote a climate justice approach (MRFCJ n.d.), while some maintain a securitized discourse despite the general movements away from this discourse (EJF 2014).

The many reports, briefings and press releases, which have originated from all of the actors discussed in this section over the last years, make up a large part of this discourse. Many of these documents are written as part of collaborations between several actors as part of organized networks or groups. Examples of this include the (now somewhat defunct) Climate Change, Environment and Migration Alliance (CCEMA), the partnership of UNU-EHS and Care International that produced the prominent 'Where the Rain Falls' report (Warner *et al.* 2012) and the Global Knowledge Partnership on Migration and Development (KNOWMAD) Working Group 11 on Environmental Change and Migration. Many academics also work closely with these organizations, assisting with the development of policy or writing policy reports, sometimes blurring the lines between academics and IOs or NGOs.

Other coalitions or groups are forming around particular international policy processes, in particular the Advisory Group on Climate Change and Human Mobility, which is constituted to inform 'several major interrelated policy processes on climate change, disaster risk reduction (DRR) and sustainable development that are expected to culminate in agreements in 2015', in particular the United Nations Framework Convention on Climate Change (UNFCCC) process, a post-2015 DRR framework, and Sustainable Development Goals

(SDGs). Over the past few years, briefing documents on the topic of migration have been submitted to the UNFCCC (IOM 2012a; UNHCR *et al.* 2012) and side events have also been hosted during the COP meetings (UNFCCC 2014). A prime example of this has been the COP20 of the UNFCCC that took place in December 2014. An organized effort was made in order to increase the visibility of migration as an issue of relevance to the climate change negotiations, with side events being organized by coalitions, and briefing documents being released. This included a series of recommendations from the Advisory Group on Climate Change and Human Mobility for the COP20 (Advisory Group on Climate Change and Human Mobility 2014) and a separate briefing document from IOM, which outlines the various ways in which the issue of migration may be integrated in the UNFCCC, and advocates for this. Another new aspect that emerges within this document is the stated aim of opening 'access for climate funding mechanisms' (IOM 2014d: 1).

A discursive turn in environmental migration advocacy?

This chapter has now outlined the key storylines within the environmental migration management discourse and the way in which migrants are portrayed within it, as well as highlighting some of the main actors that are active in this discourse and in other (potentially complementary) discourses, particularly emanating from organizations working from a protection perspective. The presence of the environmental migration management discourse is not in question here, however whether it constitutes a discursive turn away from the securitized discourse towards a more managerial approach can be discussed.

For the purposes of this chapter, the term 'discursive turn' has been used to describe the tipping point when one discourse obtains dominance over another, becoming the foremost discourse in a given area. Therefore, the question of whether the rise of the environmental migration management discourse represents a discursive turn in discussions related to climate change and migration can also be formulated as follows: Has the environmental migration management discourse become the foremost discourse in discussions related to climate change and migration?

This chapter has already argued that within IOM in particular, the environmental migration management discourse has become embedded and is actively promoted (IOM 2014a). However, this is not the case for all organizations. In particular, UNHCR has taken on this discourse to a lesser extent. Although adopting this discourse in joint documents, it is not present when UNHCR acts alone. Here, the protection mandate of UNHCR comes to the forefront and labour migration is less frequently considered overall. Similar comments can be made regarding the Nansen Initiative, which is steered away from considering labour migration due to its disasters and cross-border displacement focus.

While the detailed mapping of other active discourses in the area of environmental migration is beyond the scope of this chapter, others have undertaken this task of mapping (and sometimes also evaluating) the discursive field. Mayer identifies four different 'framings' of environmental migration: humanitarian assistance; forced migration; environmental sustainability; and international security (Mayer 2014). McAdam also breaks the issue of environmental migration down by issue type, arguing that:

> at the macro level, climate change-related movement can be categorized and responded to in a variety of ways – for instance, as a protection issue, a migration issue, a disaster issue, or a development issue. Each 'lens' contains an implicit set of assumptions that motivates different policy outcomes.
>
> (McAdam 2012: 212)

One of the challenges with these assessments of the discursive landscape is the pace with which it is developing. As different actors respond to ongoing policy processes, more precisely target their advocacy work and develop coalitions with other actors, their discourses are undergoing changes. Keeping up with these changes is a big challenge for academic commentators.

The emerging empirical academic literature, however, seems to have adopted the environmental migration management discourse to a large extent. This is, in part, a reaction to the critiques that work aligned with a securitized discourse attracted. In particular, recent empirical studies that have utilized a livelihoods approach to ascertain more details about the dynamics of migration in the context of climate change have included migration as a potential adaptation strategy (Warner 2014).

Conversely, and partly in reaction to the increasing prominence of the environmental migration management discourse, a corpus of critical academic work is also emerging, which highlights some of the potential pitfalls of the environmental migration management discourse (Bettini 2013; Felli 2012). The environmental migration management discourse transforms migrants into entrepreneurial individuals, to whom responsibility for adaptation is transferred. According to the logic of the environmental migration management discourse this is to be achieved via participation in the labour market. As Felli puts it:

> primitive accumulation, understood as the development of capitalist social relations, is at the very heart of the discourse on climate migration, which seeks to produce individuals who not only should individually 'adapt' to the effects of climate change (instead of contesting these effects by waging collective demands) but also, ultimately, should be integrated within capitalist social relations, albeit in a mostly informal and degraded form of waged labour.
>
> (Felli 2012: 357)

The potential therefore exists for the reinforcement of existing equalities, poverty and exploitation due to reliance on a neoliberal capitalist system of labour for achieving climate change adaptation (of which migration is a strategy).

Methmann and Oels argue that the emerging discourse on climate change and migration 'deprives subjects of their rights', as the 'loss and damage caused by global warming is redefined as an opportunity for affected countries' (Methmann and Oels 2015: 62). They also argue that responsibility is shifted from the North to the South, as 'populations that will potentially be affected by climate change [are made] responsible for securing themselves' (Methmann and Oels 2015: 63). A third critique presented by Methmann and Oels is that 'governing climate-induced migration through resilience presupposes that climate change is an unavoidable reality and fact that needs to be lived with', eliminating 'the political space for addressing the root causes of global warming' (Methmann and Oels 2015: 63). Some of these critiques are leading to calls for the pluralization of the debate on climate change and migration, which can 'help us better appreciate the political, ethical, legal and cultural dimensions of the relation between climate change and migration' (Baldwin 2014: 516).

The ongoing focus on forced migration and protection regimes, particularly by those organizations with strict mandates, suggests that the environmental migration management discourse has not reached complete saturation. Given the mandates of these organizations and the nature of the challenges accompanying forced migration in contrast to labour migration, this is perhaps not surprising. However, there has been a clear and targeted move away from the securitized discourse which previously dominated discussions concerning climate change and migration.

The environmental migration management discourse is gaining ground, and the other discursive elements, in particular calls for 'climate justice' and protection concerns which are present in discussions concerning forced migration and disasters are not as coherently promoted as the environmental migration management discourse. These discourses should be monitored further in order to establish whether the environmental migration management discourse reaches saturation or whether the other more nuanced discourses which are at play gain traction. As the different discursive elements are not necessarily incompatible (and indeed actors which are central to the propagation of the environmental migration management discourse continue to collaborate with those which have a greater focus on protection), it could be that the discursive constellation does not alter significantly, but remains fragmented.

Options for political action

Discourse is 'constitutive both in the sense that it helps to sustain and reproduce the status quo, and in the sense that it contributes to transforming it' (Wodak and Fairclough 1997: 258). Discourse is inherently of a social nature and thus 'an exploration of discourse asks for the social and political effects that result from using a particular vocabulary on the one hand and the productive effects of particular constructions of reality on the agency and identity of individuals and groups' on the other (Holzscheiter 2013: 144). Therefore, this chapter will now consider the (potential) productive effects of the environmental migration management discourse. The question here is: What options for political action are included or excluded by this discourse? This question is important as political decisions taken in this area could directly impact the way that those migrating due to environmental factors are treated and what options are open to them.

The environmental migration management discourse moves the potential options for political action away from a focus on military action and the tightening of borders, which were the feared responses with the securitized discourse (Hartmann 2010; Martin 2010). The environmental migration management discourse instead emphasizes circular and temporary migration, the preferred option for destination states, partially allaying fears that the discourse could feed into anti-migrant sentiments. However, it remains less clear what alternatives for political action become possible when military actions, the tightening of borders and anti-migrant rhetoric are excluded (at least partly) from the range of potential actions.

The type of migration that is being proposed within the environmental migration management discourse is labour migration; therefore actions that involve the international labour market are a potential avenue deserving exploration. There has already been interest in this area from the International Labour Organization (ILO 2013) and from The World Bank (Barnett and Webber 2010). Some of the suggestions that have been made for maximizing the positive impacts of migration include structured visa schemes to allow those affected by climate change to migrate in a managed manner. Current migration schemes have also been targeted as a potential avenue for orderly migration. In particular, the government of Kiribati's 'Migration with Dignity' involves ensuring that citizens are equipped with the skills required to be able to take part in migration schemes as highly-skilled migrants (Office of the President – Republic of Kiribati 2013). This strategy requires little input from other states, whose existing schemes are simply being employed.

Another policy recommendation that is frequently touted within the environmental migration management discourse is the maximization of remittance flows, particularly through the minimizing of costs for transferring funds, allowing migrants to send money with more ease. In addition to being outlined in policy documents directly regarding migration and climate change (IOM 2014a; cf. Bendandi *et al.* in this volume), increasing the efficiency of remittances transfers is highly likely to feature within the SDGs that are to be finalized in 2015 (Open Working Group on the Sustainable Development Goals 2014).

The international policy processes, which are culminating in 2015, will provide opportunities for this political action to take place (cf. Thomann in this volume). Migration in relation to climate change has already featured within the UNFCCC in the Cancún Agreement, where 'climate change induced displacement, migration and planned relocation' entered the text (UNFCCC 2010: 14[f]). In addition, the Zero Draft of the SDGs includes several goals that relate to climate change and migration, although the two are not explicitly connected. While any assessments of post-2015 policy in relation to climate change and migration is purely speculative at this time, it is worthy of further monitoring. Finally, a post-2015 framework for DRR, a successor to the Hyogo Framework for Action on DRR (HFA), should also be adopted in 2015.

Conclusion

This chapter has outlined the central components of the environmental migration management discourse, including the central storylines that identify migration as a potential climate change adaptation strategy. Environmental migration is no longer a phenomenon to be avoided at all costs, but is perceived as normal and potentially positive.

This signifies a distinct move away from the securitized discourse which has previously dominated, and emphasized the potential for conflict and instability that would accompany the 'huge' predicted population movements which would take place. However, it does not mean that there is complete discursive agreement among actors. Within academia, there is an emerging critical discourse in response to the environmental migration management discourse, and among actors having a specific protection mandate, there is still a focus on the protection regimes for forced migrants. In particular in relation to disasters this is still highly visible.

Discourses are productive, and therefore through discourse different alternatives for political action are included or excluded from the range of possibilities. The military responses that were feared would be utilized in response to the securitized discourse are largely excluded as possibilities when the environmental migration management discourse is employed. Instead, there is a distinct possibility that certain policies in the field of labour migration will be developed, which aim to increase the positive impacts of migration, in particular the efficiency of remittances or designing particular skilled migration schemes.

While these measures are refreshing for many as they remove the military aspect of the opportunities for political action, a critical eye should be kept on developments. If the focus remains on remittances and self-help on the part of migrants, who have to take on responsibility for their own adaptation, this could distract attention from other actors, in particular states, and their responsibilities towards adaptation efforts.

References

Advisory Group on Climate Change and Human Mobility (2014) *Human mobility in the context of climate change: recommendations from the Advisory Group on Climate Change and Human Mobility COP20 Lima, Peru* [online]. Available: https://www.iom.int/files/live/sites/iom/files/pbn/docs/Human-Mobility-in-the-context-of-Climate-Change.pdf [Accessed 13 March 2015].

Baldwin, A. (2014) Pluralising climate change and migration: an argument in favour of open futures. *Geography Compass*. 8(8): 516–28.

Barnett, J. and Webber, M. (2010) *Accommodating migration to promote adaptation to climate change*. Background paper to the 2010 World Development Report. Washington D.C.: The World Bank.

Bettini, G. (2013) *Climatised moves: climate-induced migration and the politics of environmental discourse.* Lund: Lund University Faculty of Social Sciences and LUCSUS.

Black, R. (2001) *Environmental refugees: myth or reality? New issues in refugee research.* Geneva: United Nations High Commissioner for Refugees.

Black, R., Bennett, S.R.G., Thomas, S.M. and Beddington, J.R. (2011) Climate change: migration as adaptation. *Nature.* 478: 447–449.

Boucher, G. (2009) A critique of global policy discourses on managing international migration. *Third World Quarterly.* 29(7): 1461–1471.

Center for American Progress (2007) *Climate change, migration and violent conflict: addressing complex crisis scenarios in the 21st century.* Washington D.C.: Center for American Progress and Heinrich Böll Stiftung.

Center for American Progress (2009) *Climate change on the move: climate migration will affect the world's security* [online]. Available: http://americanprogress.org/issues/green/report/2009/12/08/7075/climate-change-on-the-move/ [Accessed 27 February 2015].

Christian Aid (2007) *Human tide: the real migration crisis.* London: Christian Aid.

Environmental Justice Foundation (EJF) (2014) *The gathering storm: climate change, security and conflict.* London: Environmental Justice Foundation.

Felli, R. (2012) 'Managing climate insecurity by ensuring continuous capital accumulation: 'climate refugees' and 'climate migrants'. *New Political Economy.* 18(3): 337–63.

Foresight (2011) *Migration and global environmental change.* Final project report. London: The Government Office for Science.

Geiger, M. and Pécoud, A. (2010) *The politics of international migration management.* Basingstoke: Palgrave Macmillan.

Gemenne, F. (2011) Why the numbers don't add up: a review of estimates and predictions of people displaced by environmental changes. *Global Environmental Change.* 21(1): 41–9.

Georgi, F. (2010) For the benefit of some: the international organization for migration and its global migration management. In *The politics of international migration management,* eds. M. Geiger and A. Pécoud. Basingstoke: Palgrave Macmillan.

Ghosh, B. (2012) A snapshot of reflections on migration management: is migration management a dirty word? In *The new politics of international mobility, migration management and its discontents,* eds. M. Geiger and A. Pécoud. Osnabrück: Institut für Migrationsforschung und Interkulturelle Studien.

Hartmann, B. (2010) Rethinking climate refugees and climate conflict: rhetoric, reality and the politics of policy discourse. *Journal of International Development.* 22(2): 233–46.

Holzscheiter, A. (2013) Between communicative interaction and structures of signification: discourse theory and analysis in international relations. *International Studies Perspectives.* 15(2): 142–62.

Homer-Dixon, T. (1999) *Environment, scarcity and violence.* Princeton: Princeton University Press.

Inter-Agency Standing Committee (IASC) (2006) *IOM and camp co-ordination and camp management (CCCM) cluster – update* [online]. 64th working group meeting, WO/0603/1399/7. Available: http://idp-key-resources.org/documents/2006/d04101/000.pdf [Accessed 27 February 2015].

Intergovernmental Panel on Climate Change (IPCC) (2014) *Climate change 2014: impacts, adaptation, and vulnerability* [online]. IPCC working group II contribution to AR5, summary for policymakers. Available: http://ipcc-wg2.gov/AR5/ [Accessed 27 February 2015].

International Labour Organization (ILO) (2013) *Enhancing the capacity of Pacific island countries to address the impacts of climate change on migration* [online]. Available: www.ilo.org/suva/what-we-do/projects/WCMS_191552/lang--en/index.htm [Accessed 27 February 2015].

International Organization for Migration (IOM) (2011a) *Disaster risk reduction and climate change adaptation in IOM's response to environmental migrants.* Geneva: IOM.

International Organization for Migration (IOM) (2011b) *Climate change and migration: IOM's approach.* Geneva: IOM.

International Organization for Migration (IOM) (2012a) *International Organization for Migration (IOM) submission to the UNFCCC concerning draft decisions 23 and 24 of -/CP17 of the National Adaptation Plans (NAPs)* [online]. Available: http://unfccc.int/resource/docs/2012/smsn/igo/85.pdf [Accessed 27 February 2015].

International Organization for Migration (IOM) (2012b) *The International Organization for Migration in brief: managing migration for the benefit of all.* Geneva: IOM.

International Organization for Migration (IOM) (2014a) *IOM perspectives on migration, environment and climate change.* Geneva: IOM.

International Organization for Migration (IOM) (2014b) *Capacity-building activities on migration, environment and climate change.* Geneva: IOM.

International Organization for Migration (IOM) (2014c) *Programmatic activities on migration, environment and climate change.* Geneva: IOM.

International Organization for Migration (IOM) (2014d) *What is at stake on migration and for IOM at COP20? 20th Conference of the Parties (COP), United Nations Framework Convention on Climate Change (UNFCCC) Lima, Peru, 1–12 Dec 2014.* Geneva: IOM.

Jakobeit, C. and Methmann, C. (2012) 'Climate refugees' as dawning catastrophe? A critique of the dominant quest for numbers. In *Climate change, human security and violent conflict: challenges for societal stability*, eds. J. Scheffran, M. Brzoska, H.G. Brauch, P.M. Link and J. Schilling. New York: Springer.

Kniveton, D., Schmidt-Verkerk, K., Smith, C. and Black, R. (2008) Climate change and migration: improving methodologies to estimate flows. *IOM Migration Research Series.* (33). Geneva: IOM.

Laczko, F. and Aghazarm, C. eds. (2009) *Migration, environment and climate change: assessing the evidence.* Geneva: IOM.

Martin, S. (2010) Climate change, migration, and governance. *Global Governance.* 16(3): 397–414.

Mary Robinson Foundation for Climate Justice (MRFCJ) (n.d.) *Principles of climate justice* [online]. Available: www.mrfcj.org/pdf/Principles-of-Climate-Justice.pdf [Accessed 13 March 2015].

Mayer, B. (2014) 'Environmental migration' as advocacy: is it going to work? *Refuge: Canada's Journal on Refugees.* 29(2): 27–41.

McAdam, J. (2012) *Climate change, forced migration, and international law.* Oxford: Oxford University Press.

McLeman, R. (2012) Developments in modelling of climate change-related migration. *Climatic Change.* 117(3): 599–611.

Methmann, C. and Oels, A. (2015) From 'fearing' to 'empowering' climate refugees: governing climate-induced migration in the name of resilience. *Security Dialogue.* 46(1): 51–68.

Morrissey, J. (2012) Rethinking the 'debate on environmental refugees': from 'maximalists and minimalists' to 'proponents and critics'. *Journal of Political Ecology.* 19. 36–49.

Myers, N. (1993) Environmental refugees in a globally warmed world. *BioScience*. 43(11): 752–61.

Myers, N. (1997) Environmental refugees. *Population and Environment*. 19(2): 167–82.

Myers, N. (2002) Environmental refugees: a growing phenomenon of the 21st century. *Philosophical Transactions of the Royal Society*. 357: 609–13.

Nansen Initiative (2013) *The Nansen Initiative: towards a protection agenda for disaster-induced cross-border displacement*. Information note. Geneva: The Nansen Initiative Secretariat.

Newland, K. (2011) *Climate change and migration dynamics*. Washington D.C.: Migration Policy Institute.

Ober, K. (2014) *Migration as adaptation: exploring mobility as a coping strategy for climate change* [online]. Briefing paper for United Kingdom Climate Change and Migration Coalition. Available: http://climatemigration.org.uk/wp-content/uploads/2014/02/migration_adaptation_climate.pdf [Accessed 27 February 2015].

Office of the President – Republic of Kiribati (2013) *'I-Kiribati want to migrate with dignity'* [online]. Available: www.climate.gov.ki/2013/02/12/i-kiribati-want-to-migrate-with-dignity/ [Accessed 27 February 2015].

Open Working Group on the Sustainable Development Goals (2014) *Introduction and proposed goals and targets on sustainable development for the post 2015 development agenda* [online]. Available: http://sustainabledevelopment.un.org/owg.html [Accessed 27 February 2015].

Scheel, S. and Ratfisch, P. (2014) Refugee protection meets migration management: UNHCR as a global police of populations. *Journal of Ethnic and Migration Studies*. 40(6): 924–41.

Smit, B., Pilifosova, O., Burton, I., Challenger, B., Huq, S., Klein, R.J.T and Yohe, G. (2001) Adaptation to climate change in the context of sustainable development and equity. In *Climate change 2001: impacts, adaptation, and vulnerability. Contribution of working group II to the third assessment report of the Intergovernmental Panel on Climate Change*, eds. A. Patwardhan and J.F. Soussana. Cambridge: Cambridge University Press.

Suhrke, A. (1994) Environmental degradation and population flows. *Journal of International Affairs*. 47(2): 473–96.

United Nations Framework Convention on Climate Change (UNFCCC) (2010) *Report of the conference of the parties on its sixteenth session, held in Cancún from 29 November to 10 December 2010* [online]. FCCC/CP/2010/7/Add.1. Available: http://unfccc.int/resource/docs/2010/cop16/eng/07a01.pdf [Accessed 27 February 2015].

United Nations Framework Convention on Climate Change (UNFCCC) (2014) *Side event summaries: addressing climate change while improving the lives of the urban poor* [online]. Available: http://unfccc.int/meetings/bonn_jun_2014/items/8392.php [Accessed 27 February 2015].

United Nations General Assembly (UNGA) (1950) *General assembly resolution 428 (V) of 14 December 1950: statute of the Office of the United Nations High Commissioner for Refugees* [online]. Available: www.unhcr.org/3b66c39e1.pdf [Available 27 February 2015].

United Nations High Commissioner for Refugees (UNHCR) (2006) *High-level dialogue on international migration and development: UNHCR's observations and recommendations*. Geneva: UNHCR.

United Nations High Commissioner for Refugees (UNHCR) (2011) *Climate change, natural disasters and human displacement: a UNHCR perspective*. Geneva: UNHCR.

United Nations High Commissioner for Refugees (UNHCR) (2014) *UNHCR: the environment & climate change – an overview*. Geneva: UNHCR.

United Nations High Commissioner for Refugees (UNHCR), United Nations University (UNU), Norwegian Refugee Council (NRC), Internal Displacement Monitoring Centre (IDMC), United Nations Special Rapporteur on the Human Rights of Internally Displaced Persons and International Organization for Migration (IOM) (2012) *Human mobility in the context of loss and damage from climate change: needs, gaps, and roles of the convention in addressing loss and damage* [online]. Submission to the SBI Program on Loss and Damage. Available: www.refworld.org/pdfid/5153ffac2.pdf [Accessed 27 February 2015].

United Nations Security Council (UNSC) (2007) *Security Council hold first-ever debate on impact of climate change on peace, security, hearing over 50 speakers* [online]. Security Council 5663rd Meeting. SC/9000. Available: www.un.org/News/Press/docs/2007/sc9000.doc.htm [Accessed 27 February 2015].

US Department of Defense (2010) *Quadrennial defense review report* [online]. Available: www.defense.gov/qdr/images/QDR_as_of_12Feb10_1000.pdf [Accessed 27 February 2015].

Warner, K. ed. (2014) Special issue: connections between (changing) rainfall patterns, food and livelihood security, and human mobility: evidence and a new analytical framework. *Climate and Development*. 6(1).

Warner, K., Afifi, T., Henry, K., Rawe, T., Smith, C. and de Sherbinin, A. (2012) *Where the rain falls: climate change, food and livelihood security, and migration*. Global policy report. Bonn: UNU-EHS.

Wodak, R. and Fairclough, N. (1997) Critical discourse analysis. In *Discourse as Social Interaction*, ed. T.A. van Dijk. London: Sage.

15 International epistemic organizations and their role in shaping the politics of environmental migration

Angela Pilath

Introduction

Over the last decade, environmental migration has evolved into a key issue-area of international environmental governance despite the concept's significant analytical and conceptual challenges. In order to understand this evolution, this chapter introduces and conceptualizes the notion of international epistemic organizations (IEOs) and examines their role in shaping the politics of environmental migration.

IEOs are organizational hybrids and can be understood as the institutionalized form of an epistemic community. They constitute an interface between a research community and an autonomous international organization (IO). In order to account for the recent evolution of environmental migration into an international policy field, it is crucial to examine the role of IEOs. They hold significant explanatory value as to why and how the issue of environmental migration moved up the international political agenda even though the concept's analytical capacity continues to be extremely limited. Examining the role of IEOs in institutionalizing causal claims offers innovative insights into how claims that are essentially contested come to impact international politics and cause normative change in the international system. An analysis of the role of IEOs in the politics of environmental migration thus holds wider analytical relevance for our understanding of how politics in essentially contested issue-areas evolve.

The empirical analysis of this chapter focuses on the United Nations University Institute for Environment and Human Security (UNU-EHS), an international organization that has been vocal in environmental migration politics. UNU-EHS qualifies as an organizational hybrid: by mandate it is both an autonomous research institution and UN organization. On the basis of its distinct organizational characteristics, UNU-EHS has been selected as the conceptual archetype of an IEO for the purpose of this study. UNU-EHS is often mentioned in association with the evolution of catalytic paragraph 14(f) in the Cancún Adaptation Framework (CAF) that marked a milestone in the advancement of environmental migration politics. When 14(f) CAF was adopted in December 2010, it constituted the first legal recognition in an internationally recognized agreement to pertain to the interconnections between environmental change and migration.

Any influence of UNU-EHS on the politics of environmental migration in general, and paragraph 14(f) CAF in particular, seems surprising given the IEO's lack of significant funding, a normative mandate, and the material capacity to influence states. The chapter seeks to shed light on this puzzle by addressing the following research question: *How has UNU-EHS influenced the politics of environmental migration?*

Two mechanisms by which IEOs, such as UNU-EHS, exert influence on the politics of environmental migration are identified: *expert authority* and *loyalty networks*. It is argued that, through the dual exploitation of both mechanisms, UNU-EHS has been able to establish itself as a highly influential actor within the politics of environmental migration despite its lack of material capacity to influence states.

The chapter follows a tripartite structure. Section one offers a conceptualization of IEOs and their potential mechanisms of influence. Section two sketches out the anatomy of UNU-EHS as an IEO. Section three provides the empirical analysis and investigates how UNU-EHS has influenced the evolution of paragraph 14(f) CAF.

Theoretical framework: IEOs and their mechanisms of influence

IEOs: a conceptualization

IEOs occupy a particular political space among IOs in world politics. They are organizational hybrids. On the one hand, they are established as IOs by treaty or other formal political agreement between sovereign states. On the other, contrary to regular intergovernmental organizations, IEOs are not mandated with formal political decision-making power. IEOs are autonomous research institutions that function under the auspices of one or more intergovernmental organizations. They can be understood as the institutionalized form of an epistemic community at the international level. Haas first defined an epistemic community as:

> a network of professionals with recognized expertise and competence in a particular domain and an authoritative claim to policy-relevant knowledge within that domain or issue area.
>
> (1992: 3)

Haas' Epistemic Community Theory offers an ideational dimension to formerly rigidly material conceptions of power in International Relations by introducing epistemic actors as players to the political centre stage. According to Haas, experts may exert political influence on policy outcomes by interpreting and shaping information for policymakers in complex issue-areas (Haas 1992). Building on Epistemic Community Theory, the political influence of IEOs is derived from the logic that knowledge generates power and policy influence based on the assumption that policymakers are information seekers and scientists are information providers. IEOs offer *expert authority* in areas of political uncertainty that opens up room to influence the attitudes, and ultimately behaviour, of policymakers. This offers insights into why, in light of complex issue-areas such as environmental migration,

> hard to grasp decisions may move actual, although not necessarily formal, power from elected representatives (...) to elites acquainted with the subject in a transnational setting.
>
> (Sundström 2000: 1)

IEOs have been widely ignored by the International Relations literature even though they form a structurally distinct category of IOs. The place of IEOs in the scholarly literature is largely limited to the acknowledgement that epistemic communities may reside in domestic organizations and that IOs are the recipient of intellectual innovations, which epistemic communities help produce (Adler 1992: 373). However, the question that has been neglected is how the potential for policy influence is affected when an epistemic community is congruent with the structures of a research institution (e.g. universities, think tanks, etc.) that operates and is recognized as an IO. The argument put forward here is that due to their international mission and mandate and their proximity to and cooperation with other IOs, IEOs are arguably more durable and more influential in international politics than 'regular' epistemic communities.

Due to their institutionalized connections to intergovernmental organizations, IEOs frequently encounter state actors in the international arena. Consequently, one could expect that a higher frequency of interaction between state and IEO actors increases opportunities for IEOs to effectively disseminate their knowledge to policymakers and thereby frame state interests. Regarding the persistence of their influence, the predominant opinion concerning epistemic communities in the political arena is that 'their life is limited to the time and space defined by the problem and its solutions' (Adler 1992: 371). Epistemic communities are issue-specific. Due to their lack of institutional organization and coordination, they usually disintegrate when their focus is no longer of relevance to policymakers. IEOs have the competitive advantage of operating as autonomous organizations. Their mandate and mission are not bound to one single issue-area. As such they have the ability to shift their research focus to other more policy-relevant issue-areas should the need arise. This enables IEOs to maintain their networks with policymakers over time, which could translate into increased policy influence.

Expert authority

In line with Epistemic Community Theory, IEOs derive policy relevance from their *expert authority*. *Expert authority*, however, is no 'manna from heaven' but is distilled from an authoritative claim to scientific knowledge. 'Scientific truths are those that enjoy a consensus within a scientific community' (Litfin 2000: 130). Consensus is usually found when the academic community is in agreement about the causal-positivistic nature of a phenomenon. Problematically, environmental migration remains contested due to a range of conceptual and methodological shortcomings, including issues of quantifiability, predictive value, and generalizability of the environmental change–migration nexus. A consensus of the lowest common denominator recognizing the multi-causal nature of the phenomenon has emerged in recent years (Betts 2010; Castles 2002; McAdam 2012; Zetter 2008, 2009). Unfortunately, reaching the conclusion that all factors are interrelated in a complex system is, of course, true but effectively tautological and thus meaningless. The consensus in place does not help us understand the causal relationship in question and how it can be differentiated from others. Stating that some people will migrate due to environmental pressures while others will not is a meaningless truth that can neither be refuted nor inform policy-making on the issue (Nicholson 2014). Consequently, it would be an overstatement to claim that an authoritative claim to knowledge has yet been able to take form in this area of forced migration research. Therefore, it must be concluded that given that *expert authority* rests on unsettled grounds, it is rather questionable to what extent IEOs may be able to use this mechanism to exert influence in the politics of environmental migration.

Loyalty networks

Due to the methodological and conceptual shortcomings of the environmental migration concept, which might limit the extent to which *expert authority* can yield policy influence, alternative mechanisms of IEO policy influence need to be explored. It is suggested that social network structures, particularly the emergence of *loyalty networks*, establish an important second mechanism of IEO influence. *Loyalty networks* describe structures (social ties) that form when connections between nodes within a network are created, and due to continuous interactions generate relationships of trust, credibility, and loyalty, which help foster IEO relevance and influence in international politics. They open up room for manoeuvre for IEOs to infiltrate the policy process more deeply by ensuring access to the policy debate, empowering the dissemination of knowledge into the policy cycle, and helping to overcome part of the challenges IEO *expert authority* faces in the area of environmental migration.

The logic that *loyalty networks* yield particularly positive effects for IEOs is based on their ability to create social capital. While the concept has been applied to diverse contexts during its evolution in sociological theory, Portes underlines that its most common function is as a source of network-mediated benefits (1998: 12). The argument of this chapter is that IEOs strategically seek to create and exploit *loyalty networks* with policymakers and those agents that can enable their influence on the policy process.

Following a social capital logic, the idea of *loyalty networks* draws on social network analysis as it is applied in the International Relations discourse to examine the influence of networks on world politics. Networks have been identified as prominent actors in international politics by a number of scholars (e.g. Hafner-Burton *et al.* 2009; Kahler 2009; Lake and Wong 2009). 'Defined in simplest form, networks are ubiquitous: any set of interconnected nodes' (Kahler 2009: 5). Nodes are agents such as individuals, groups, organizations, or states. In the past, network research has primarily focused on examining networks' effects on their environments while 'the effect of network structures on actors and outcomes within those networks' has not been a research priority (Hafner-Burton *et al.* 2009: 561). Only recently has International Relations theory accepted networks as 'sets of relations that form structures, which in turn may constrain and enable agents' (Hafner-Burton *et al.* 2009: 561).

It is specifically the effect of network structures upon IEO policy influence that the concept of *loyalty networks* aims to capture. Network theorists posit that network structures and the associations between network nodes have a strong effect on a network's ability to exert influence on a given debate. This concept offers valuable insights as to how and with what effect IEO influence on international politics in general and the politics of environmental migration in particular is established.

UNU-EHS: an IEO anatomy

The first section offered a conceptualization of IEOs and their two dominant mechanisms of policy influence. This second section maps the IEO concept onto the United Nations University Institute for Environment and Human Security. It will outline the structures through which UNU-EHS is able to exert *expert authority* and create *loyalty networks* that allow for its influence on the politics of environmental migration.

UNU-EHS and the United Nations University: authority by association

When trying to understand the nature of the IEO that is UNU-EHS and the role that it plays in the international politics of environmental migration, one is obliged to recognize its deep embeddedness in the United Nations (UN) system. UNU-EHS pertains to the United Nations University (UNU) as one of its independent research institutes and forms an integral part of the UN system. UNU was founded in 1973 as 'an autonomous organ of the General Assembly of the United Nations' designed to take the form of an independent research institution (UNU 1973: art. XI). Established by the General Assembly on the consensual basis of its member states, UNU enjoys the same rights and privileges as any other UN organization that falls under articles 104 and 105 of the UN Charter (UN 1945). UNU and its institutes form particular kinds of IOs, which are not intergovernmental but epistemic in nature and were designed to function as the 'academic arm of the United Nations' (UNU 1973: art. I, para. 1). It is the institutionalization of a research institute into a UN organization, with a distinct mission and mandate that gives UNU-EHS its particular IEO character.

When UNU-EHS took up its work in 2003, its mission was to '[spearhead] UNU's research and capacity development activities in the broad interdisciplinary field of risk and vulnerability' specifically with regards to the environment

(UNU-EHS 2015). In this context, one key thematic area of UNU-EHS's research concerns internal displacement and transboundary migration due to environmental push factors. Like all UNU institutes, UNU-EHS is mandated to develop policy-relevant research that aims to support policy- and decision-makers within the UN system.

Located in Bonn, UNU-EHS consists of four academic sections. The Environmental Migration, Social Vulnerability and Adaptation Section (EMSVA) led by Dr Koko Warner, is of particular interest to this study as it undertakes empirical research with a specific focus on environmentally induced migration and social vulnerability. Though the other three sections remain of significant importance, it should be stressed that Warner's academic section is in the vanguard of UNU-EHS's ambitions to place environmental migration on the agenda of political actors and policymakers.

It is important to note that UNU-EHS's embeddedness in the UN system, and its status as an official UN institution, imbues the IEO with considerable legitimacy. While recognition as a UN research institution may increase UNU-EHS's scientific legitimacy in the eyes of policymakers and could enhance its voice in policy negotiations, it arguably is also to no small part the 'UN label' that fosters relationships with other UN institutions such as UNFCCC. UNU-EHS's 'UN label', mission, and mandate put it in a unique position, particularly in comparison with other research institutions involved in the issue of environmental migration, as it distinguishes UNU-EHS as an interface between science and politics at the UN level. This ostensibly establishes a competitive advantage for UNU-EHS over other research institutions in the global policy discourse. In a world where resources are limited but social problems are endless, universities and research centres are fiercely competing for funding. Researchers, particularly in the Social Sciences, increasingly need to justify themselves by demonstrating the political impact and relevance of their work. UNU-EHS's relationship to the UN might increase the likelihood of gaining access to negotiation tables and being heard in the political debate. UNU-EHS's power as a UN institution should not be overstated. UN association is not tantamount to authority and influence in UN negotiations.

UNU-EHS and UNFCCC: the playing field

In what follows, the partnership between the United Nations Framework Convention on Climate Change (UNFCCC) and UNU-EHS is evaluated. The argument advanced here is that UNFCCC structurally facilitates UNU-EHS's potential to influence the politics of environmental migration. It thus constitutes the main political arena to which UNU-EHS channels its knowledge dissemination.

UNU-EHS is situated in close proximity to the UNFCCC Secretariat in Bonn. This spatial proximity is of strategic significance when explaining the close cooperation between both institutions. UNU-EHS is a small institute with approximately 60 staff members, and constitutes one of 18 UN agencies situated in Bonn. Based on its material capacity alone, it is very unlikely that UNU-EHS would ever be able to exert any influence, let alone a significant one, on the politics of environmental migration.

However, through the selection of the appropriate political arena, IEOs, such as UNU-EHS, can maximize their influence on the policy process. Conveniently, UNFCCC constitutes the domain in which both IEO mechanisms of influence meet. It forms an ideal playing field for UNU-EHS to create *loyalty networks* and demonstrate *expert authority*. Four reasons can be identified that make the UNFCCC an ideal playing field for UNU-EHS's endeavour to influence the politics of environmental migration:

1   *Congruence of research agendas.* UNU-EHS's work on risks and vulnerability assessments related to linked human–environment systems as well as its research in the area of environmental migration resonates with the UNFCCC context and logically forms part of the climate change discourse. The research undertaken by Warner's EMSVA academic section is particularly congruent with the research interests of many other actors engaging in the context of UNFCCC.
2   *Existence of an environmental migration network.* UNFCCC negotiations involve a diverse range of actors allowing UNU-EHS to interact and cooperate with IOs, non-governmental organizations (NGOs), and state partners as well as private sector actors and academics that are fighting for the prevention or mitigation of environmental migration. Moreover, UNFCCC offers the opportunity to directly engage with parties to the Convention, which allows UNU-EHS to disseminate knowledge to those who exercise decision-making power. This is an essential prerequisite for the translation of epistemic knowledge into policy influence.
3   *Acceptance of the environmental migration phenomenon.* The acknowledgement of environmental migration in political discourse seems nowhere more appropriate than in environmental policy and in relation to combatting climate change. Recognition of 'climate change refugees' under the current refugee regime through an expansion of the 1951 Geneva Convention is highly unlikely. Redirecting the climate change debate in order to achieve political recognition of the environmental migration phenomenon and the need to protect people displaced by natural disasters under the UNFCCC seems to be the second-best option available.
4   *Increased organizational profile.* While *de jure* non-governmental in nature, there seems to be some *de facto* scope as to what kind of organization UNU-EHS is *perceived* to be within UNFCCC. Tracing UNU-EHS submissions to UNFCCC shows that the institute is commonly ranked with other intergovernmental organizations such as the World Bank or UNDP. By tailoring its work to ongoing UNFCCC negotiations and through its close cooperation with intergovernmental organizations, UNU-EHS raises its organizational profile and achieves greater circulation of its work among the representatives of nation states.

UNU-EHS and the 'environmental migration network': strategic cooperation

This section identifies five groups of actors that advocate a political response to environmental migration. They all operate in the context of the UNFCCC and form part of UNU-EHS's 'environmental migration network'. These actors significantly enable the IEO to influence the politics of environmental migration. Over the course of the negotiations on 14(f) CAF under UNFCCC, UNU-EHS cooperated extensively with the following: (1) *States* (Parties to the Convention); (2) *IOs* such as The Office of the United Nations High Commissioner for Refugees (UNHCR), the International Organization for Migration (IOM) or the World Bank; (3) *NGOs* such as Germanwatch or CARE International; (4) *Private sector actors* such as the Munich Re Foundation; and (5) *Academics* such as François Gemenne, Andras Vag, and Roger Zetter. Together they construct a star-shaped network, in which UNU-EHS seeks to establish itself as the central vertex in order to ensure the network's dependence on it for maintaining connectedness. In fact, most actors are connected *to* and *because of* UNU-EHS. Koko Warner, head of UNU-EHS's EMSVA section, can be identified as the network's central node; the networker and stability guarantor of *loyalty networks* within the 'environmental migration network' (Interviews with Anonymous AWG-LCA Party, 17 April 2012; François Gemenne, 30 April 2012; Vikram Kolmannskog, 23 April 2012; Thomas Loster, 23 April 2012; Andras Vag, 20 April 2012).

The environmental migration network results in three forms of network-mediated benefits for all actors involved. The mutually beneficial nature of the network ensures the support of the actors and thus the continuity of the network itself. The following network benefits can be observed: (1) The *establishment of UNU-EHS as a valuable partner in negotiations*. Through cooperation with a diverse range of actors, UNU-EHS is recognized as relevant and influential within the debate. This is due to its particular IEO character that is distinct from the characteristics of the other actors. The five remaining actors subsequently profit from UNU-EHS's *expert authority*, which allows them to legitimize policy decisions in areas of contested knowledge such as environmental migration (Interview Andras Vag, 20 April 2012). (2) The ability to *act in concert with other actors* invested in the issue of environmental migration. The network allows groups of actors to present a more united front with regards to environmental migration. This increases the political weight of statements advocating environmental migration as an issue of political concern, benefiting the agendas of all actors within the network. (3) The *facilitation of knowledge dissemination*. Given UNU-EHS's central network position, it is able to enforce its own viewpoints on environmental migration within the network. However, other actors also profit from UNU-EHS's scientific insights. It broadens their knowledge base on environmental migration, without requiring them to agree with or endorse the viewpoints of UNU-EHS.

The individual cooperative relationships with the five groups of actors do, however, create specific network benefits for UNU-EHS, which can significantly facilitate its influence on the political process. The cooperation with other *academics* advances the creation of scientific knowledge, which in turn can be disseminated to policymakers. Cooperation with academics in the field of environmental migration is crucial for increasing UNU-EHS's academic profile as a representative of the whole academic environmental migration community. A stronger academic profile increases the IEO's *expert authority*, and thereby its potential to influence the policy process on the basis of being consulted to give policy advice. Similarly, the cooperation with NGOs can increase the IEO's profile and help identify it as a valuable partner in the debate. It also can help raise the IEO's level of *expert authority* (e.g. when internationally-operating NGOs partner with the Institute on particular research projects). It is the idea of 'endorsement' that makes partnerships with NGOs so valuable. Connections with *private sector actors* do not directly strengthen the expert authority of UNU-EHS. They do so indirectly by constituting a main source of research funding. In the case of UNU-EHS, the close cooperation with the Munich Re Foundation has resulted in augmented support from the Foundation for research projects (Interview Thomas Loster, 23 April 2012). More research creates more knowledge, which in turn bolsters UNU-EHS's expert authority and advances its academic leadership in the issue-area of environmental migration. IOs, due to their intergovernmental nature, can fulfil powerful bridge-building functions between UNU-EHS and state parties, creating greater possibilities for cooperation between the IEO and state actors in the UNFCCC context.

It needs to be recognized that, among the five groups of actors, states arguably constitute the most valuable network connection for UNU-EHS. Ultimately, the interaction with states is crucial: they hold the decision-making power in the formation of global public policy. Cooperation and communication with Parties to the negotiations can thus be expected to form a priority for UNU-EHS in order to achieve policy influence. According to UNU-EHS's discussed mandate, the Institute seeks to function as a think tank for state parties, and to offer them policy advice. If such advice is accepted and becomes part of a state's political agenda, UNU-EHS can indirectly influence public policy through the state proxy.

From the considerations above it can be concluded that the 'environmental migration network' is of crucial importance for UNU-EHS's ability to influence the politics of environmental migration. *Loyalty networks* established with each of the five groups of actors – *academics*, NGOs, *actors of the private sector*, IOs and *state parties* – yield distinct benefits that facilitate UNU-EHS's actions as an environmental migration policy entrepreneur in the political arena.[1] They either strengthen the IEO's expert authority and voice in the policy process or improve its chances of cooperation with state actors in one way or another. The following empirical analysis will reveal what effects the cooperation with each of the actors has yielded with regards to the evolution of paragraph 14(f) CAF.

UNU-EHS and the evolution of paragraph 14(f) CAF

In this chapter's empirical case study, the two identified mechanisms of IEO influence, *expert authority* and *loyalty networks*, will be mapped onto UNU-EHS, investigating its influence on the evolution of paragraph 14(f) CAF under the UNFCCC in order to answer the research question: *How has UNU-EHS influenced the politics of environmental migration?*

Paragraph 14(f) CAF[2] constitutes the first legal recognition in an internationally-binding agreement to pertain to the interconnections between environmental change and migration and highlights the importance of addressing environmental migration as part of a global adaptation strategy. The relevance of this agreement is threefold as it: (1) recognizes the humanitarian consequences of climate change as an adaptation challenge; (2) envisages environmental migration to become part of national adaptation plans thereby providing an entry point for protection issues; and (3) outlines internal and cross-border displacement as issues that not only concern the national level of government but equally require regional and international cooperation efforts (Kälin 2011: 32).

Case selection, methodology and data

Given the importance of 14(f) CAF as a milestone in the politics of environmental migration, the examination of the paragraph's policy evolution constitutes a pertinent case study. Based on preliminary research, UNU-EHS appeared to be one of the most vocal actors advocating the policy-relevance of environmental migration. However, its policy influence seemed unlikely given the Institute's limited material capacity to influence states and the knowledge contestation surrounding the issue of environmental migration. Therefore, the study sought to investigate how and to what degree UNU-EHS managed to yield political influence on the evolution of paragraph 14(f) CAF.

This study's empirical analysis is based on data obtained through qualitative elite interviews with UNU-EHS personnel, academics, NGO, state, and IO partners of UNU-EHS as well as partners from the private sector. Eight interviews were conducted between 11 April 2012 and 30 April 2012. The analysis applies a process-tracing method in order to establish the independent causal effects UNU-EHS (independent variable) has had on the policy evolution of paragraph 14(f) CAF (dependent variable).[3] However, this is not to suggest that a counterfactual causation between UNU-EHS and the creation of 14(f) CAF can be established beyond doubt. Yet, based on the findings of the process-tracing method and the exploration of alternative actor influence, e.g. state parties, the evidence strongly suggests that paragraph 14(f) CAF is indeed a manifestation of UNU-EHS's influence on the politics of environmental migration.

The evolution of paragraph 14(f) CAF

Politically, the inclusion of paragraph 14(f) in the CAF was the result of three years of negotiations on climate change adaptation under the Ad Hoc Working Group on Long-term Cooperative Action under the Convention (AWG-LCA), following the adoption of the Bali Action Plan at the 2007 Climate Change conference in Bali, Indonesia (Conference of the Parties [COP] 13 / Conference of the Parties serving as the meeting of the Parties to the Kyoto Protocol [CMP] 3). The Bali Action Plan created the AWG-LCA, a subsidiary body intended to prepare the basis for a successful climate agreement to succeed or complement the Kyoto Protocol (Warner 2011a: 4). AWG-LCA quickly emerged as the epicentre of negotiations that ultimately resulted in the CAF and marks the primary forum towards which UNU-EHS channelled its efforts to lobby for an inclusion of environmental migration in the negotiation text. During climate change negotiations in Bali, and later in Accra, Poznań, Copenhagen and finally in Cancún, AWG-LCA discussed the issue of adaptation in a total of 13 sessions. UNU-EHS, as one of the observer organizations, was present at every single meeting, represented by Koko Warner, head of UNU-EHS's EMSVA section that spearheads the IEO's research on environmental migration.

The evolution of paragraph 14(f) CAF and UNU-EHS's influence on the process can broadly be separated into two distinct mobilization phases. The first phase involves the *mobilization of the academic community* with regards to the issue of environmental migration. Between late 2006 and mid-2009, a research base was created that established environmental migration as an 'empirical reality' sound enough to trigger the interest of policymakers. The second phase concerns the *mobilization of policymakers*, beginning with the adoption of the Bali Action Plan in December 2007 that tuned international political agendas towards 'adaptation' and led to the creation of the AWG-LCA. Through the AWG-LCA, environmental migration was raised as an issue of international concern. It subsequently entered the UNFCCC policy process and was ultimately legally recognized through 14(f) CAF.

While both phases cannot be understood in isolation from each other, they are addressed in turn in order to offer a clearer understanding of a highly complex process.

Academic mobilization: UNU-EHS emerges as an expert authority

When UNU-EHS took up the topic of environmental migration in 2005, it joined an academic debate on a burgeoning but yet highly contested area of knowledge. Discussions on the issue had begun to pick up momentum in the early 2000s, when Myers's catastrophic enumerations of 'environmental refugees' stirred up academic interest but failed to create noteworthy political recognition (Myers 2002, 2005). Empirical evidence investigating the causal relationship between environmental change and migration was meagre. This left the scientific community somewhat paralyzed, resulting in largely sterile discussions of conceptual and methodological concerns that only empirical research could clarify. Before political recognition of the environmental migration concept could be achieved, extensive empirical evidence needed to be gathered that could establish environmental migration as an empirical reality in order to demonstrate its relevance to policymakers and global public policy.

Rather coincidentally, UNU-EHS was favourably positioned when the environmental migration discourse took its empirical turn. UNU-EHS had only recently appointed Dr Koko Warner, the key figure who later came to represent the academic community in the AWG-LCA negotiations. Admittedly, '[t]here was a little bit of element of accident' in UNU-EHS's initial involvement in the issue (Interview Koko Warner, 11 April 2012). When UNU-EHS first approached environmental migration as a research subject in 2005, Warner had just been working for the institute for a few months and was given the responsibility of exploring the issue (Interview Koko Warner, 11 April 2012). Shortly after, an immense research opportunity presented itself: the EACH-FOR project. Through the Sixth Framework Programme of the European Commission, EACH-FOR became the first global study to investigate the correlations between climate change and migration, and was given a budget of €800,000.

EACH-FOR can be claimed to have initiated the empirical turn in environmental migration research and marked the issue's transformation into one of political concern. It also turned UNU-EHS into a policy entrepreneur on environmental migration issues. François Gemenne, who was part of EACH-FOR's managing board and supervised the research clusters on Asia-Pacific and Central Asia during the project, agreed that 'EACH-FOR really put UNU-EHS on the map' (Interview François Gemenne, 30 April 2012). Between January 2007 and March 2009, 23 case studies were conducted, making EACH-FOR the first consistent global study investigating the causal relationship between environmental change and migration. EACH-FOR quickly evolved into the dominant empirical study in environmental migration research. It managed to attract the interest of policymakers as it 'was used as a proof that climate change migration was happening' (Interview François Gemenne, 30 April 2012).

EACH-FOR was set up as an exploratory, policy-oriented research project, designed to inform and make recommendations to policymakers. While this direction was inscribed in the project from the start due to its support from the European Commission, UNU-EHS significantly contributed to the policy oriented-nature in line with its mandate to produce policy-relevant research. Consequently, EACH-FOR was criticized for a purportedly unsound methodology that was said to be too tailored towards policy advice and hence failed to fulfil academic standards (Interview Roger Zetter, 20 April 2012). Gemenne admits that given the immense volume of case studies, the budget of the project was limited and the project itself might have been too broad (Interview François Gemenne, 30 April 2012). 'The methodology wasn't perfect, but we were still learning,' Warner acknowledges (Interview Koko Warner, 11 April 2012). Despite this criticism, EACH-FOR was still regarded as a pioneering project in the field of environmental migration and received immense attention in the academic community. Due to the attention it received, EACH-FOR 'set the agenda' (Interview Koko Warner, 11 April 2012) and established the basis on which political mobilization around the environmental migration concept was achieved (Interview Thomas Loster, 23 April 2012).

EACH-FOR put UNU-EHS in a leadership position in the academic community, which formed a stepping-stone towards the IEO's current political recognition and influence. UNU-EHS came to represent EACH-FOR in the academic community, investing it with considerable *expert authority* in the field of environmental migration. UNU-EHS demonstrated its leadership position in environmental migration research with the organization of the first international conference on the issue entitled 'Environmentally Forced Migration and Social Vulnerability' (EFMSV) in Bonn, in October 2008. EFMSV presented the preliminary findings of EACH-FOR to the academic as well as the political world and marked an important point in UNU-EHS's development into an environmental migration policy entrepreneur. While 'the conference aimed to get the academic community going', it also helped to promote UNU-EHS's *expert authority* among policymakers in the UNFCCC negotiations (Interview Koko Warner, 11 April 2012).

This initial assumption of *expert authority* can be said to mark the beginning of UNU-EHS's policy influence. However, *expert authority* derived from the academic mobilization of the environmental migration concept alone is insufficient in accounting for the IEO's influence on paragraph 14(f) CAF. While mobilizing academics was arguably sufficient to trigger the interests of policymakers, convincing them to include the issue in the negotiation text 'required the back up of a diverse range of actors' (Interview Koko Warner, 11 April 2012). The story of how that 'range of actors' was mobilized is the story of UNU-EHS's creation and exploitation of *loyalty networks*, as outlined in the following section.

Political mobilization: Loyalty networks yield policy influence

This section highlights the political mobilization of the environmental migration concept under the UNFCCC during the three years of negotiations leading up to the adoption of paragraph 14(f) in the CAF in December 2010. It demonstrates how UNU-EHS managed to create and exploit *loyalty networks* that helped to continuously strengthen its *expert authority*, ensured access to the negotiation tables, and facilitated the dissemination of knowledge to policymakers. Two types of *loyalty networks* were central to UNU-EHS's influence on the evolution of paragraph 14(f) CAF: (1) those it maintained with a particular group of AWG-LCA Parties; and (2) those that embedded the IEO in the 'humanitarian community' involved in the negotiations consisting of IOs, NGOs, and private sector actors. Both types of *loyalty networks* will be explored in turn.

The first category of *loyalty networks*, those that UNU-EHS established with AWG-LCA Parties over the duration of the UNFCCC negotiations, began to form immediately after the Bali Action Plan had created the AWG-LCA as a subsidiary body in December 2007. From the start, Warner represented UNU-EHS in its capacity as an observer organization in all 13 negotiations of the AWG-LCA that led up to the 2010 Cancún Climate Change Conference, which adopted the CAF and paragraph 14(f). After Bali (COP 13), Michael Zammit Cutajar, chair of AWG-LCA, invited Parties and observer organizations to the AWG-LCA to contribute ideas as to what issues could fall under the newly-envisaged global climate change adaptation strategy that COP 13 had laid out. Presented with this unique opportunity, UNU-EHS, under the management of Warner, wrote the first submission that was presented to UNFCCC delegates in August 2008 at the Accra, Ghana session of the AWG-LCA. The submission introduced the Parties to the first preliminary findings of the EACH-FOR project, presenting the idea of environmental migration at a time when:

> Parties were gearing up under AWG-LCA to approach a variety of adaptation issues. This position made Parties receptive to research-supported submissions, and supported them in bringing questions about migration and displacement into their early informal discussions in Accra.
>
> (Warner 2011a: 6)

With UNU-EHS's first submission to the UNFCCC, the Institute began to create *loyalty networks* with policymakers, researchers and other humanitarian actors aiming to promote the issue of environmental migration. Parties were looking to applied research for guidance as to what would fit under the envisaged adaptation framework and Warner 'saw that as an opportunity to bring in environmentally-induced displacement, which had never been mentioned before in an international negotiation setting' (Interview Koko Warner, 11 April 2012).

UNU-EHS continued to strengthen and enlarge its *loyalty networks* during this initial phase of the negotiations, through which more and more information on environmental migration was progressively inserted into the political debate. The promotion of EACH-FOR's results among policymakers steadily reinforced UNU-EHS's *expert authority* and leadership position in environmental migration research in the political arena through which Warner came to represent the academic community in the negotiations.

More submissions to UNFCCC regarding the issue of environmental migration were made after August 2008, including submissions by the International Labour Organization (ILO), IOM, and another joint submission by the UNHCR and UNU-EHS. For the AWG-LCA's fourth session in Poznań, 'Chair Michael Zammit Cutajar had compiled an assembly text from all submissions between Bali (COP 13) and September 30, 2008' (Warner 2011a: 8). The document mentioned migration and displacement in the context of climate change for the first time reflecting UNU-EHS's submissions and those of other humanitarian organizations. UNU-EHS's submission was further discussed and promoted in Poznań, where Warner had the rare opportunity as the representative of an observer organization to address the Parties to the negotiations in a plenary session during which she spoke on the subject of EACH-FOR (Interview Vikram Kolmannskog, 23 April

2012). Warner continued to promote the Institute's submission and the results of EACH-FOR among a core group of Parties. Through the continuous interaction between UNU-EHS and the AWG-LCA Parties, *loyalty networks* emerged that ensured mutual respect and trust.

The vital link between these *loyalty networks* and UNU-EHS's policy relevance was revealed over the course of 2009. After Accra and Poznań, the subsequent three sessions of the AWG-LCA in the lead-up to Copenhagen (COP 15) were held at UNFCCC in Bonn. The importance of UNU-EHS's geographic proximity to UNFCCC in Bonn should not be underestimated here as it placed the Institute closer to the negotiation site and over time made UNFCCC the closest working partner of UNU-EHS (Interview Koko Warner, 11 April 2012). With COP 15 drawing closer, negotiations over adaptation and the inclusion of environmental migration in the framework reached their peak.

At this point, it is crucial to mention the importance of the second type of *loyalty networks* UNU-EHS created over the course of the negotiations, namely those it upheld with actors within the 'humanitarian community' (Warner 2011a: 7). It is important to note that UNU-EHS embedded itself into the humanitarian community by creating relationships with many influential IOs and NGOs, such as CARE International, UNHCR, IOM, and parties to the IASC Task Force on Climate Change. The mobilization of the humanitarian community is central to the political mobilization around the environmental migration concept in the UNFCCC negotiations. Together with humanitarian actors, UNU-EHS presented 'a united front' that helped convince policymakers of the importance of environmental migration (Interview Koko Warner, 11 April 2012). Warner admitted:

> It was crucial not to work in isolation but in a larger group of humanitarian organizations that were also looking towards COP 15 to emphasize the human face of climate change. (…) We are a super small UN organization, we have a particular mandate to do research and bring it to policy but that is not enough. You have to have the big operational organizations that also chime in, like IOM, and many NGOs, like CARE and Oxfam.
>
> (Interview Koko Warner, 11 April 2012)

The need to provide a united front as one community invested in the topic of environmental migration and to convey a consistent message to UNFCCC delegates was central in convincing Parties to the negotiations of the importance of the issue in a future climate change adaptation framework.

Warner fulfilled a key role in facilitating and managing the communication within the 'humanitarian community'. She maintained close connections with the Inter-Agency Standing Committee (IASC) Task Force on Climate Change, particularly with its subgroup on migration and displacement, and communicated regularly with representatives of IOM, OCHA, UNHCR, UNDP and the World Bank. 'We could always rely on Koko to arrange things, to bring people together. (…) Koko has this almost magical ability of networking with delegations', explained Jean-François Durieux, who represented UNHCR in the IASC subgroup on migration and displacement (Interview Jean-François Durieux, 30 April 2012). It is also important to note that the *loyalty networks* UNU-EHS maintained always consisted of a small and stable group of people, in which everyone seemed to know each other. The networks 'were tight and effective' and the IASC subgroup on migration and displacement was no exception in this regard (Interview Vikram Kolmannskog, 23 April 2012). 'Koko was always there, at the centre, talking to everyone and connecting everyone' (Interview François Gemenne, 30 April 2012). 'She had good relations with many stakeholders (…) and made UNU-EHS what it was, a factor in the negotiations that couldn't be simply ignored' (Interview Thomas Loster, 23 April 2012).

From Poznań (COP 14) onwards, 'migration and displacement' entered and remained in the draft negotiating text. However, it was in Copenhagen that environmental migration became firmly established in the negotiation text in a way that closely resembled the wording of future paragraph 14(f) CAF (Interview Koko Warner, 11 April 2012). The period prior to Copenhagen marked the peak of the dissemination of EACH-FOR's research results into UNU-EHS's *loyalty networks*. This period was also defined by additional research activities that often included demand-driven research that UNU-EHS conducted in response to the questions posed by delegates during the AWG-LCA negotiations. In its cooperation with delegates,

> [a] big part of what we [UNU-EHS] were hoping to do was to shape and understand what delegate questions were and then in some ways have a common response.
>
> (Interview Koko Warner, 11 April 2012)

Case studies initiated on the basis of *loyalty networks* with Parties to the negotiations allowed UNU-EHS to create a feedback loop that constantly helped reinforce its *expert authority* and Parties' dependency on the knowledge that the IEO provided. Warner admitted that once delegate questions were identified '[w]e often went back and conducted a case study on it, which we then took back to them (…) and delegates greatly appreciated that' (Interview Koko Warner, 11 April 2012). Such behaviour likely maximized delegates' confidence in the issue's relevance and arguably made it more likely for them to include environmental migration in the draft negotiation text.

When the Copenhagen Climate Change Conference finally took place in December 2009, the political community had been successfully mobilized around the environmental migration concept during the two previous years of negotiations. The power of *loyalty networks* was clearly demonstrated when, despite the general breakdown in negotiations during COP 15, delegates laid the groundwork for what later became 14(f) CAF. Despite the fact that the conference finished on 15 December 2009 and the mandate of AWG-LCA delegates had ended, delegates continued working on elements of a broader adaptation framework (Interview Koko Warner, 11 April 2012). Their work was based on a bullet point list of potential adaptation strategy elements, which had been prepared and worked into a previous assembly document by UNU-EHS and the humanitarian community. This list, including the issue of 'migration and displacement', was ultimately inserted into the negotiation text. 'Migration and displacement' eventually featured in paragraph 14(f), while the other adaptation elements found expression in paragraphs 14(a)–(e) (Interview Koko Warner, 11 April 2012).

Conclusion

This chapter introduced the notion of IEOs and developed a conceptualization of IEOs as political actors. It did so through a focus on the role of UNU-EHS, an IEO that is highly influential in the politics of environmental migration. The analysis centred on the question: *How has UNU-EHS influenced the politics of environmental migration?* The empirical analysis focused on UNU-EHS's role in the evolution of paragraph 14(f) CAF, which constituted the first legal recognition of the environmental change–migration nexus.

Two mechanisms of IEO influence were identified, *expert authority* and *loyalty networks*, in order to explain the independent causal effects of IEOs on international politics in general and UNU-EHS's influence on the politics of environmental migration in particular. The empirical findings contribute to a better conceptual and practical understanding of IEOs as a group of under-researched but highly influential actors in international politics, especially within areas of contested knowledge, such as environmental migration. It was argued that while *expert authority* is commonly identified in the International Relations literature as the main driver of epistemic influence in global politics, *expert authority* alone is insufficient in explaining the influence of IEOs on the politics of environmental migration. Only by examining the creation and exploitation of *loyalty networks* can IEO policy influence be sufficiently explained.

UNU-EHS built its *expert authority* through its leadership role in the EACH-FOR project, the first global empirical study on environmental migration. It then used this *expert authority* to gain access to the negotiating tables of UNFCCC. Through Warner's continuous promotion of the EACH-FOR results on both an academic and political level, UNU-EHS came to represent the academic community as a whole on the issue of environmental migration within the negotiations.

UNU-EHS managed to maintain its relevance as a policy advisor by conducting demand-oriented research based on the questions of UNFCCC delegations. UNU-EHS strategically created *loyalty networks* with AWG-LCA Parties and humanitarian organizations active under UNFCCC through the dissemination of knowledge and the networking efforts of Warner. It utilized these *loyalty networks* to ensure continuous access to the political debate, increase knowledge dissemination to policymakers and create opportunity-structures to integrate its views on environmental migration within the policy process. In particular, the experience of COP 15 demonstrated the power of such networks. Here,

AWG-LCA delegates that had been in close contact with UNU-EHS and Warner used an assembly document that reflected the Institute's position on environmental migration to create a rough draft of what would later become paragraph 14(f) CAF.

The results presented in this chapter contain important implications for the literature on environmental migration. Moving beyond the predominant focus of existing works on causal and methodological debates, these results show that environmental migration is highly political. Moreover, this chapter builds on existing accounts on the politics of environmental migration (Betts 2010; Bristow 2007; Gemenne 2009; McNamara 2007; Piguet 2008; Warner 2011a, 2011b), by showing the role of IEOs in shaping an area of contested causal knowledge. Beyond its empirical focus, this research has implications for International Relations theory. Combining literature on epistemic communities (Haas 1989, 1992, 1993; Ruggie 1975, 1978, 1983) with work on IOs (Barnett and Finnemore 1999, 2004; Oestreich 2012), it highlights the important and academically neglected role of IEOs. The explored mechanisms of *expert authority* and *loyalty networks* further demonstrate the unique nature of IEOs as a particular type of political actor. Last but not least, by exploring UNU-EHS's particular influence in the politics of environmental migration, this study has implications for the role of the other 14 United Nations University Institutes. Each constituting IEOs in their specific issue-areas, this study provides a guide for future research on IEOs as neglected actors in the study of world politics.

Notes

1 For the literature on policy entrepreneurs see Sabatier 1988; Sabatier and Jenkins-Smith 1993; Mintrom and Vergari 1996.
2 Paragraph 14(f) CAF reads: '14. Invites all Parties to enhance action on adaptation under the Cancún Adaptation Framework, taking into account their common but differentiated responsibilities and respective capabilities, and specific national and regional development priorities, objectives and circumstances, by undertaking, inter alia, the following: (…) (f) Measures to enhance understanding, coordination and cooperation with regard to climate change induced displacement, migration and planned relocation, where appropriate, at national, regional and international levels' (UNFCCC 2011).
3 For a definition of process tracing see George and Bennett 2005.

References

Adler, E. (1992) The emergence of cooperation: national epistemic communities and the international evolution of the idea of nuclear arms control. *International Organisation.* 46(1): 101–45.

Barnett, M.N. and Finnemore, M. (1999) The politics, power, and pathologies of international organizations. *International Organization.* 53(4): 699–732.

Barnett, M.N. and Finnemore, M. (2004) *Rules for the world: international organizations in global politics.* Ithaca and London: Cornell University Press.

Betts, A. (2010) Substantive issue-linkage and the politics of migration. In *Arguing global governance*, eds. C. Bjola and M. Kornprobst. London: Routledge.

Bristow, S.D. (2007) The political ecology of environmental displacement and the United Nations' response to the challenge of environmental refugees. PhD Thesis, Department of International Politics, Aberystwyth University.

Castles, S. (2002) Environmental change and forced migration: making sense of the debate. *UNHCR Working Paper.* (70). Geneva: UNHCR.

Gemenne, F. (2009) *Géopolitique du changement climatique.* Paris: Armand Colin.

George, A.L. and Bennett, A. (2005) *Case studies and theory development in the social sciences.* Cambridge and London: MIT Press.

Haas, P.M. (1989) Do regimes matter? Epistemic communities and Mediterranean pollution control. *International Organization.* 43(3): 377–403.

Haas, P.M. (1992) Introduction: epistemic communities and international policy coordination. *International Organization.* 46(1): 1–36.

Haas, P.M. (1993) Epistemic communities and the dynamics of international environmental cooperation. In *Regime theory and international relations*, ed. V. Rittberger. Oxford: Clarendon Press.

Hafner-Burton, E.M., Kahler, M. and Montgomery, A. (2009) Network analysis for international relations. *International Organization.* 63(3): 559–92.

Kahler, M. (2009) Networked politics: agency, power, and governance. In *Networked politics: agency, power, and governance*, ed. M. Kahler. Ithaca: Cornell University Press.

Kälin, W. (2011) *Climate change induced displacement: a challenge for international law* [online]. Available: www.mcrg.ac.in/DL3.pdf [Accessed 6 May 2015].

Lake, D.A. and Wong, W. (2009) The politics of networks: interests, power, and human rights norms. In *Networked politics: agency, power, and governance*, ed. M. Kahler. Ithaca: Cornell University Press.

Litfin, K.T. (2000) Environment, wealth, and authority: global climate change and emerging modes of legitimation. *International Studies Review.* 2(2): 119–48.

McAdam, J. (2012) Conceptualizing climate change-related movement. *American Society of International Law Proceedings.* 106: 433–36.

McNamara, K. (2007) Conceptualizing discourses on environmental refugees at the United Nations. *Population and Environment.* 29(1): 12–24.

Mintrom, M. and Vergari, S. (1996) Advocacy coalitions, policy entrepreneurs and policy change. *Policy Studies Journal.* 24(3): 420–34.

Myers, N. (2002) Environmental refugees: a growing phenomenon of the 21st century. *Philosophical Transactions of the Royal Society of London – Series B: Biological Sciences.* 357(1420): 609–13.

Myers, N. (2005) *Environmental refugees and emergent security issue*, 13th Economic Forum, 23–27 May 2005.

Nicholson, C.T.M. (2014) Climate change and the politics of causal reasoning: the case of climate change and migration. *The Geographical Journal.* 180(2): 151–60.

Oestreich, J.E. ed. (2012) *International organizations as self-directed actors: a framework for analysis.* New York: Routledge.

Piguet, E. (2008) *Climate change and forced migration: how can international policy respond to climate-induced displacement?* Geneva: UNHCR Evaluation and Policy Analysis Unit.

Portes, A. (1998) Social capital: its origins and applications in modern sociology. *Annual Review of Sociology.* 24: 1–24.

Ruggie, J.G. (1975) International responses to technology. *International Organization.* 29: 557–84.

Ruggie, J.G. (1978) Changing frameworks of international collective behavior. In *Forecasting in international relations*, eds. N. Choucri and T.W. Robinson. San Francisco: W.H. Freeman.

Ruggie, J.G. (1983) Continuity and transformation in the world polity. *World Politics*. 35: 261–85.

Sabatier, P. (1988) An advocacy coalition framework of policy change and the role of policy-oriented learning therein. *Policy Science*. 21: 129–68.

Sabatier, P. and Jenkins-Smith, H. (1993) (eds.) *Policy change and learning: an advocacy coalition approach*. Boulder: Westview Press.

Sundström, M. (2000) *A brief introduction: what is an epistemic community?* [online]. Available: www.svet.lu.se/joluschema/epistcomm.pdf [Accessed 6 January 2012].

United Nations (UN) (1945) Charter of the United Nations. *1 UNTS XVI* [online]. Available: www.refworld.org/docid/3ae6b3930.html [Accessed 6 May 2015].

United Nations Framework Convention on Climate Change (UNFCCC) (2011) *The Cancún Agreements: outcome of the work of the Ad Hoc Working Group on Long-term Cooperative Action under the Convention* [online]. Available: http://unfccc.int/resource/docs/2010/cop16/eng/07a01.pdf [Accessed 6 May 2015].

United Nations University (UNU) (1973) *UNU charter* [online]. Formally adopted by the United Nations General Assembly on 6 December 1973. Available: http://unu.edu/about/charter#overview [Accessed 6 May 2015].

United Nations University Institute for Environment and Human Security (UNU-EHS) (2015) *Goals and objectives* [online]. Available: https://www.ehs.unu.edu/article/read/about-us [Accessed 6 May 2015].

Warner, K. (2011a) *Climate change induced displacement: adaptation policy in the context of the UNFCCC climate negotiations*. Bonn: UNU-EHS.

Warner, K. (2011b) *Climate and environmental change, human migration and displacement: recent policy developments and research gaps*. Bonn: UNU-EHS.

Zetter, R. (2008) Legal and normative frameworks. *Forced Migration Review*. (31): 62–3.

Zetter, R. (2009) The role of legal and normative frameworks for the protection of environmentally displaced people. In *Migration and environment research: state of the art review*. Geneva: International Organization for Migration.

16 Conclusion

The actors involved in the environmental migration complex

François Gemenne and Kerstin Rosenow-Williams

Introduction

While an increasing number of empirical studies have been conducted clearly establishing the impact of changing climate patterns on local responses, with migration emerging as one adaptation strategy across the globe (see Introduction in this volume), fewer studies have analysed the influence and rhetoric of various types of organizations in the debates on environmental migration. To close this research gap this volume has gathered both researchers and practitioners in a joint volume that aims at comparing different points of views on the role organizations play and have played in this dynamic and emerging policy field.

Combining various disciplines and research perspectives, as well as research methods ranging from classic document analyses and expert interviews to participatory observations, court case analyses, and self-observations from within the organizations under discussion, this volume provides a new insider perspective on organizational developments. Some contributions advance theoretical debates while others provide the reader practical insights into the challenges faced by organizations that are now dealing with a phenomenon that was not always within their organizational mandate or that even triggered the creation of a new organization or advocacy coalition.

The variety of actors analysed throughout this volume also reflects the spectrum of organizations that take part in the various discourses surrounding environmental migration at the advocacy, policy, media, legal and societal levels.

An evolving organizational landscape

In general, it took quite some time for organizations – be they intergovernmental or non-governmental – to take the full measure of the challenges brought upon by environmental migration. It was not until the mid-2000s, when the human impacts of climate change became more visible and obvious, that organizations started to earnestly position themselves on the subject. They flocked to attend the different rounds of United Nations (UN) climate negotiations and were increasingly keen to present their work and activities on the subject to audiences as diverse as possible.

Yet before the mid-2000s, the perspectives of organizations on the subject were rather timid. In the 1970s and 1980s, the issue of environmental migration was emerging. It was first discussed in several papers from environmental think-tanks, such as the Worldwatch Institute (Jacobson 1988), and gained further ground with the United Nations Environment Programme (UNEP) commissioning an influential report entitled 'Environmental Refugees' (El-Hinnawi 1985). However, by the early 2000s, major intergovernmental organizations in the field of migration like the United Nations High Commissioner for Refugees (UNHCR) and the International Organization for Migration (IOM) were still in the process of defining how they would address environmental migration. Back then, the environment–migration nexus was mostly referred to with regard to the environmental impacts of migration. The 2004 Indian Ocean tsunami caught both organizations somewhat by surprise, and forced them to deploy operational resources to assist those displaced by the disaster. Now, ten years later, both UNHCR and IOM are driving forces in the debate on how to better assist and protect those displaced by environmental events. IOM has even created, in early-2015, a specific division to coordinate the organization's work on the issue.

UNHCR and IOM are however not alone in this endeavour. As the chapters in this volume show, a growing number of international organizations including among others the International Red Cross/Red Crescent Movement, the Inter-Agency Standing Committee (IASC) for the coordination of humanitarian assistance, the Norwegian Refugee Council (NRC), the intergovernmental Nansen Initiative and the United Nations Convention to Combat Desertification (UNCCD) have moved the issue of environmental- or disaster-related migration onto their agendas. They have often forged new coalitions among each other to support their advocacy work and their programmes on the ground via knowledge exchange and the pooling of resources to generate greater attention for the issue from national and international policy-makers.

This increase in attention towards environmental migration as an advocacy issue can also be observed in a growing number of non-governmental organizations (NGOs). The very first NGO dedicated to this issue 'Living Space for Environmental Refugees' (LiSER) was created in 2002 and discontinued in 2011. It was a Dutch NGO born out of the goodwill of one man, Harry Wijnberg.[1] Since then, most major humanitarian NGOs, with the possible exception of Doctors Without Borders, have developed a position on the issue. Climate-related NGOs have joined forces with development-related NGOs since the Copenhagen summit of 2009, and some, such as the UK Climate Change and Migration Coalition, have been newly created to lead advocacy work on the issue. The articles from Bangladesh and Zimbabwe in this volume, as well as the case study on West Africa by IOM and UNCCD, also indicate that the issue elicits not only international attention but also local responses in those places where environmental migration takes place. However, more research on local civil society responses worldwide remains desirable.

The mutual influence between organizations and academics

All in all, the organizational landscape has witnessed some major evolutions over the last decade. This volume has sought to describe these evolutions, but also to show how organizational perspectives had an impact not only on the policy debates, but also on the academic and public debates. The topic of environmental migration is a rare example of the mutual influence of researchers and policy-makers on each other. Overall, there are very few areas of policy-making where researchers and policy-makers interact so regularly, attending the same conferences, sitting in the same committees and developing common work together. Interestingly, the workshop from which this volume stems is a very example of such interactions, as it gathered researchers, practitioners and activists. Throughout the years, many such interactions occur, to the point that it can become difficult to disentangle research perspectives from organizational perspectives. It shows that organizational perspectives on environmental migration are not shaped solely within the organizational context, but they are informed by research directions, policy context and public and media perceptions. But organizations do not just seek to shape policy evolutions: they also steer, in turn, research directions.

A clear example of this mutual influence can be found in the evolution of the migration–adaptation nexus. Initial conceptions of environmental migration viewed the latter as a solution of last resort, a humanitarian crisis in the making, an option that migrants would choose if and only if they had exhausted all other possibilities to adapt to their changing environment. Then different research endeavours, and collaborative empirical projects in particular,[2] highlighted that migration could also be an adaptation strategy for the migrants rather than only a failure to adapt. This perspective was soon embraced by IOs and promoted in the international negotiations on climate change. At the policy level, migration became recognized as an adaptation strategy that should be addressed at the regional, national and international level according to the Cancún Adaptation Framework (see article 14f of the 2010 Cancún Agreements of the Conference of the Parties to the United Nations Framework Convention on Climate Change: UNFCCC 2010).

Since then, different research efforts have sought to evaluate under which circumstances migration could serve as a successful adaptation strategy. Overall, it was acknowledged that migration could support adaptation through the diversification of income sources, the provision of remittances for those who stayed, or the alleviation of pressure on resources (Black *et al.* 2011; McLeman and Smit 2006; Webber and Barnett 2010). More recently, the MECLEP project (Migration, Environment and Climate Change: Evidence for Policy) seeks to assess the impacts of migration on the adaptive capacity of the communities of origin and of destination of the migrants.[3]

This mutual influence between epistemic communities made up of various organizations including academic actors, indeed, is not without risk for the integrity of scholarly work: increasingly, research is being pushed towards policy-relevance, and oftentimes research agendas are modelled on policy agendas.

Framing environmental migration

Different contributors in this volume have outlined different framings for the conceptualization of environmental migration. Some stressed the link to climatic changes that cause an increase in displacement in areas that are negatively affected, e.g. by rising sea levels or increased droughts. Other organizations focus on the issue of environmental degradation that can be caused by humans, e.g. in the exploitation of natural resources for monetary benefits causing large displacement that might be supported by regional and national state authorities. The intergovernmental Nansen Initiative, moreover, addresses the need for protection for those people being forced to migrate across state borders due to natural disasters. All three scenarios are included in the term environmental migration, as it has been discussed throughout this volume.

In addition to the question, what types of triggers are referred to when speaking about environmental migration, the question of framing also concerns the type of discourse in which the issue is embedded. Security considerations have long dominated the debates led by nation states with regard to the possible increase in migration due to environmental changes. The question who is legally responsible for the protection of those seeking refuge abroad due to environmental or climate change-induced changes in their countries of origin is currently discussed at the level of national courts since an international law framework that recognizes state responsibility is not yet in place and not likely to develop in the near future.

In addition to the security and the protection discourse, the issue of migration management has evolved in the context of a development discourse. This discourse advocates the framing of migration as an adaptation strategy rather than as an option of last resort. The mutual influence between organizations and academic research concerning this frame was discussed above.

Moreover, both environmental activists, as well as the humanitarian community, are now engaged with the topic of environmental migration. It is this broad scope of actors that contribute to the large variety of framings on environmental migration presented in this book. To a certain extent, these framings compete with each other in the way we conceptualize environmental migration. And most are the outcomes of research and policy interactions.

The analyses show that organizational perspectives matter, as they contribute to the very conceptualization of what we have come to know as environmental migration. Studying the different organizational perspectives, indeed, is important not just to understand how policy debates are shaped, but more generally how the very topic of environmental migration is being conceptualized. Even the very wording of this is influenced by organizational perspectives, as intergovernmental organizations, such as UNHCR and IOM (among others), have insisted that the expression 'environmental refugees' be dropped.

Among the different framings of environmental migration and the different discourses linked to it, it is not obvious which one shall prevail in a common conceptualization, nor which one shall yield the most significant policy results. In that regard, it will be fascinating to observe not only how organizational perspectives evolve in the future, but also – and perhaps more interestingly – how they influence and shape each other. It will also be interesting to compare the presented organizational perspectives to those of other actors that were not analysed within this volume. And it will remain a task for all actors involved to trace new developments as policy debates will evolve globally, nationally, and locally as both the natural environment and the global climate keep changing with migration being one possible response option among others.

Notes

1   www.liser.eu/en/liser/about-us/history-and-statutes [Accessed 16 April 2015].
2   Examples of such projects include EACH-FOR (Environmental Changes and Forced Migration Scenarios), which sought to test the influence of environmental changes as drivers of forced migration (Entzinger *et al.* 2010), or Where the Rain Falls, where a key component of the project looked at the impacts of droughts on mobility (www.wheretherainfalls.org).
3   See www.iom.int/cms/meclep [Accessed 16 April 2015].

References

Black, R., Bennett, S.R.G., Thomas, S.M. and Beddington, J.R. (2011) Migration as adaptation. *Nature.* 478: 447–9.

El-Hinnawi, E. (1985) *Environmental refugees.* Nairobi: United Nations Environment Programme.

Entzinger, H., Jäger, J. and Gemenne, F. (2010) Le projet EACH-FOR. *Hommes & Migrations.* 1284: 10–15.

Jacobson, J. (1988) *Environmental refugees: a yardstick of habitability. WorldWatch Paper.* (86). Washington, D.C.: WorldWatch Institute.

McLeman, R. and Smit, B. (2006) Migration as an adaptation to climate change. *Climatic Change.* 76(1–2): 31–53.

United Nations Framework Convention on Climate Change (UNFCCC) (2010) *Report of the Conference of the Parties on its sixteenth session, held in Cancún from 29 November to 10 December 2010* [online]. FCCC/CP/2010/7/Add.1. Available: http://unfccc.int/resource/docs/2010/cop16/eng/07a01.pdf [Accessed 27 February 2015].

Webber, M. and Barnett, J. (2010) Accommodating migration to promote adaptation to climate change. *World Bank Policy Research Working Paper.* (5270). Washington, D.C.: World Bank.

Index